Memory Across Borders
Nabokov, Perec, Chamoiseau

LEGENDA

LEGENDA is the Modern Humanities Research Association's book imprint for new research in the Humanities. Founded in 1995 by Malcolm Bowie and others within the University of Oxford, Legenda has always been a collaborative publishing enterprise, directly governed by scholars. The Modern Humanities Research Association (MHRA) joined this collaboration in 1998, became half-owner in 2004, in partnership with Maney Publishing and then Routledge, and has since 2016 been sole owner. Titles range from medieval texts to contemporary cinema and form a widely comparative view of the modern humanities, including works on Arabic, Catalan, English, French, German, Greek, Italian, Portuguese, Russian, Spanish, and Yiddish literature. Editorial boards and committees of more than 60 leading academic specialists work in collaboration with bodies such as the Society for French Studies, the British Comparative Literature Association and the Association of Hispanists of Great Britain & Ireland.

The MHRA encourages and promotes advanced study and research in the field of the modern humanities, especially modern European languages and literature, including English, and also cinema. It aims to break down the barriers between scholars working in different disciplines and to maintain the unity of humanistic scholarship. The Association fulfils this purpose through the publication of journals, bibliographies, monographs, critical editions, and the MHRA Style Guide, and by making grants in support of research. Membership is open to all who work in the Humanities, whether independent or in a University post, and the participation of younger colleagues entering the field is especially welcomed.

ALSO PUBLISHED BY THE ASSOCIATION

Critical Texts
Tudor and Stuart Translations • New Translations • European Translations
MHRA Library of Medieval Welsh Literature

MHRA Bibliographies
Publications of the Modern Humanities Research Association

The Annual Bibliography of English Language & Literature
Austrian Studies
Modern Language Review
Portuguese Studies
The Slavonic and East European Review
Working Papers in the Humanities
The Yearbook of English Studies

www.mhra.org.uk
www.legendabooks.com

TRANSCRIPT

Transcript publishes books about all kinds of imagining across languages, media and cultures: translations and versions, inter-cultural and multi-lingual writing, illustrations and musical settings, adaptation for theatre, film, TV and new media, creative and critical responses. We are open to studies of any combination of languages and media, in any historical moments, and are keen to reach beyond Legenda's traditional focus on modern European languages to embrace anglophone and world cultures and the classics. We are interested in innovative critical approaches: we welcome not only the most rigorous scholarship and sharpest theory, but also modes of writing that stretch or cross the boundaries of those discourses.

Editorial Committee
Chair: Matthew Reynolds (Oxford)
Robin Kirkpatrick (Cambridge)
Laura Marcus (Oxford)
Patrick McGuinness (Oxford)
Ben Morgan (Oxford)
Mohamed-Salah Omri (Oxford)
Tanya Pollard (CUNY)
Yopie Prins (Michigan)

Advisory Board
Jason Gaiger (Oxford)
Alessandro Grilli (Pisa)
Marina Grishakova (Tartu)
Martyn Harry (Oxford)
Linda Hutcheon (Toronto)
Calin-Andrei Mihailescu (London, Ontario)
Wen-Chin Ouyang (SOAS)
Clive Scott (UEA)
Ali Smith
Marina Warner (Birkbeck)
Shane Weller (Kent)
Stefan Willer (Berlin)

Managing Editor
Dr Graham Nelson
41 Wellington Square, Oxford OX1 2JF, UK

www.legendabooks.com/series/transcript

TRANSCRIPT

1. *Adapting the Canon: Translation, Visualisation, Interpretation*, edited by Ann Lewis and Silke Arnold-de Simine
2. *Adapted Voices: Transpositions of Céline's Voyage au bout de la nuit and Queneau's Zazie dans le métro*, by Armelle Blin-Rolland
3. *Zola and the Art of Television: Adaptation, Recreation, Translation*, by Kate Griffiths
4. *Comparative Encounters between Artaud, Michaux and the Zhuangzi: Rationality, Cosmology and Ethics*, by Xiaofan Amy Li
5. *Minding Borders: Resilient Divisions in Literature, the Body and the Academy*, edited by Nicola Gardini, Adriana Jacobs, Ben Morgan, Mohamed-Salah Omri and Matthew Reynolds

Memory Across Borders

Nabokov, Perec, Chamoiseau

Sara-Louise Cooper

LEGENDA

Transcript 6
Modern Humanities Research Association
2016

Published by Legenda
an imprint of the Modern Humanities Research Association
Salisbury House, Station Road, Cambridge CB1 2LA

ISBN 978-1-910887-08-0 (HB)
ISBN 978-1-78188-351-8 (PB)

First published 2016

All rights reserved. No part of this publication may be reproduced or disseminated or transmitted in any form or by any means, electronic, mechanical, photocopying, recording or otherwise, or stored in any retrieval system, or otherwise used in any manner whatsoever without written permission of the copyright owner, except in accordance with the provisions of the Copyright, Designs and Patents Act 1988, or under the terms of a licence permitting restricted copying issued in the UK by the Copyright Licensing Agency Ltd, Saffron House, 6–10 Kirby Street, London EC1N 8TS, England, or in the USA by the Copyright Clearance Center, 222 Rosewood Drive, Danvers MA 01923. Application for the written permission of the copyright owner to reproduce any part of this publication must be made by email to legenda@mhra.org.uk.

Disclaimer: Statements of fact and opinion contained in this book are those of the author and not of the editors or the Modern Humanities Research Association. The publisher makes no representation, express or implied, in respect of the accuracy of the material in this book and cannot accept any legal responsibility or liability for any errors or omissions that may be made.

Trademark notice: Product or corporate names may be trademarks or registered trademarks, and are used only for identification and explanation without intent to infringe.

© Modern Humanities Research Association 2016

Copy-Editor: Dr Susan Wharton

CONTENTS

	Acknowledgements	ix
	A Note on Translation	xi
	List of Abbreviations	x
	Introduction	1
1	The Portrayal of Home	17
2	Writing Between Languages	53
3	Traces of Trauma	84
4	Literary Thinking as Conscious Memory	114
	Conclusion	141
	Bibliography	147
	Index	159

To my parents

ACKNOWLEDGEMENTS

I should like to record my thanks to the Arts and Humanities Research Council and the John W. Kluge Centre at the Library of Congress for funding the doctoral research on which this book is based. I am also grateful to Brasenose College, Oxford and Oriel College, Oxford for supporting my research.

During the doctorate, Julie Curtis offered expert supervision, hospitality and kindness. Patrick McGuinness was a source of excellent advice. I am grateful to Philip Bullock and Charles Forsdick for making the viva such a stimulating and encouraging experience and for offering very helpful advice about developing the project. Matthew Reynolds and Graham Nelson at Legenda have made the preparation of the manuscript as easy as it could have been and I thank them for their support. I am grateful to the anonymous reviewer for offering helpful and constructive comments on the first draft. Any errors remain, of course, entirely my responsibility. Part of Chapter Three and Four appeared in a different form in my earlier 'Writing Selves, Written Selves: Spiralling Paths from Past to Present in Patrick Chamoiseau's *Une Enfance créole*', *Wasafiri*, 31 (2016), 52–58 and I thank the editors of *Wasafiri* for their advice in the writing of that paper.

I could not have written this book without knowing many excellent teachers along the way: I am grateful to Cathérine Sands, Sean Treanor, Cristina Gaillard, Mary Bell, Amelia Stevenson, Richard Cooper, Carole Bourne-Taylor and Mike Nicholson for everything they taught me.

At the Taylor Institution, Dora Grindrod, Magda Kalinowska, Mark Cooper and Piotr Szkonter were always helpful and flexible colleagues. Richard Stayt was a wonderful boss and I am grateful to him for everything he did to support me and my work. Katherine Lunn-Rockliffe at Hertford has been a kind and supportive colleague during the later stages of completion of the manuscript. I have many happy memories of the time shared with Oriel students 2013–2016 and Hertford students 2015–2016. At Oriel, Louisiane Ferlier, Claire Deligny and Emma Claussen made Wednesday lunch times a bright spot in my week. Special thanks to Francesco Manzini and Richard Scholar for their boundless warmth and generosity, and for introducing me to the theory and practice of 'pure space'.

My friends helped me so much, either by discussing the book, or by not discussing it, and I thank Rachel Benoit, Sarah and Dominic Cherry, Claire De Carlo, Jonathan Edwards, Harry Ford, Camilla Gruffydd-Jones, Aisling Hollowood, Judy McElroy, Tamara Moellenberg, Claire Mullen, Eleanor Parker, Jane Rooney, Kelsey Rubin-Detlev, Hannah Sikstrom-Walker and Helena Clare Wilding.

Upon hearing I was writing a book, my mother made a horrified request: 'Don't put us in it'; I have complied with the letter of that request, but of course my parents' wisdom and love is in everything I do and I dedicate this book to them. Thanks also to my brothers and sisters, Kerri, Helen, Bernard and Patrick, for offering a healthy sense of perspective ('Who's going to read it? Other academics?') and for making me laugh. My love and thanks go to my husband, Joseph, for encouraging me to begin and for everything since.

S.-L. C., Oxford, July 2016

A NOTE ON TRANSLATION

Translations of Patrick Chamoiseau, *Antan d'enfance* (Paris: Gallimard, 1990) are adapted from Patrick Chamoiseau, *Childhood*, trans. by Carol Volk (London: Granta, 1999).

The translation of Charles Baudelaire, *Les Fleurs du mal*, ed. by Jacques Dupont (Paris: Flammarion, 1999) is adapted from Charles Baudelaire, *Selected Poems*, trans. by Geoffrey Atheling Wagner (London: Falcon, 1946).

Translations of Patrick Chamoiseau, *Chemin-d'école* (Paris: Gallimard, 1996) are adapted from Patrick Chamoiseau, *School Days*, trans. by Linda Coverdale (London: Granta, 1997).

Translations of Georges Perec, *W ou le souvenir d'enfance* (Paris: Denoël, 1975) are adapted from Georges Perec, *W or the Memory of Childhood*, trans. by David Bellos (London: Vintage, 1996).

Translations of Georges Perec, *Penser/Classer* (Paris: Hachette, 1985) are adapted from Georges Perec, *Thoughts of Sorts*, trans. and ed. by David Bellos (London: Notting Hill Editions, 2011)

All other translations are my own.

LIST OF ABBREVIATIONS

DB   Vladimir Nabokov, *Другие берега*. Ann Arbor: Ardis, 1978.
SM   Vladimir Nabokov, *Speak, Memory: An Autobiography Revisited*. London: David Campbell, 1999.
W   Georges Perec, *W, ou le souvenir d'enfance*. Paris: Denoël, 1975.
Antan   Patrick Chamoiseau, *Antan d'enfance*. Paris: Gallimard, 1990.
Chemin Patrick Chamoiseau, *Chemin-d'école*. Paris: Gallimard, 1996.
A bout Patrick Chamoiseau, *A bout d'enfance*. Paris: Gallimard, 2005.

INTRODUCTION

In Fort-de-France, Martinique, in the middle of the last century, a child rummaged in a wardrobe and found a box of books. Half a century later, the author Patrick Chamoiseau recalls his impressions of the books:

> Ils semblaient provenir, presque intacts, d'un autre âge. Le négrillon avait parfois l'impression qu'ils avaient glissé des mondes fabuleux dont leurs images attestaient l'existence. Quand on en soulevait un, il s'accrochait aux autres par des fils d'araignée. Et quand on les ouvrait, quand on les ouvrait, le papier dérangé exhalait comme une haleine ancienne; *oh, quand on les ouvrait...*[1]

> [The books seemed to have come almost intact from a different age. Sometimes the little boy had the impression they had emerged from the fabulous worlds whose existence their illustrations proved. When you picked one up, it clung to the others with spider webs. And when you opened them — when you opened them, the ruffled paper breathed a sort of ancient sigh, *oh, when you opened them...*]

In this moment of encounter, both child and books are changed. Opening the books' stiff pages brings other worlds into the 1950s Martinican house and the child's touch disturbs the fragile but sticky strands of the spiders' webs which hold the books together. Like the spiders' webs, the language here stretches and contracts, recreating the child's excitement at contact with literature, an excitement so intense and enduring that it moves the narrator into alexandrines at the beginning and end of the last sentence, and finally leaves him wordless.

The ellipsis seems to evoke the silence of an overwhelmed imagination, but overwhelmed in what sense? The conjuring of the 'mondes fabuleux' points towards two kinds of journeys triggered by reading. On the one hand, 'fabuleux', in its meaning of 'irréel, féerique, merveilleux', suggests a trajectory towards an imaginary world. This meaning of 'fabuleux' is reminiscent of Chamoiseau's commitment to 'l'émerveille', a mode of being and perception open to phenomena rendered invisible by ruling conventions.[2] For Chamoiseau, 'l'émerveille' is both the source and goal of a fruitful politics and aesthetics. Contact with 'mondes fabuleux' through the books in the wardrobe is then a kind of opening of the worlds the author will continue to explore and imagine during his long career as a novelist, essayist, dramatist and activist. Yet the second meaning of 'fabuleux', 'tiré d'une fable' [drawn from a fable], suggests another kind of trajectory. It points the reader back to the origin of the worlds the child encounters in the books. These worlds emerge out of the particular stories narrated in each book, and these stories in turn emerge out of European literary culture where the world known to the child is often absent or erased. The books are given as prizes to his older siblings at school, a frightening place where the child will suffer physical pain and be forbidden from speaking Creole, his mother tongue. The peculiar fascination books exercise on the child speeds the alienation he undergoes at school, which leaves literary worlds seeming more real than his own experience. The moment when the child opens the books is then ambivalent, the crossing of a threshold into a literary space which is both liberating and oppressive.

The duality of this encounter poses a challenge to the literary critic, which forms the central question of this book: how to read a literary tradition in the light of histories of mobility. Accounting for both the freedom and oppression experienced in and evoked through literature here involves thinking through what it means for a Martinican child to begin reading a European canon and so to encounter a foreign literary culture, in a moment marked by the resonating histories of violence and oppression that have characterized the French presence in Martinique. The relationship between the aesthetics and the politics of this moment is tied to the question of the forces at play in a moment of contact between two cultures. Yet though I write 'two cultures', addressing this question is challenging precisely because both European and Caribbean culture emerge out of histories of travel, real and imagined, which leave their borders shifting. Even a brief look at the authors the child reads complicates the idea that European and Caribbean culture are entirely foreign to one another. The child reads '[d]es ouvrages de Jules Verne, de Daniel Defoe, d'Alexandre Dumas, de Lewis Carroll, de la comtesse de Ségur, de R. L. Stevenson'. The lives and works of these authors point to the multiple forms of intercultural contact existing within European culture and reveal the extent to which the European canon is shaped by the experience of colonial conquest abroad. While Defoe, Verne and Stevenson draw on histories of imperial conquest of 'new' worlds to write their stories, Alexandre Dumas bears the trace of these histories in his name, which he took from his grandmother, Louise-Céssette Dumas, who had been bought as a slave by his grandfather for his estate in Saint-Domingue (now Haiti). The European children's canon which reaches the child in Martinique is the product of a long history of contact between Europe and the Americas, whose cultures, bound into unequal relationships through conquest, resistance and trade, have been shaping each other since the fifteenth century.

A look at the reception of this children's canon by another twentieth-century French-language writer reveals the degree to which these transatlantic histories make themselves felt in the literary culture of the former empire's centre, just as much as on its furthest reaches. Georges Perec, who lived all but one year of his life in France, draws on Jules Verne's transatlantic fictions to narrate a life-story shaped by a family history of intra-European migration and oppression in his haunting 1975 autobiography, *W ou le souvenir d'enfance*. The narrative has two alternating strands, the first a fictional tale reminiscent of Verne's fiction, the second a halting narration of the author's difficulties recalling with any certainty the details of his wartime childhood. The subject-matter of the autobiographical strand, which addresses the silences left in Perec's family history by his mother's deportation to Auschwitz and his father's death as a soldier in the French army, is so painful that the reader is initially glad of the respite the fictional chapters seem to offer. These are written at first from the perspective of a man who has gone in search of a shipwrecked child. The man, who fled conscription, was given a false name by a charitable organization. His new name is Gaspard Winckler, the name of the lost child whom a stranger sends him to find.

Halfway through the autobiography, the reader comes to a blank page with an ellipsis in brackets at its centre. After this the first-person voice disappears from the fictional strand and it is narrated in the third person. The new, apparently impersonal voice describes an island in the Atlantic called W. It appears to be a Verne-esque utopian society devoted to sport, but over the course of the narration, it gradually becomes clear that the island is a totalitarian landscape all too reminiscent of the Nazi camp in Poland where Perec's mother probably lost her life. The spatiotemporal dynamics of the imagined island are not straightforward, however. Just as the allusions to the Nazi camps reach a critical mass which would encourage the reader to map the island space on to the European wartime history of the camps, Perec disrupts any such stable rooting of the concentrationary universe, drawing attention to its contemporary echoes in a society on the other side of the Atlantic, Pinochet's Chile.[3] Throughout the narration, Perec draws on the indeterminacy of the utopian (then dystopian) island space to layer references to European colonialism abroad with the language of racial exclusion in contemporary France and Holocaust imagery.

Whether we read Chamoiseau, Verne or Perec, we enter into a literary tradition that is implicated in, emerges from and engages with transatlantic histories of travel and conquest. Reading that literary tradition involves consideration of the particular ways in which those transatlantic histories reverberate through the work of each author. This can occur in surprising ways, as when transatlantic histories become a way of talking about events in Europe for Perec, or European histories become a way of talking about events in the Americas for authors like Chamoiseau, or his Caribbean contemporaries Maryse Condé and Gisèle Pineau.[4] We have touched briefly on Perec's intertwining of Holocaust and colonial histories in his creation of the W island. Such intertwinings are also found in Chamoiseau's work. In his autobiography, the children's school playground acts as an echo-chamber for violent histories which have taken place all over the world.[5] The author speaks of his interactions with other children in terms which call up both colonial histories and intra-European histories of genocide.[6] The fusing of resonances of different histories in Chamoiseau's language is in line with an argument he makes elsewhere about modernity as a 'magma' of memory where unnameable crimes intermingle.[7] Such literary connections between transatlantic and European histories of course draw on and reflect the intertwined nature of these histories. They also reflect the fact that in a globalized world, narrations of other people's experiences of displacement are available to the imagination of those who seek to explore the resonances of histories of migration in their own lives.

Connected at the level of thought in the work of an author like Perec, movements within Europe and across the Atlantic are connected in the life experiences of Vladimir Nabokov. We see this if we look at his reception of another of the authors from the box in the wardrobe, the Comtesse de Ségur. In *Speak, Memory: An*

Autobiography Revisited, Nabokov remembers his uncle Ruka reading the Comtesse de Ségur's *Les Malheurs de Sophie* in Russia in the early years of the twentieth century. Reading this book in his nephew's nursery takes the uncle back to his own childhood. Nabokov deploys this memory to make an argument about the presence of Russian realities in French writing. The Comtesse de Ségur, Nabokov suggests, did not write of French childhoods, but rather, as she wrote, she 'was Frenchifying the authentic surroundings of her Russian childhood which preceded mine by exactly one century'.[8] Nabokov here creates an unlikely literary predecessor for himself, situating his own recollections of childhood in a foreign language as part of Russian literary genealogy. Nabokov too would go on to 'Frenchify' his Russian childhood when he wrote 'Mademoiselle O', the French-language sketch about his Swiss governess he published in 1936.[9] This sketch marked the beginning of his autobiographical project, as it led him to make a plan for the full-length work he would complete after his move to America in 1940. Nabokov's rendering of childhood memories in French was the first step in an autobiographical enterprise that lasted three decades, encompassing the creation of a full-length English autobiography,[10] its revision and translation into Russian,[11] and a revision of the first English version that drew on the development of the Russian version.[12] Nabokov's allusion to Mme de Ségur's 'Frenchifying' calls up his own shifts between Russia, England, France and Germany, and his forays into writing about his youth in French. All these moves are evoked from an American vantage point, as Nabokov writes this episode after his emigration from Europe. For Nabokov, the Comtesse de Ségur is a pivot which allows him to gesture towards the potential Russianness of non-Russian texts; for Chamoiseau, her work is connected to metropolitan Frenchness. In Chamoiseau's 1992 novel, *Texaco*, Martinican children about to undertake a journey to France expect to find it bristling with 'des Comtesses de Ségur'.[13] In the novel the phrase evokes the unreality of a country only known to the children through the alien images that emerge from French children's literature. But France is also a country of Comtesses de Ségur in the sense that it is a country whose literary tradition is infused with re-imaginings of French spaces by people from outside of hexagonal France. Looking at the autobiographical work of Nabokov, Perec and Chamoiseau makes France visible as a country of Comtesses de Ségur in this second sense, as each author in different ways explores points of contact between the idea of a French childhood and languages and literatures from other places.

These authors' complex relationship to the language and literature of childhood is due to history, history in Georges Perec's sense of 'l'Histoire avec sa grande hache', history as a severing touch which ends life rather than creating it, breaking links between the individual and the world in the process, not least the link of language.[14] Each author tussles with the difficulties of writing about the past through a language and literary tradition which is the most vivid sign of his exclusion from it. Nabokov charts his movement from the Russian to the English language (via French) against the backdrop of the October Revolution, the Second World War and the Cold War. Perec attempts to tell the story of a life lived in the aftermath of a family history of movement between religious affiliations, countries, alphabets and languages, triggered by multiple waves of anti-Semitism, culminating with his mother's death in the Holocaust. Chamoiseau explores the ambivalent cultural and linguistic affiliations produced by a postcolonial childhood in Martinique. In each case, the link of language and culture which would normally embed the author's individual life within a group becomes problematic. When language becomes problematic, so does the question of memory and belonging to a national literary tradition.

The memory in these texts crosses the borders of literary community, language and self, as each author creates a memorial to the language and cultures of his forebears. Another kind of border crossing occurs when each author links his own wounds from the axe of history to its blows in seemingly distant lives. I touched briefly on Perec's intertwining of Holocaust and colonial histories in his creation of the W island and on Chamoiseau's linking of colonial oppression with violence occurring within Europe's borders. Nabokov, too, links racial, colonial and anti-Semitic violence in statements like the following, where he recalls his abhorrence of Lenin's revolutionary terror and his efforts to convince his 1920s Cambridge acquaintances that it was an old form of oppressive state rather than anything novel:

> Indeed, I pride myself with having discerned even then the symptoms of what is so clear today, when a kind of family circle has gradually been formed, linking representatives of all nations, jolly empire-builders in their jungle clearings, French policemen, the unmentionable German product, the good old churchgoing Russian or Polish *pogromshchik*, the lean American lyncher, the man with the bad teeth who squirts anti-minority stories in the bar or the lavatory, and, at another point of the same subhuman circle, those ruthless, paste-faced automatons in opulent John Held trousers whom — or shall I say which? — the Soviet State began to export around 1945[15]

The movement of Nabokov's sentence from distant to personal history suggests something of the purpose of such historical comparisons. As this study will go on to explore, the particular history which has led each author to language change is out of reach for him, for his reader or both. This leads him to approach the near history of his family through more spatially distant histories which are nonetheless within easier reach of memory. Such multiple crossings of borders pose significant challenges to the literary critic. These texts situate themselves relationally, exploring points of contact and severance between the author's life, those of his ancestors, his local literary tradition and distant histories. Each calls for ways of reading attentive to the crossing of geographical and linguistic boundaries. Though there are significant differences between them, each text reaches backwards to family histories lived in other languages, in the process creating connections between modernity's violent histories and rewriting national literary traditions themselves shaped by migration. The border-crossing forms of memory in these texts mean they sit uncomfortably within the national and the local. How then to read them? This is the central question of this study. It explores the kinds of literary conversations these texts set up and asks how these conversations should relate to those we have as readers and critics.

★ ★ ★ ★ ★

The questions raised by Chamoiseau's memory of opening the books from the wardrobe are issues that have been the subject of increasing preoccupation amongst literary scholars for the last several decades. As Alec G. Hargreaves, Charles Forsdick and David Murphy note, 'questions of travel and mobility have been at the heart of a desire on the part of many French/Francophone studies scholars to de-centre a model of French studies that was focused exclusively on the hexagon'.[16] The project of decentring French studies involves finding a way beyond the centre/periphery logic present in the division of the discipline's object of study into 'French literature' (literature written in French in France) and 'Francophone literature' (literature written in French outside of France, usually in France's former colonial territories). Yet as the use of the term French/Francophone in the quotation indicates, such a division is difficult to do away with without also losing much that is valuable. Scholars have long been aware of the problems inherent in the term 'Francophone' and the arguments against its use are by now familiar. Firstly, it elides the vast differences between parts of the world where French is spoken. Secondly, because it tends not to be applied to foreign authors like Beckett or Ionesco though it is used for authors who are technically French citizens like Chamoiseau, it can serve more to mark literary production as 'peripheral' rather than pointing to the geographical origin or linguistic history of the author. Thirdly, the institutional forces of Francophonie maintain a troubling continuity with colonial practices of 'soft power', where the idea of cultural fraternity masks a quest for political dominance.[17]

In the face of such concerns, one might have expected the concept of 'world literature in French' proposed by the signatories of the 2007 *littérature-monde* manifesto to be welcomed with open arms. Yet it was met with a raft of scholarship pointing out the way its apparently more open vision of French-language literature subtly replicated the same exclusionary logic present within the concept of a 'Francophone' text.[18] The response to the manifesto illustrated the scholarly community's continued investment in, and need for, the idea of the Francophone, even as it acknowledges all the problems it brings in its wake. Perhaps the most persuasive and most frequently voiced reason for preserving the idea of a separation between 'French-French' and 'Francophone' writing is the argument that erasing the divisions between writing produced in metropolitan France and that produced in France's former colonies runs the risk of passing over in silence the particular histories that have led 'Francophone' writers to the French language.[19] Postulating a borderless literary space ignores the continuities between the violent extension of national boundaries in the era of colonial expansion and the unequal distribution of economic and political power in the present world. In the light of the lethal policing of national borders, it seems at best naive and at worst wilfully complicit to assert that the literary sphere operates apart from such political divisions.

The idea of a borderless literary space is untenable, but zooming in to consider French-language works solely in their own localities also poses significant though lesser problems. Sandy Petrey, in an article urging caution towards the centrifugal energies inherent in the study of literature produced in French outside the hexagon, warns of a curriculum which 'will inevitably be an endless series of snapshots with zero chance of becoming an album'. Though I am sceptical of Petrey's argument that reading literature produced in French outside of France will end the discipline of French studies, I see merit in his point about the need to think through what binds the corpus of literature read within French studies even as the discipline is decentred. Even reading French-language texts on their own terms requires an engagement with the idea of national history, national language and national literature, as such questions take on a charged presence in much writing from within and without the hexagon. The approach evoked through Petrey's metaphor of the snapshot means neglecting the way in which authors writing in French outside the hexagon engage with the hexagonal literary tradition, which, as we have touched on briefly, is itself shaped by contact between metropolitan and overseas 'France'. It also evades the question of whether one language creates a common literary tradition, and, if so, how such a tradition might be read. Though Petrey's vision of 'an endless series of snapshots' is perhaps more of an alarmist fantasy than a description of current scholarship, it is still useful as a reminder of the importance of thinking about the space between the various zones examined within French studies.

There is, then, a need to think through ways of reading literary texts produced in French in different parts of the world without losing sight of the oppressive histories which lead authors from colonized countries to the French language. This study responds to this dilemma by asking what it means to come to a language through violent histories in the colonial centre (Perec), on its peripheries (Chamoiseau), and outside its national territories (Nabokov). It seeks to interrogate the links between France, the French and the Francophone by foregrounding the processes by which each author comes to the language in which he writes, the same processes which challenge the contemporary critic to find ways of reading beyond and across national boundaries: modernity's histories of travel. In doing so, it experiments with modes of reading which understand the Francophone as referring to 'linguistic contact zones all over the world in which French, or some kind of French, is one of the languages in play', and it sees hexagonal France as one of those 'linguistic contact zones'.[20] In an investigation which takes me into French-language literary space, but also through it and beyond it, I ask: how are lives shaped by histories of displacement written, and how should they be read? I engage with the challenge posed by questions of mobility to literary study, not by constructing an all-embracing category for writing arising from histories of travel, nor by zooming in to consider individual texts in a local context. Rather, I experiment with modes of reading attentive to the multiple, imbricated memories of mobility which criss-cross French-language literature and reverberate beyond it.

★ ★ ★ ★ ★

Multiple meanings are at play in the word 'mobility'. Like the journey begun by the child opening the books, travel can be both freeing and oppressive. A person's forced movement from one place to another is a visible sign of his or her subjection at another's hands, but chosen forms of travel can be one of the fullest expressions of freedom. To engage with the challenge posed by questions of mobility to literary study, the critic must think through the relationship of literature to travel as gain and travel as loss. When scholars debate the possibility of representing experiences of mobility within literary texts, the distinction between travel as gain and travel at loss is often at play. George Steiner argues that a writer who has had to change language at some point in his lifetime can represent the losses of the many people forced to leave their homes in recent history. He offers Nabokov as an example:

> It seems proper that those who create art in a civilization of quasi-barbarism which has made so many homeless, which has torn up tongues and peoples by the root, should themselves be poets unhoused and wanderers across language. Eccentric, aloof, nostalgic, deliberately untimely as he aspires to be and so often is, Nabokov remains, by virtue of his extraterritoriality, profoundly of our time, and one of its spokesmen.[21]

Edward Said disagrees with Steiner's view of Nabokov as a representative figure. He argues that only travel as freedom can be expressed through literary forms and that travel as loss is by definition unrepresentable:

> To understand exile as a contemporary political punishment it is necessary to map territories of experience beyond those mapped by literature. It is necessary to set aside Nabokov and Joyce and even Conrad who wrote of exile with such pathos, but of exile without cause or rationale. Think instead of the uncountable masses for whom UN agencies have been created, of refugees without urbanity, with only ration cards and agency numbers.[22]

Caren Kaplan sounds a note of caution about this division between travel as gain (literary) and travel as loss (non-literary). She argues that by suggesting that the experiences of mass displacement or migration are 'irrecoverable', Said actually participates in the silencing he identifies.[23]

At its heart, this debate is about the relationship of lived experience to the literary, the kinds of communities created by reading and writing, and the articulation or suppression of other voices within a literary text. These are the questions that are present when the child opens the books from the wardrobe, and the critic must think through them to develop a way of reading this moment. Because the three texts which are the subject of this study, Vladimir Nabokov's *Speak, Memory: An Autobiography Revisited*, Georges Perec's *W ou le souvenir d'enfance*, and Patrick Chamoiseau's *Une enfance créole* fall within the autobiographical genre, they offer a rich corpus for thinking through these problems. All autobiographers face the question of whether and how lived experience can be faithfully narrated through literary forms. The lived experience of these writers is shaped by histories of displacement, so each tussles with the points of contact and severance between mobility and the literary medium. They look in two directions, as each looks back towards one linguistic community but is read in another. Addressing the readership then involves reflection on the risks and rewards of portraying one cultural community to another. This study draws out ideas about mobility, literary community and others' voices that emerge from readings of Nabokov, Perec, and Chamoiseau and seeks to move from them to develop new ways of reading that grapple with the challenge of mobility to the idea of a national literature.

Two ideas lie behind my approach. The first is that the question of language change is also a question of a relationship between a speaker and a listener. To shift from one language to another is to trigger a shift in the persons one can address, and the way one can address them. In the case of these authors, meditating on language change involves thinking through a changing relationship to their communities of origin, and in particular changes in the linguistic life of the family between one generation and the next. These authors remember the languages of the familial past and mourn the passing of the parents who were, or would have been, the author's interlocutors in a language he has left behind. Writing in the elegiac mode involves giving the absent loved one a voice within a text addressed to a linguistic community of which s/he was not a part. My emphasis on parental voices is influenced by John Paul Eakin's argument for attention to the role of the 'proximate other' in autobiographical texts. Eakin uses this term to refer to a close friend or family member, (usually the latter) who plays an important role in an autobiography.[24] Eakin's emphasis on the importance of such figures is part of a broader movement in autobiographical criticism away from seeing the genre as a privileged space for the portrayal of the sovereign self and towards attention to the interstices of self and other in life-writing. The relationship between the author and his proximate others is decisive in understanding the linguistic dynamics of the texts under discussion, because each author speaks a different language to his parents. In each case, the space between self and proximate other is also a transitional current between one language and culture and another. If, as Eakin convincingly argues, selfhood emerges in relationship, what kind of selfhood emerges in the relationship between two or more languages?

The second idea behind my approach is that language change does not emerge in a vacuum, but is brought about by history. In this I follow Edward Said, who writes, 'Modern exile is irremediably secular and unbearably historical. It is produced by human beings for other human beings'.[25] Though only Nabokov fits the definition of an exile, the language change that echoes through each author's life is certainly produced by human beings. The sense of history as a lacerating force is present in all three texts, from Nabokov's 'fool-made history' to Perec's 'l'Histoire avec sa grande hache' to the schoolmaster's whips in Chamoiseau's texts, which are given names drawn from French official history.[26] When these authors respond to language change, they must also write about the histories that brought it about. In fact, the writing of each autobiography can be seen as a kind of wresting of speech from 'l'Histoire avec sa grande hache', a creative search for a linguistic mode where the past's presence can be articulated in the aftermath of silencing histories. To seek to understand the ways in which these texts situate themselves in relation to the idea of a national language or national literary community involves studying the particular ways in which each man's approach to these questions is interwoven with a response to violent histories.

My reader at this point might wish to object that the particular violent histories which make the question of language a painful one for each author are very different in scope, duration and date. In particular, a comparative approach to the Holocaust might seem to be problematic ethically. My examination of the ways in which the Russian Revolution and Second World War, the Holocaust and French imperialism inflect these three authors' conceptions of the link between language, nation and literary community is not intended to establish any kind of equivalency between the very different histories each author experiences. This study is based on the belief that modes of comparison are possible where respect is retained for irreducible difference. Moreover, the history of thought on the Holocaust suggests that refusals of comparison can be implicated in the minimization of historical violence just as much as commitments to comparison. On a conceptual level, situating the Holocaust as a historical event entirely unlike any other works to remove it from the sphere of history. It becomes a kind of transcendental evil, a view which discourages investigation of its historical causes.[27] This conceptual move does not in fact end comparative approaches to the Holocaust, but rather situates it as the genocide against which all others must be judged. Objections to comparative approaches to the Holocaust rely on what Michael Rothberg has called the 'zero sum' approach to memory, which says that to remember one event is necessarily to diminish the supply of attention available for another.[28] As we touched on briefly above, each of these authors is committed to a comparatist approach to the historical violence which inflects his literary language. By comparing the long resonances of imperialism and the Second World War in each author's life, this study is faithful to the links set up between these histories in each text.

Each author is at a different generational distance from the history which makes the question of literary language and community problematic. As well as this, the kind of community these authors belong to and their relationship to literary language differs greatly. Nabokov was in his early forties when he made the definitive move into the English language. He had had a whole career as a Russian-language author, publishing eight novels as well as poetry, theatre and literary criticism. The whole of his career as a Russian-language author took place outside Russia in the Russian émigré literary community with its centres in Berlin and Paris. His move into English was triggered by the definitive blow dealt to this community by the outbreak of the Second World War. This move was not inevitable; Nabokov also experimented with writing in French in the same period when he first began writing seriously in English. He was able to do so because he had heard, spoken and written French and English from his earliest childhood. As well as employing native speakers of French and English as governesses, his family spoke French and English amongst themselves. In the original French piece on his Swiss governess, Nabokov writes that French was passed on from father to son in his family, and in the English-language autobiography he writes that his uncle's French was much better than his Russian.[29] Nabokov's forays into writing French and English in his late thirties speak of the cosmopolitan privilege of his upbringing as a 'perfectly normal trilingual child in a house with a large library'.[30]

This cosmopolitan upbringing resonates through his relationship to the historical events which led to his move away from writing in Russian. These historical events came in two swathes: the first began with the October Revolution in 1917; the second in the 1930s with Hitler's rise to power. The new Bolshevik state opposed all forms of anti-autocratic politics but its own, which put Nabokov's father, a leader of the Constitutional Democratic party, in danger, and so the family fled their home in Petrograd for the Crimea. Early in 1919 it became apparent that it, too, was no longer safe in the face of the advancing Bolshevik army, and they left Russia entirely for Western Europe. Nabokov completed a degree in French and Russian at the University of Cambridge while his family set up home in Berlin, where his father was killed by a right-wing Russian monarchist in 1922. From 1922 Nabokov lived in Berlin and was part of the thriving literary scene of the Russian émigré community. He married Véra Slonim in 1925 and they had a son, Dmitri, in 1934. Hitler's rise to power made the Nabokov family situation in Berlin increasingly dangerous, as Nabokov's wife Véra was Jewish, and he began to look for a way out. The family moved first to France and then, in May 1940, shortly after the Nazi invasion, to America.

As an adult, Nabokov consciously experienced the histories which led him to stop writing in his native tongue. This is true both for his departure from Russia aged nineteen and for his departure from Russia Abroad aged forty-one. Nabokov constantly opposes the material losses he experienced through his exile from Russia to the aesthetic, intellectual and psychological gains it brought. His ability to move freely in language and literature mitigates against the force of the moves from one place to another he felt compelled to make. In this he appears to fit within Kaplan's definition of a Euro-American modernist writer as someone who experiences exile as a paradoxical form of aesthetic gain and is 'nostalgic about an irreparable loss and separation from the familiar or beloved'.[31] In fact, Nabokov unites these two facets of Euro-American modernism when he writes of nostalgia as 'a peculiarly fertile emotion', which he can draw on to create works of fiction.[32] Nabokov's writing explores a mode of migration which is intimately connected with creativity, with linguistic and psychological enrichment and with full consciousness of the histories which bring about the migration.

Georges Perec explores the afterlives of a very different mode of migration. In May 1940, when the Nabokov family boarded the Champlain for America, Georges Perec was four years old, living with his parents in Paris, both immigrants from Eastern Europe who had met in the city. Unlike Nabokov, Perec's literary career was conducted almost entirely in Paris and in the French language. Like Nabokov, Perec would have heard languages other than French during his early childhood, but in contrast to the Russian-American writer, Perec's early experience of other languages did not lead to an adult ability to speak or write in those languages. Where Nabokov's multilingual childhood environment arose from privilege and offered him resources when twentieth-century history scattered his first literary community, Perec's relationship to the languages of the family past is marked by dispossession. Unlike Nabokov, who as a child learned to speak French and English, two imperial languages with global reach, the languages Perec heard, Polish, Yiddish and Hebrew, were the languages of migrant communities with marginalized places within the nation-state. This marginalization was part of Perec's family history and had played a role in bringing both of his parents from an increasingly hostile Eastern Europe to Paris.

Perec's father died in 1940 fighting as a foreign soldier in the French Army. Three years later, Perec's mother was interned in Drancy and then deported to Auschwitz. In an irony Perec brings out in his autobiography, her journey towards her death was also a journey back to the country where she had been born.[33] Perec was four when his father died and six when his mother was deported to Auschwitz. He was still living in Paris at the time of his father's death, but when his mother was interned he was living in Villard-de-Lans in the Dauphiné, where he had been sent as part of a Red Cross evacuation. He joined members of his extended family who had also fled there to escape the dangers of Paris, and was under the care of his father's sister, Esther. As a child during the war, he was not fully conscious of the history he was living through. A persistent uncertainty about his mother's fate complicated the process of telling her son the news of her probable death. This shadowy form of knowledge of his mother's death continues in a way into the author's adulthood, as an absence of accurate record of the circumstances of her death, and the fact that she does not have a grave, means her death can never be known fully. There are more details available about Perec's father's death, and the author's visit to his father's grave is presented as a moment which allows him some relief from the previously unnameable quality of his grief.[34] Nonetheless, the author has very few memories of his father, and his narration of them retains a quality of melancholic frustration over his inability to call his father to mind accurately. In sharp contrast to Nabokov, then, Perec's relationship to the historical events which shape his family history is haunted by an awareness of the inadequacy of an individual memory in the face of the destructive power of twentieth-century history. From the publication of his first novel in 1965 to the posthumous publication of the novel he was writing when he died in 1982, much of Perec's work can be read as an exploration of what it means to create and inhabit communities of memory.

In 1966, when Perec published his second work, *Quel petit vélo à guidon chromé*, a comic engagement with the recently ended Algerian War of Independence, Chamoiseau was only thirteen, and beginning to feel the full force of French imperialism in another guise. He was a child when he began to make the transition from Creole to French, which came when he entered the French education system. He remembers this transition, but did not choose it, and as a child could not have been consciously aware of the history and politics which brought it about. Much of his literary work, however, is an exploration of this history and the ways in which it resonates in the life of an individual in community. His three-volume autobiography, *Une enfance créole*, is part of this exploration. The first volume, *Antan d'enfance,* was published in 1990, followed in 1994 by *Chemin-d'école*. The trilogy was completed in 2005 by *À bout d'enfance*. The trilogy gestures towards the child's place in Caribbean history by setting up a series of echoes between moments of cultural and linguistic change brought about by colonial history of Martinique. Thinking through the child's shift from Creole to French becomes a way of thinking through the economic and social changes which followed 1946, when Martinique became a French *département*. Chamoiseau sees this moment as a trigger for greater Martinican assimilation to French ways of living. He also reaches further back beyond 1946 to connect the imposition of French in school with older forms of colonial violence that deprive the colonized subject of a voice, and sets up oblique echoes between his experience of school and the Middle Passage. Though Chamoiseau, like Perec, writes a life lived mostly in the city where he was born, tracing his linguistic history becomes for him a way of tracing the afterlives of the 'crime fondateur' of Atlantic slavery and the colonization of Martinique.[35]

These variations in each author's linguistic history and life experiences might be seen as too great to permit a meaningful comparison. But the object of this study is not to argue that each writer's approach to language is the same; rather it is to bring out the various ways in which voices and histories lived outside France and French might be spoken through an engagement with the French literary tradition. The differences between each author's linguistic lives allow me to shed light on the multiple borders present within the French language, and to study the range of ways in which they might be crossed. The authors' different generational distances from the histories which trigger the language change they address in their writing permit an exploration of questions of inter-generational transfer of memory. The differences in the author's degrees of consciousness of the histories which led to language change offers a way into an investigation of the relationship between memory and imagination in constructing knowledge of the past.

The first half of the book draws out aspects of these authors' work which encourage a decentred approach to the connection between the French language and literary community, while the second part considers the risks and rewards of reading these authors together. The first chapter argues that each author's situation in a local literary tradition ties his life to histories of border crossing. It looks at the way each author's portrayal of his childhood home(s) roots him in a tradition which is situated at an angle to the idea of a national literary tradition. The home for each author is a place of convergence of multiple languages, histories and cultures. Changes to the home between childhood and adulthood raise questions about how to preserve memory in a context of linguistic and cultural change and point towards the problematic role of the nation-state in erasing or damaging repositories of memory. The second chapter moves on to consider in more detail the presence of multiple languages within each text. It studies the way these authors' literary practice allows other languages to echo through their written language. It looks at the range of ways in which the connections between the French language, nation and literary tradition can be complicated by lives lived across its boundaries.

Having studied the presence of multiple linguistic and cultural histories within the authors' homes and texts, the second part of the book considers comparative approaches to these authors' presentation of the resonances of modernity's histories of travel. It asks: what can comparative readings tell the critic that she could not know otherwise? What do we learn about the texts from comparative readings, and what do we learn about our own critical practice? The third chapter investigates whether the concept of trauma is valuable in reading the resonances of modernity's painful histories together. It argues that comparative readings of these texts in the light of recent debates in trauma theory have the potential to nuance those debates while illuminating the portrayal of psychic pain in each text. The fourth chapter looks at aspects of these texts which challenge the trauma paradigm, in particular its emphasis on the unknowability of traumatic events. It considers whether these texts can be read together in the light of their shared commitment to literary thinking as a form of heightened consciousness. It brings out the importance of literal and figurative modes of displacement in the genealogy of this conception of literary thinking.

I employ different methods in each chapter, and sometimes within chapters. I draw on Gaston Bachelard's writing on space when I look at these authors' depictions of childhood homes, Jean Piaget's theories of childhood consciousness when I consider their exploration of the child's mind, translation theory when I consider language, trauma theory when I look at memory, and Russian formalist literary theory when I examine the question of the literary. This methodological eclecticism is motivated by a view of comparative criticism as 'a method of using diverse methods' which is mindful of Gayatri Chakravorty Spivak's emphasis on 'nonexhaustive taxonomies' and 'provisional system making' in a comparative practice which is open to future shifts in the discipline away from European national languages.[36] Rather than assuming these texts are comparable in a certain way, I test out the kinds of comparability that arise from different modes of critical practice. As I shift between methods, I ask what each critical lens can tell us about the texts in their own right, what the kind of comparison it enables reveals about ways of creating relationships between these texts, and what such relationships say about the idea of a national literature and ways of reading beyond it. Although my methodology is inflected by the distinctive qualities of the works under discussion, because each text explores histories whose resonances are also traced by a wide range of recent authors, the ideas that arise from this study are relevant beyond the work of Nabokov, Perec and Chamoiseau. In the final, concluding, chapter I reflect on this question of moving between methods and the connections between the study of these three authors and the wider field of French Studies. This chapter returns to the question of the relationship between lived histories of displacement and literary writing in the light of the previous four chapters to establish how attention to the transcultural and translingual aspects of these texts can inform recent debates about the object of study in French studies. It argues that attention to the multiple migrations memory makes across the borders of language, self and nation into the literary text is valuable in developing ways of reading now.

Notes to the Introduction

1. *Chemin*, 198, italics in original.
2. Wendy Knepper charts the beginnings of Chamoiseau's concept of the 'émerveille' in Wendy Knepper, *Patrick Chamoiseau: A Critical Introduction* (Jackson: University Press of Mississippi, 2012), pp. 158–61.
3. *W*, 220. I use 'concentrationary' as a translation of the term deployed in David Rousset's 1946 memoir of his time as a political deportee in a Nazi camp, *L'Univers concentrationnaire*. In this I am following Griselda Pollock and Maxim Silverman, 'Series Preface', in *Concentrationary Memories: Totalitarian Resistance and Cultural Memories*, ed. by Griselda Pollock and Maxim Silverman (London: I. B. Tauris, 2014), pp. xv–xix (p. xvi), who define the term as referring to 'the political/industrial/military complex which underpins totalitarian rule', so that it embraces the camp experience while maintaining focus on the broader social structures which support the creation of the camps. I use this term to refer to Perec's depiction of the island space because at the end of *W ou le souvenir d'enfance*, Perec cites a passage from Rousset's *L'Univers concentrationnaire*, which serves to root his fictional creation in a documentary source.
4. For more on this, see Celia Britton, *Language and Literary Form in French Caribbean Writing*

(Liverpool: Liverpool University Press, 2014), pp. 61–76; Maeve McCusker, *Patrick Chamoiseau: Recovering Memory* (Liverpool: Liverpool University Press, 2007), pp. 4–6; Sara-Louise Cooper, '"Des fils invisibles nous relient": Comparative Memory in Caribbean Life-writing', *Francosphères*, 5 (2016), 29–43.
5. *A bout*, 102–03.
6. *A bout*, 141.
7. *De la mémoire obscure à la mémoire consciente* (Paris: Gallimard, 2010), p. 5
8. *SM*, 56.
9. V. Nabokoff-Sirine, 'Mademoiselle O', *Mesures*, 2 (1936), 143–72.
10. *Conclusive Evidence* (New York: Harper, 1951).
11. *Другие берега* (Ann Arbor: Ardis, 1978).
12. *Speak, Memory: An Autobiography Revisited* (London: David Campbell, 1999).
13. *Texaco* (Paris: Gallimard, 1992), p. 280.
14. *W*, 13.
15. *SM*, 206.
16. 'Introduction: What Does Littérature-monde Mean for French, Francophone and Postcolonial Studies?', in *Transnational French Studies: Postcolonialism and Littérature-monde* (Liverpool: Liverpool University Press, 2010), ed. by Alec G. Hargreaves, Charles Forsdick and David Murphy, pp. 1–11 (p. 2).
17. Here I am summarizing arguments against the term 'Francophonie' laid out in Roger Little, 'World Literature in French; or, Is Francophonie Frankly Phoney?', *European Review*, 9 (2001), 421–36.
18. Camille de Toledo, *Visiter le Flurkistan, ou, les illusions de la littérature-monde* (Paris: Presses universitaires de France, 2008); *Transnational French Studies: Postcolonialism and Littérature-monde*, ed. by Alec G. Hargreaves, Charles Forsdick and David Murphy (Liverpool: Liverpool University Press, 2010); Maria Chiara Gnocchi, 'Du Flurkistan et d'ailleurs: Les Réactions au manifeste "Pour une littérature-monde en français"', *Francofonia*, 59 (2010), 87–105.
19. Emily Apter, 'Afterword: The "World" in World Literature', in *Transnational French Studies: Postcolonialism and Littérature-monde* pp. 287–95 (p. 288).
20. Emily Apter, *The Translation Zone: A New Comparative Literature* (Princeton, NJ: Princeton University Press, 2006), p. 87.
21. George Steiner, *Extraterritorial: Papers on Literature and the Language Revolution* (London: Faber, 1972), p. 11.
22. Edward W. Said, 'The Mind of Winter: Reflections on Life in Exile', *Harper's Magazine*, September 1984, 49–55 (p. 50).
23. Caren Kaplan, *Questions of Travel: Postmodern Discourses of Displacement* (Durham, NC: Duke University Press, 1996), pp. 120–21.
24. *How Our Lives Become Stories: Making Selves* (Ithaca, NY: Cornell University Press, 1999), p. 86.
25. Said, p. 50.
26. *SM*, 240; *Chemin*, 97–98.
27. Roger Luckhurst, *The Trauma Question* (London: Routledge, 2008), pp. 65–67.
28. *Multidirectional Memory: Remembering the Holocaust in the Age of Decolonization* (Stanford: Stanford University Press, 2009), p. 3.
29. 'Mademoiselle O', p. 166; *SM*, 51.
30. *Strong Opinions* (London: Weidenfeld & Nicolson, 1974), p. 43.
31. Kaplan, p. 28.
32. *SM*, 35.
33. *W*, 53.
34. *W*, 54.
35. *De la mémoire obscure à la mémoire consciente*, p. 14; Gayatri Chakravorty Spivak, *The Wellek Library Lectures: Death of a Discipline* (New York: Columbia University Press, 2003), p. 6.
36. Xiaofan Amy Li, *Comparative Encounters between Artaud, Michaux and the Zhuangzi* (Oxford: Legenda, 2015), p. 161.

CHAPTER 1

The Portrayal of Home

This chapter examines the portrayal of childhood homes in Vladimir Nabokov's *Speak, Memory: An Autobiography Revisited*, Georges Perec's *W ou le souvenir d'enfance* and Patrick Chamoiseau's *Une enfance créole*. The particular ways in which childhood homes are portrayed are revealing of these authors' relationship to linguistic, cultural and geographical points of origin. Each author's portrayal of the buildings where he lived as a child draws attention to the histories of mobility which shape his experience of 'home'. These histories are portrayed through the material traces they leave in the buildings where the author lived and the psychic traces which inflect each author's sense of his place in the world. The childhood home acts, or at least has the potential to act, as a visible trace of the author's past. This opens up questions about the relationship between writing, memory and the physical world in each text. This relationship, in turn, inscribes the author's work within a broader, generational literary tradition of writing which explores the legacy of violent histories. The generational literary tradition to which each author belongs exists within national literary traditions but looks outwards to histories which have occurred across the borders of the nation. This chapter uses the portrayal of home as a way to explore the nuances of Nabokov's location within the Russian émigré tradition, Perec's place in the 1.5 generation and Chamoiseau's position within contemporary Caribbean writing in French.[1] Though these authors belong to very different local traditions, looking at the ways childhood homes are portrayed brings out a range of concerns common to all three: inter-generational shifts in language; their implications for the author's relationship to the previous generation; anxiety about access to the past in the aftermath of histories of state-sponsored oppression. If the portrayal of home gestures toward this common set of concerns, then the particular ways in which damage to the home is portrayed indicate the specificities of each author's engagement with this common set of issues. This chapter seeks, then, to bring out points of convergence and divergence in each author's relationship to traces of the past, in the light of painful family histories of migration and linguistic change.

Gaston Bachelard speaks of the home as 'notre premier univers'.[2] For each of these authors, the first world represented by the childhood home(s) is associated with languages different from the one each author is writing in. The departure from the childhood home is, to a certain extent, associated with a move away from the languages spoken in early childhood. Nabokov's departure from his Northern

Russian homes marks the first of multiple journeys which will lead him to write in English rather than Russian. Perec's departure from Paris and his mother marks the deepening of his loss of connection to an ancestral culture that begins with his parents' emigration from Eastern Europe.[3] When Chamoiseau leaves the intimate world of the home and enters into contact with the French state through the public education system, he discovers that Creole and French are separate languages, and that Creole is his first language, though he must speak French in school.[4] Because the author's earliest homes are associated with the language of the previous generation, returning to, or re-imagining, early homes leads to a reflection on the possibility or impossibility of return to the languages of childhood and the cultural context associated with them. As the child does not absorb a language in a vacuum, but rather learns to speak through relationships with the people around him, questions of linguistic change are also tied up with issues of inter-generational communication. The portrayal of home involves addressing the connections between linguistic change, geographical movement and changing ways of life from one generation to the next.

Broadly speaking, the figure of home is approached in two ways in these texts. Either it is evoked as seen from the outside by the adult narrator, or as experienced from within by the childhood self. The house seen from without sometimes functions as a repository of memory. Where this is the case, relationships of analogy or contrast can be drawn between the author's mind and the house as two sources of memory in the text. Images of homes as repositories of memory also call up metaphors of entry, exclusion and the crossing of boundaries. The presence of the author on the threshold of childhood dwelling-places, unwilling or unable to enter, occurs in some way in all three authors' work. Such images dramatize tensions present in the autobiographical enterprise, where the author seeks imaginative re-entry into spaces inhabited by the child-self, a quest complicated in these cases by linguistic and spatial change. As well as acting as a vessel which contains traces of the past, the childhood home itself is sometimes portrayed as a trace. In this case, its depiction sparks reflection on the interaction between interior, psychological traces of the past and its exterior, material remnants. The particular relationship constructed between interior and exterior traces of the past inscribes each author's work within a generational literary tradition.

Nabokov's text can be read alongside other autobiographical writing by authors born at the turn of the century whose work records the upheaval of the Revolution and the subsequent development of Russian literary life outside Russia. The trope of turning away from the material world and relying on the inner resources of memory and imagination recurs across this body of texts.[5] Reliance on the portable traces preserved by the mind becomes a matter of necessity in the context of the rapid change in post-revolutionary Russia and of the difficulties of returning after emigration. Nabokov's turn inwards has been read as part of a modernist focus on the psychological and aesthetic effects of displacement and a retreat from a consideration of its historical causes and consequences.[6] Yet a close reading of the portrayal of homes in these texts calls into question this interpretation, situating the boundaries of the home as a filter which allows the absorption of both beauty and violence into the self.

Perec has been identified as part of the 1.5 generation, the generation who were children during the Second World War and Holocaust, but little extended work has been done on how his work fits within this generation.[7] This chapter explores his place within this body of texts, beginning with his portrayal of home. Perec's narrative of his childhood, like that of other writers of the 1.5 generation, involves multiple moves between different dwelling-places, in an attempt to avoid deportation. These physical moves are often accompanied by changes of name and assumed identities. The place of deceptive narrations at the heart of family identity is reflected in the portrayal of domestic spaces. These become places where the child moves between different identities, rather than stable signifiers of a unitary identity and past.[8] The return to pre-war homes, like the movements between different dwelling-places during the war, is also associated with the painful grafting on of identity. Where one or both parents have been killed during the war, going back home involves the realization that the parent will not return. The return to the domestic space is thus associated with the period when the temporary absence of the parent or parents begins to take on a permanent quality.[9] This also leads to a recomposition of family dynamics through adoption, or remarriage by the surviving parent, so that the child takes on a new role within the family.[10] In this way, the portrayal of home locates loss and shifting identity at the origins of the individual's life. It draws attention to the unreliability of internal traces of the past as it brings out the child's confusion over the different places he lived during the war. Material traces of the past are no more promising than mental record; former homes tend to be figured as mute or unreliable witnesses to the past, in this way mirroring the often absent or distorted record of the parent's deportation.

Maeve McCusker and Louise Hardwick have convincingly argued for the place of Chamoiseau's autobiographical trilogy within a late twentieth-century 'boom' in life-writing in the French-speaking Caribbean.[11] McCusker writes that the recent coincidence of several historical anniversaries, such as the 'discovery' of the Caribbean and the abolition of slavery, led to a reflection on questions of individual and historical memory amongst contemporary authors.[12] McCusker and Hardwick also identify the autobiographical trilogy as a contribution to the *créolité* project elaborated by Chamoiseau along with Raphaël Confiant and Jean Bernabé in 1989.[13] The three writers advocate the rediscovery of an interior view of Antillean culture and an appreciation of its interwoven African, Asian and European strands. Chamoiseau's depiction of his childhood home acts as a way of exploring the specificities of Creole modes of dwelling in the world. The home's porous boundaries come to stand for the passages between self and world, interior and exterior that Chamoiseau suggests are characteristic of Creole culture. There is a twilight quality about Chamoiseau's evocation of the old house as an artefact of Creole culture. A parallel is drawn between the growing rarity of the old wooden houses and the child's increasing assimilation to French culture. The text thus suggests that the disappearance of external traces of the past goes hand in hand with the diminishing presence of Creole culture in the inner world of Martinique's inhabitants. Its lament over the destruction of external traces of the past also functions as a way of pointing toward cultural and economic changes that have taken place in Martinique in the last fifty years.

Though the portrayal of houses where the author lived as a child does allow an exploration of contrasts between material traces of the past (or their absence) and interior, psychic traces, the figure of the home is valuable precisely because it complicates the boundaries between the material and the psychological, interior and exterior, self and world. Bachelard speaks of the home as 'le non-moi qui protège le moi', drawing out the role of the home as a place where the boundaries of the self are both established and crossed.[14] Because the home is often the scene of the first contact between self and other, portrayals of the child-self within the home act as ways of exploring the early relationship established between the child and the surrounding world. Though not the case in Perec's text, in Nabokov and Chamoiseau's work, the interior space of the home is figured as secure to a certain extent. Here, the walls of the home exclude the more threatening aspects of the outside world and with these aspects excluded, the walls of the self soften to allow it to fuse with others and the world. The interior space of the home becomes the scene of fusion between the self and the mother, the natural world, and beauty in various forms. Portraying the home then becomes a way of evoking the open-ended boundaries of the self.

It is the protective walls of the home which create the possibility of the self's fusion with the proximate other, if it does occur. Because of this, any threat or damage to the walls of the home, and the accompanying loss of protection from the dangers of the outside world, carries much weight. The significance of breached boundaries varies depending on the meaning given to the domestic interior. The inner space of the home can be mapped on to a range of different spaces; it can act as a kind of extended version of the child's inner world or of the artist's mind, a larger version of the maternal body or a smaller version of the nation. These images can be read as representations of the place of histories of violence within the 'premier univers', the intimate world of the family, the self and the first language(s). Looking at the particular kinds of incursion into the protective space of the home, or at the absence of protection within the home, offers a way of distinguishing between the different places given to the legacy of violent histories in each author's narration of his life.

The Adult Narrator on the Threshold of the Childhood Home(s)

The Nabokov family homes, one on Morskaya Street in St Petersburg, and three family estates just south of St Petersburg, Vyra, Batovo and Rozhestveno, play an important role in *Speak, Memory*. While working to create a full-length autobiographical work from a series of short sketches, Nabokov thought about entitling the work 'The House Was Here', and wrote a foreword which begins with those words. The Vladimir Nabokov Papers in the Library of Congress preserve this discarded foreword, which I will study here as it concentrates aspects of the relationship between physical place, memory and history that run throughout the text. This brief piece of prose features an imagined return to what used to be Morskaya Street, re-named Herzen Street during the Soviet period. There, Nabokov and his companion, Hopkinson, look briefly at the author's former home before turning and fleeing the suspicious look of a passer-by. Although Nabokov chose not to use the foreword, the image of the house seen from without recurs in the last version of the autobiography, which features a photograph of 47 Morskaya Street taken in 1955 by Andrew Field.[15] The photograph is accompanied by a long caption which revives and reshapes elements of the discarded foreword. Looking at the relationship between the two pieces of text allows an exploration of the role Nabokov gives to material traces of the past compared to images of the past which are generated by the mind.

This is the discarded foreword:

> The house was here. Right here. I never imagined the place would have changed so completely since nineteen seventeen. How dreadful, I don't recognize a thing. No use walking any farther. Sorry, Hopkinson, to have made you come such a long way. I had been looking forward to a perfect orgy of nostalgia and recognition! That man over there seems to be growing suspicious. Talk to him. Turistï Amerikantsi. You surely know the Russian for ghost. *Mechta* [Dream]. *Prizrak* [Ghost]. *Metafizicheçky kapitalist* [Metaphysical capitalist]. Run, Hopkinson![16]

The foreword draws attention to the narrator's position outside the place where he lived as a child and, by implication, outside the past the text seeks to evoke. The two men, are, of course, physically outside the house, but the use of the emphatically non-Russian name 'Hopkinson', the mention of ghosts and Nabokov's new American nationality, and the fear of the local passer-by all mark the description of the scene as conducted from the point of view of someone who is now, perforce, a foreigner.

The references to ghosts and dreams also suggest subjective modes of vision and the presence of the mind without the body. The foreword serves, then, to remind the reader that Nabokov's return to Russia can only be accomplished through memory or imagination. By situating this passage on the threshold of the text as a whole, Nabokov would have been gesturing towards a point he makes in other ways in the body of the autobiography, which is that a blend of memory and imagination are more valuable than physical presence for revisiting the past. The retreat from the house signals a dismissal of the value of external traces of the past and a privileging of the traces it leaves on the mind. The foreword also serves another, political, purpose. It marks the author's presence outside the past, outside Russia and the Russian language, but it also marks the speaker's distance from the values of the Soviet state. The two men's fear of the suspicious passer-by evokes the pervasive sense of danger that comes with being in a place where ordinary-looking people could be informers. The preface's ending could be seen as a kind of re-enactment of the author's original flight from Petrograd and then Russia in the period after the October Revolution, and an affirmation of the necessity of that choice. In the foreword, precisely what the two men fear is left unarticulated, but it suggests that contemporary Leningrad is not very much safer than the Petrograd Nabokov and his family left behind.

In particular, the portrayal of the street is deployed as part of a mini-polemic against the Soviet state in the caption to a photograph of the St Petersburg house in the final, revised edition of the English text. The re-naming of the street from Morskaya to Herzen provides a focus for this contestation. In the Russian version of the autobiography, Nabokov only refers briefly to this name-change, writing of another street, 'куда вливается удивлённый Герцен' [into which runs a surprised Herzen Street].[17] Presumably he trusts the Russian-speaking reader to understand the reason for Herzen's surprise. He leaves nothing to chance with the English-speaking reader, however. In the caption to the 1955 photograph of his house he writes that it is taken in 'St Petersburg, now Leningrad, 47, Morskaya, now Hertzen street'. He then gives a brief biography of Herzen: 'Aleksander Ivanovich Hertzen (1812–1870) was a famous liberal (whom this commemoration by a police state would hardly have gratified).'[18] He goes on to say that Herzen's memoir was one of his father's favourite books. Laurence Petit has written of the 'power struggle' that takes place between the photographs and their captions in *Speak, Memory*, as the two compete for the role of authoritative guide to the past.[19] What is being contested in the relationship set up between the image of Nabokov's house and the caption which describes it is the inheritance of the legacy of Russian liberalism. Nabokov here wrests this legacy from the Soviet state, drawing attention to the gap between Herzen's liberalism and the repressive tactics of the contemporary Russian state. His mention of his father's admiration for Herzen's memoir also suggests that Vladimir Dmitrievich Nabokov is a more fitting heir to the Russian liberal tradition.

In *La Chambre claire*, Roland Barthes famously speaks of photography as an indexical trace of the past, comparable to a fingerprint or a footprint. According to this view, the photograph is created through the impression of light rays from a given object or person on chemical substances.[20] The photograph, then, acts as a material trace of the presence of an object or a person in the world. Nabokov's caption to the photograph of his house suggests that such material traces are less valuable than the internal traces of the past the author carries within his own mind. Nabokov uses the caption to correct elements of the photograph, nudging the reader to picture instead the image he holds in his mind: 'The lindens lining the street did not exist. Those green upstarts now hide the second-floor east-corner window of the room where I was born.'[21] The way Nabokov brings the photograph into line with his own internal image of the house could be seen as part of the turn away from the material and toward the individual and psychological that is argued to be characteristic of modernist writing on displacement.[22] Put together with the comments on the re-naming of the street, however, it begins to appear in a different light. Nabokov's critical use of the material trace of the photograph as a way into the past reflects the fact that material traces can obscure as much as they reveal, just as the trees hide the room where he was born and the naming of the street after a famous Russian liberal hides the state's eviction of another representative of the liberal tradition from the house on Morskaya Street. Nabokov's privileging of the internal and the psychological thus appears not as a turn away from the political or the historical, but is itself a political gesture, which draws attention to the deceptive quality of material traces of the past, especially when manipulated by the state.

Perec

There is also a political edge to Perec's portrayal of the relationship between his own memories and the house where he lived with his parents in early childhood, but in most other ways, Perec's text constructs a very different relationship between external and internal traces of the past from that found in *Speak, Memory*. Unlike Nabokov and Chamoiseau, Perec's autobiographical text does not portray his childhood home as a repository of memory. It is not connected with a specific family history; rather its depiction evokes the anonymity of his family history, its absence, or very faint presence, in the external world. Whereas Nabokov constructs a relationship of contrast between deceptive material traces of the past and the more accurate record of it preserved through imagination and memory, Perec establishes a relationship of analogy between external and internal remnants of the past, both of which are presented as potentially unreliable and subject to gradual erosion as well as wilful destruction.

The tenth chapter of *W ou le souvenir d'enfance* opens with a description of the rue Vilin where Perec lived with his parents, grandparents and aunt before he was evacuated to Villard-de-Lans in 1942. The rue Vilin was a place of work as well as his family's home, as his grandparents ran a grocer's shop nearby and his mother had a hairdressing business on the street.[23] Perec's description of the street brings it into dialogue with other sites of memory, both topographical and textual. The interaction between different sites of memory is an abiding concern in Perec's wider work. In *Espèces d'espaces*, a collection of essays on space, Perec writes that part of the reason for his interest in space is the lack of geographical continuity in his family history.[24] The essay evokes the absence of containing spaces of memory brought about by his family's moves from Eastern Europe to France, and his subsequent moves within France during the war. In *Ellis Island*, the text of the script Perec wrote to accompany a film about the immigration centre, he writes that the island is 'le lieu d'une autobiographie probable', further developing the theme of aleatory family geography.[25] *Ellis Island* dwells on the nature of 'le non-lieu, le nulle part', analysing the nature of the space between departure from one's former home and arrival in a new country.[26]

This interstitial position can be mapped on to the experience of the 1.5 generation, whose childhood coincides with the space between pre- and post-war periods. Because growing up during the war often involved multiple moves, a questioning, unsettled approach to space is often expressed by members of this generation. Anne Whitehead quotes Geoffrey Hartman, who was sent from Germany to England on one of the children's transports, and who went on to live in America, as saying, 'An organic relation to place is what I lacked and would never recover.'[27] Dan Bar-On, who was born in Haifa to parents who had emigrated from Germany, also speaks of 'a sense of being uprooted', shared by his generation of Israeli children of European parents.[28] It is worth noting that Perec does express a sense of familiarity with Paris in *Espèces d'espaces*, writing that he would have trouble getting lost there even if he tried because he knows its metro and bus routes so well.[29] Though this indicates knowledge of the city, it nonetheless suggests a connection to place through movement rather than rootedness. Having invoked the image of metro and bus routes as a sign of his knowledge of the city, Perec goes on to make the comment, 'le nom des rues ne m'est presque jamais étranger' [the name of the streets is almost never unknown to me].[30] This 'presque' calls up the remark in *W ou le souvenir d'enfance* where Perec says that for most of his youth he could not have placed the street where his parents lived on a map and would have looked for it near the wrong metro station.[31] Another echo between *Espèces d'espaces* and *W ou le souvenir d'enfance* adds a note of irony to *Espèces d'espaces*' expression of intimacy with Paris. In *Espèces d'espaces*, Perec writes: 'j'identifie sans trop de peine les églises et autres monuments; je sais où sont les gares'.[32] This placing of 'gares' and 'monuments' next to each other echoes Perec's return to Paris after his evacuation when he asks his aunt and uncle what the name of the monument is, only to be told that he is not at a monument but at the gare de Lyon.[33] Perec's confusion can be read as an oblique reference to the fact that the gare de Lyon was the last place he saw his mother.[34] Through the comments in *Espèces d'espaces* on the author's close knowledge of Paris run echoes of allusions to grief-stricken disorientation in the same city. Though Perec spends almost his whole life in Paris, his relationship to it is inflected by his childhood return to his mother's absence there.

Perec's interest in the spaces his parents inhabited with him is apparent in the unfinished *Lieux* project, parts of which are incorporated into *W ou le souvenir d'enfance*.[35] This project involved him visiting places which had some kind of significance in his life over the course of twelve years and jotting down what he saw. One of the places was the rue Vilin. Because the houses on the rue Vilin were demolished over the years that Perec pursued the *Lieux* project, his notes record its gradual destruction. The autobiography devotes most space to an image of the street where most of the houses have been demolished. Like Nabokov, then, Perec presents a contemporary image of his former home where it has greatly changed. Whereas Nabokov is able to dismiss the newer version of his childhood home, impressing upon the reader that his memory of it is the more important image, there is no sense of connection between Perec and the rue Vilin. Recalling a visit there in the early sixties, he writes: 'La rue n'évoqua en moi aucun souvenir précis, à peine la sensation d'une familiarité possible.'[36] He mixes up the buildings, not recognizing the one where he lived, in strong contrast with Nabokov who still recalls the exact room of the house where he was born.[37]

There is a desolate quality to Perec's description of the street, which is in the process of being demolished by the time he is writing the autobiography:

> La rue Vilin est aujourd'hui aux trois quarts détruite. Plus de la moitié des maisons ont été abattues, laissant place à des terrains vagues où s'entassent des détritus, de vieilles cuisinières et des carcasses de voitures; la plupart des maisons encore debout n'offrent plus que des façades aveugles.[38]
>
> [Today, Rue Vilin has been three-quarters demolished. More than half the houses have been razed, leaving waste ground, piling up with rubbish, with old cookers and wrecked cars; most of the houses still standing are boarded up.]

Bachelard writes that a lighted window evokes a benevolent human presence; here the boarded-up windows suggest the solitude of Perec's quest to make sense of his past, and the failure of the buildings to speak of the past.³⁹ The 'terrains vagues' created by the crumbling walls of the home give the reader a sense of the destruction of the protective qualities of a sealed domestic space, which have been swept away by a history of violence which abolishes distinctions between public and private.

The desolation of the scene can also be read as a way of evoking the destruction of many of the traces of his mother's life. It is possible to read his account of his return to the rue Vilin as a kind of attempted replacement for the impossible visit to his mother's grave, whose absence has been described in the previous autobiographical chapter.⁴⁰ The reference to the inscription 'Coiffure Dames' above the door where his mother used to work provides support for this reading.⁴¹ It is one of the few physical traces in the text of his mother's life, and the only one of her working life. It can be read as a kind of headstone, which, in the absence of a more ordinary grave, marks the fact that she lived and died. There is further evidence for this reading in the notes from the *Lieux* project which form the basis of this passage in the autobiography. They record Perec's sighting of a piece of graffiti which reads 'Travail=Torture', an inversion of the infamous motto above the gates of Auschwitz. Perec also writes that the road takes the shape of a stretched-out S, like that found in the SS sign.⁴² This observation is preserved in the autobiography, though it is made less explicit.⁴³ Read in this way, traces of the violent history which leads to the murder of Perec's mother are written into the street, and Perec's return to it is a return to a site which can be mapped on to the sites of the Nazi genocide and the likely location of his mother's remains.

If we read the rue Vilin as a kind of prosthetic final resting place for Perec's mother, then the way it is destroyed has implications for attitudes toward the various sources and traces of memory in Perec's text. Nabokov's house remains standing, but is adapted for new uses by the Bolshevik state; Perec's childhood home is simply demolished as part of a routine project of urban development. It is a gradual process whose progress is recorded over the years Perec continues with the *Lieux* project and it is integrated into the everyday life of the street. Perec's portrayal of the destruction of his childhood home thus suggests that the erasure of traces of the past is part of the quotidian, and that the interaction between humans and the world routinely produces and reinforces a diminished awareness of the past and its traces in the present. The text then unsettles any faith in the physical world as a reliable record of the past, or as a trigger for the reactivation of internal traces of the past. There is a hint, too, that the state is implicated in this everyday erasure. The demolition of the buildings is planned and carried out by local authorities, and can be read as a further step in the process of obscuring traces of Perec's mother's life and death that begins with the belated and inaccurate record of her death.⁴⁴

Looking at Perec's fictional work points up the political elements present in the depiction of the rue Vilin. In particular, Perec's 1978 novel, *La Vie mode d'emploi*, where each chapter deals with one room in a Parisian apartment block, brings out the connection between projects of urban renewal and the erasure of traces of the past. The building which gives the novel its structure is 11, rue Simon-Crubellier, and it is to be demolished and replaced by a hotel and leisure complex. As Lisa Villeneuve notes, this aspect of the novel's plot reflects the state-led drive for modernization of

French cities from the 1960s onwards, which led to widespread demolition of older buildings in Paris and other cities.[45] We can see the autobiography as depicting the aftermath of one such project of demolition, while the novel deals with the run-up to a similar project. Though *La Vie mode d'emploi* is fictional, Perec links it with contemporary building policy and practice through an allusion to Pompidou's 'Sixième Plan' for urban renewal.[46] The anticipation of the building's destruction strongly echoes the autobiographical description of the rue Vilin:

> Un à un les magasins fermeront et ne seront pas remplacés, une à une les fenêtres des appartements devenus vacants seront murées et les planchers défoncés pour décourager les squatters et les clochards. La rue ne sera plus qu'une suite de façades aveugles.[47]
>
> [One by one the shops will close and will not be replaced, one by one the windows of the newly vacant flats will be boarded up and the flooring will be torn up to discourage squatters and tramps. The street will be just a series of boarded up houses.]

The phrase 'façades aveugles' is also used in the description of the rue Vilin quoted earlier. The lack of human sympathy such images suggest is made clearer here through the references to the exclusion of squatters and tramps. *La Vie mode d'emploi* makes more explicit the idea implicit in the autobiography that the destruction of older Parisian buildings erases the histories of ordinary people and is driven by utilitarian and commercial concerns. Villeneuve cites Perec's use of advertising copy in the following passage as an example of the way the demolition of the building is associated with an impersonal, commercial view of human living spaces. The room in question belongs to a character in the novel who is a master puzzle-maker and who shares the name of the protagonist of the fictional W story. Since Winckler spends his days creating intricate puzzle pieces, each one unique, it is ironic that his own living space will be reduced to a homogenous, commercial model evoked in the truncated language of advertising copy: 'bientôt, le vieil appartement deviendra un coquet logement, double liv. + ch., cft., vue, calme'. [48]

In both the novel and the autobiography, the buildings which maintain a record of lives absent from official history do not last. There is some suggestion that writing or other forms of art might become counterweights to such destruction, but both texts undermine any unquestioning faith in such a substitution of the textual for the topographical. In one of *La Vie mode d'emploi*'s many uses of *mise en abyme*, the author's depiction of the people who live in the building echoes that of another artist-figure within the text. The painter Valène, who informs the reader that the building will be destroyed, plans to paint it and all its inhabitants, but he dies leaving an empty canvas.[49] This episode discourages optimism about the ability of art to preserve traces of the past when they disappear from the material world. A similar circumspection emerges from the incorporation of Perec's notes on the rue Vilin for the *Lieux* project into *W ou la souvenir d'enfance*. Though the notes record times when the street still had working houses and businesses on it, Perec chooses in the autobiography to focus on the image of the street almost entirely demolished, as if to suggest that the textual evocation of places associated with the past is no substitute for their presence. Writing could even contribute to the loss of memory created by demolition projects, as the *Lieux* notes suggest when a resident mistakes Perec's jottings in his notebook for the work of a building official and asks, 'Alors, vous êtes venu nous détruire? [So, you've come to demolish us?]'[50]

Perec then, like Nabokov, engages with the afterlife of his childhood home as a way of illustrating problems involved in using material remnants of the past as a trigger for memory. For both authors, the current situation of the childhood home serves to illustrate the author's distance from his past rather than fostering any sense of renewed connection to it, and both authors hint at the role of the state in distorting or removing elements of the physical world which could testify to the past. Unlike Nabokov, however, Perec does not have a tenacious inner image of the past with which to counteract its deceptive external traces. Though there are parallels between internal and external landscapes of memory, as both are riddled with gaps, the relationship between the two is distanced. Where there is a sense of connection between Nabokov's memories of his home and the 1955 photograph, even if it is one of hostility, in Perec's text the encounter with the current state of the home simply serves to confirm the difficulty of recovering the childhood world, gesturing toward the erasure of its remnants in his own mind, in the material world and in official records of the past. The text hovers between portraying such erasure as anonymous and routine and suggesting that it is part of a willed and violent attempt to suppress the past. In Chamoiseau's portrayal of his home, there is a similar ambivalence about the question of agency in the destruction of traces of the past, and comparable parallels are drawn between the destruction of internal and external traces of the past, but in contrast to Perec, these internal and external traces are bound into relationship. Their destruction is portrayed as an ambivalent process which heightens awareness of connections between self and world, rather than solely emphasizing the author's sense of alienation from his childhood.

Chamoiseau

Une enfance créole contains a pivotal image of the author's childhood home destroyed. As in Perec's text, the destruction of this outer remnant of the past is linked with the difficulty of re-entering the childhood world, but in contrast to the house on the rue Vilin, the destruction of Chamoiseau's old home is not a routine, anonymous process. Rather, it paradoxically confirms the value of the distinctive rituals of Chamoiseau's childhood that were designed to prevent fires in the wooden house.[51] It also acts as evidence of his mother's strength at a time when she is nearing death. The house only goes up in flames when she leaves, suggesting the force of her protective presence over the years.[52] Chamoiseau also suggests that the house embraces its own destruction, so the fire acts as evidence of the home as an animate space, one of the qualities the author most values about it.[53] This process of destruction is, then, portrayed in ambivalent terms. The depiction of the former home laments the loss of a material remnant of another period, deepening the rift between the author and the world of his childhood. Yet in doing so, it also offers a miniature portrait of the intertwining of internal and external worlds that will be central to the autobiography.

The trilogy opens with a preface appended in 1996 (the first volume of the trilogy was first published in 1990) which describes the recent destruction of the home in a fire. Chamoiseau hears the house is burning and rushes to the scene, but the building cannot be saved. The description of the destruction of the house in the preface undermines the body of the text, which will go on to evoke in loving detail a space the reader knows to have been destroyed. Though we might expect the loss of the house to be portrayed in uniquely negative terms, there is a kind of creativity about the fire, whose strange beauty is spoken of in terms of flowers and bees, lending paradoxical connotations of fertility to this scene of destruction.[54] The preface then suggests that the destruction of the house leads both to a diminished sense of connection with the past and to its potential renewal.

The trajectory the preface presents of the author's life suggests reasons for the adult narrator's simultaneous sense of nearness and distance to the world of his childhood. It locates Chamoiseau's childhood home in Martinique's principal city, Fort-de-France. The dated signature to *Antan d'enfance* and the fact that the author is able to come to the scene when he hears his house is burning gestures towards Chamoiseau's adult life as a writer and social worker in the area where he grew up. Though this indicates a degree of continuity between past and present, in other ways the preface suggests elements of distance in the narrator's relationship to the past. In particular, three elements suggest the difficulties of re-entering childhood through a literary text: the linguistic move from Creole to French; the problematic status of writing as a means of portraying the past; and the economic and cultural changes that have taken place in Martinique since the 1960s and 1970s.

The preface makes clear that there is a linguistic gap between the language of at least part of the author's lived experience and the language of its narration. The words which tell Chamoiseau of the fire, 'Difé, difé', are in Creole, unlike the surrounding text, which is in French.[55] This brings to the fore the difference between the language commonly spoken in Fort-de-France and the language of Chamoiseau's text. There is also a suggestion here that Creole is better at evoking the lived reality of Fort-de-France. The Creole words do the urgent communicative work of pointing out that there is a fire, while the surrounding French text could be seen as mere elaboration on this central fact. Doubts about the value of written language are reinforced by other elements of this preface. Only one fireman is able to come to the scene, because the other firemen have had to attend a funeral outside Fort-de-France. The narrator tells us that 'ils avaient sans doute publié un décret interdisant les feux et autres désagréments' [they had doubtless published a decree forbidding fires and other annoyances].[56] This episode can be seen as a satire of written, public language used to dominate other people or the natural world. It is a miniature version of the wider critique of official uses of written language which Chamoiseau undertakes in more theoretically-oriented works.[57] The lone fireman left to fight the fire, who is something of a pathetic figure, can be seen as representative of the relationship of the contemporary Caribbean autobiographer to the past. He attempts to put out the fire with his hose, but it is full of holes and twists in his hands 'comme un ver en souffrance' [like a suffering worm].[58] 'Ver en souffrance' contains several puns: the twisting line of the *ver* that represents the hose could be a worm or a line of poetry and is also a homophone of *vers*, the word for towards. 'Être en souffrance' can mean to suffer mentally when used of people, or to be pending or awaiting delivery when used in other contexts. Together these multiple meanings fuse the fireman/author's task of preserving the old house with connotations of pain, deferral and decomposition as well as creating an image of writing as a form of unpredictable forward motion which may or may not make contact with its object.

The linguistic gap between the lived experience and its narration makes recovery of the past difficult, as does the history of written records in the Caribbean and the nature of writing itself. But the way in which the author sees his old house also suggests more prosaic reasons for the separation between childhood and adulthood. The narrator tells us that he had occasionally passed the house since his mother moved out and that he had glimpsed it through its reflection in car windscreens.[59] This suggests something of the economic changes that have occurred in Martinique since he was growing up in the wooden house. Over the course of Chamoiseau's childhood, from the mid-1950s to the mid-1970s, Martinique moved from being a producer economy to being a service economy dependent on the French welfare state.[60] Because of these economic changes, the Martinique in which Chamoiseau lives as an adult is very different from the country he grew up in. Richard Price notes that the economic changes of the 1960s and 1970s were seen as bringing about the end of a period which had stretched from the abolition of slavery to the mid-twentieth century.[61] Raphaël Confiant argues this sense of transformation gives members of his generation a particular relationship to their own childhood, which comes to represent a lost world just before the contemporary Martinique came into being.[62] For this generation, recalling the passage from childhood to youth to adulthood also involves portraying Martinique's movement to new economic structures and the changes in everyday life these bring. Chamoiseau uses the changes in the way homes are built and lived in in Martinique as a way of conveying such changes. The disappearance of external traces of an older culture is recorded as a way of gesturing towards a concrete manifestation of more intangible change in modes of relationship between self and world in Martinique.

Each of these authors, then, uses an image of himself outside a childhood home as a way of exploring his position in relation to the early period of his life. In each case, his location outside the past is emphasized, and the means of bridging the distance between past and present is called into question, but this takes different forms in each text. Nabokov's unpublished preface and its echoes in the caption to Andrew Field's photograph draw attention to the impossibility of physical return to the house where he was born because of Russia's regime change and Nabokov's own change of nationality. Yet this physical distance from Russia does not prevent re-entry through memory and imagination, a mode of entry which is figured as more valuable than physical return in any case. Perec, by contrast, is able to return to the street where he began his life, but in spite of this has a more distanced relationship with it. His failure to recognize his childhood home indicates his alienation from this period in his life. Chamoiseau, like Perec, still lives in the same city where he grew up. Though in a more attenuated sense than is the case with Perec, his ability to return physically to the house only draws attention to the changes in his mind which have introduced distance between his childhood and current life. These changes are in part a result of the move from childhood to adulthood, but are intertwined with economic and cultural changes in Martinique which leave ever-diminishing space for the Creole culture the house represents.

Though the reasons for each author's sense of distance from the past are different, each sets up tensions between images of their former homes as they were in the past and their changed or destroyed forms in the present. These images of destruction or change suggest a certain level of suspicion about the role of the state in relation to the memory of the past. Nabokov's text brings out his disapproval of the Soviet state's co-opting of Herzen as a predecessor; Perec's image of the routine destruction of the last traces of his mother's life recalls the complicit role of the French state in her death; Chamoiseau's depiction of the fire which ruins the old house gestures toward the personal and cultural losses involved in the disappearance of older ways of life hastened by increasing dependence on the French state. These images of damage inflicted in the contemporary period and the hints at the indifferent and even falsifying role of the state in relation to traces of the past call up questions about what it means to live in the aftermath of state-sponsored histories of oppression and violence, questions which recur insistently throughout these texts. This suggests that the focus of their autobiographical enterprise extends beyond recording the distance opened up between childhood and adulthood through contact with violent histories. Rather, the scope of their project includes reflection on the ways in which the legacies of those histories continue to influence internal and external traces of the past in the present. These texts then focus on the specificities of the aftermath of such histories as well as their immediate effects. In order to construct the idea of an aftermath, some sense of 'before' is necessary, and evocations of the child's experience of the domestic interior are central to the portrayal of such a period, where it exists.

The Child's Perception of the Home

Looking at the portrayal of the child's perception of home is revealing of the meanings accorded to childhood experience in each author's work. Nabokov and Chamoiseau mobilize elements of the child's perception of the domestic interior as a way of building a portrait of the child's world as animate and benevolent. The child's experience of the world is interwoven with a particular linguistic and cultural milieu in each text, and this contributes to Chamoiseau's portrayal of the Creole language and culture as favourable to a nourishing relationship between self and world, and to the idyllic qualities in Nabokov's depiction of his childhood in the last days of Imperial Russia. The connections established between a given historical period and the child's imaginative relationship with a living, benevolent world work to create a sense of a protected time before the experience of violence or oppression, though in other ways the texts undermine clear oppositions between the periods before and after the experience of violent histories. Perec, unlike the other two authors, does not portray his childhood world as animate, and this element of his autobiography contributes to the reader's sense that there is no 'before' which precedes his contact with history; rather, the early incursion of violence into his family life precludes the early, protected relationship between self and world which undergirds the other two authors' nostalgic depiction of a living childhood world.

The home is the place where the child comes to consciousness. Jean Piaget argued in 1929 that the child ascribes life to inanimate objects as his mind is developing and that in the very early years, the child even perceives a continuity between his own conscious life and the life of other objects and beings.[63] Piaget called this aspect of child development 'animism', though he did not intend by this any overlap with the use of the term in anthropology.[64] Though Piaget's argument has been the subject of much debate in developmental psychology, it finds striking anticipations and echoes in literary portrayals of childhood perception. Walter Pater's 1895 *The Child in the House* articulates the way the child's animism makes his first domestic surroundings come to seem alive, interwoven with the child's own inner life. The subject of Pater's story, Florian, has a dream where he sees the house where he grew up. Pater connects Florian's gaze on the house with an inward examination of his own soul as it has developed over time:

> In that half-spiritualised house he could watch the better, over again, the gradual expansion of the soul which had come to be, there — of which indeed, through the law which makes the material objects about them so large an element in children's lives, it had actually become a part; inward and outward being woven through and through each other into one inextricable texture[65]

Pater's lines evoke the softening of boundaries between the child and the material world that takes place within the home and suggest that remembering the home can act as an avenue into an exploration of the formation of the child's mind. Piaget and Pater's insights into the interaction of the child's mind with the world around him are helpful in interpreting the ways in which the domestic interior functions in *Speak, Memory* and *Une enfance créole,* where the portrayal of the home from the child's point of view allows an exploration of his developing mind.

In both texts, the space of the home is portrayed as animate. Ideas, sensations and feelings seem to cross freely from the living space of the home into the inner life of the child. The portrayal of home is joined to a portrayal of the open boundaries of early selfhood. These open boundaries are important in two ways: they make possible a very close relationship between the child and his mother, and they allow the child to have a rich, imaginative relationship with the physical world. These two aspects of the child's openness to the surrounding world are linked because the relationship with the mother acts as a kind of filter which allows the child to absorb the world around him. The child's experience of the home is inflected by his mother's perception and memory of it, and this enriches his experience of the home and nourishes his imagination. The porous boundaries between child and world within the home are thus associated with the transmission of ways of thinking from the previous generation and with the beginnings of the child's imaginative life.

Though Piaget and Pater's observations on childhood animism might seem distant from the concerns of twentieth-century autobiographies confronting violent histories, Edward Said uses a comparable passage from George Eliot as an epigraph to an essay on the specificities of twentieth-century experiences of political and economic exile:

> There is no sense of ease like the ease we felt in those scenes where we were born, where objects become dear to us before we had known the labour of choice, and where the outer world seemed only an extension of our personality.[66]

The effortless continuity between the child and the surrounding world is here contrasted with the greater degree of exteriority in the individual's later relationship to the world. The quotation offers a counterpoint to the essay's evocation of the distanced relationship between the exiled individual and the world that arises from the break with the place of birth and childhood. The position of this quotation on the threshold of Said's essay and its role as a point of contrast gesture toward the significance of conceptions of the childhood home as animate in these narratives. The idea of childhood as a time where the world is animate takes on greater significance in the light of changes of location, language or culture which make return to the spaces associated with early childhood difficult. Where adult life differs from childhood in language, culture or physical surroundings, the early relationship to the surrounding world characteristic of childhood becomes associated with the older language or place. Because of Nabokov's early trilingualism, he tends to connect animism less with the experience of speaking a particular language and more with his perception of the physical spaces he inhabited as a child. Chamoiseau, whose acquisition of French is portrayed as traumatic, places more emphasis on animism connected with speaking his first language and so being in a close relationship with the previous generation, especially his mother. In both cases, depictions of childhood animism grant the spaces of the past considerable power; such portrayals suggest the world is more alive when experienced through modes of being and thinking available to the child but lost to the adult.

Linking childhood animism with an early language and culture, a particular physical space, and close contact with the previous generation thus works to create a striking contrast between past and present relationships between self and world. Portrayals of the childhood home take on this function in Nabokov and Chamoiseau's work, but what of the absence of animate domestic spaces in *W ou le souvenir d'enfance*? One obvious reason for their absence is that, unlike Nabokov and Chamoiseau, Perec does not have any memories from his early life at home before the war. He tells the reader that his first clear memories are of his time at school, after his first displacement from his family home in 1940.[67] This difference between Perec and the other two authors also throws light on the generational literary traditions to which each belongs. Suleiman identifies the primary characteristic of the 1.5 generation as the experience of trauma 'before the formation of stable identity that we associate with adulthood, and in some cases before any conscious sense of self'.[68] The lack of childhood animism in Perec's text can be seen as a result of the disruption to his developing sense of self by wartime upheaval and his early bereavement. In *Speak, Memory* and *Une enfance créole*, the portrayal of the child's experience of home acts as a way for the author to evoke the living connection with the world forged through a language and culture he has left behind to a certain extent. Perec's memories of his child-self's experience of different dwelling places speak of the experiences which hampered any such immersion in an ancestral language, culture or physical place. Each author's portrayal of his child-self's experience of domestic spaces then offers a way into the text's location in relation to cultural, familial and literary pasts.

The Home as an Animate Space

The home is portrayed as animate in *Speak, Memory* and *Une enfance créole*. Home as a living space is valued because it allows the child to pass beyond the bounds of his own mind in various ways. One of the most striking ways in which the child goes beyond the boundaries of his mind is through his relationship with his mother. The child's experience of domestic space is strongly inflected by his mother's perception of it. He experiences it for himself, but he also absorbs her memories of it so that it becomes a 'temporally layered' space, holding several different periods within it.[69] Each author links the child's ability to enter into the mental worlds of his loved ones with an enriched memory that expands his experience of the home.

For Nabokov, the world of his childhood home is living and responsive. Everything on his family's estates is infused with spirit — furniture, plants, air and light seem to have moods and opinions and they participate in his life, swaying it this way or that. Though Piaget argues that animistic beliefs are characteristic of early childhood, and will gradually taper off as the child becomes an adolescent, in Nabokov's autobiography, home retains its animate qualities throughout his youth. Indeed, these become particularly striking during his early adolescence. When he looks up erotic words in his family's eighty-volume encyclopaedia on rainy days, he writes of the 'poor light that did all it could to discourage my furtive inquiry'.[70] Light is attributed agency, and so is darkness. When Nabokov describes cycling home from nightly trysts with Tamara, one of his first loves, he remembers his 'slow, laboriously pedaling feet trying to press down the monstrously strong and resilient darkness that refused to stay under'.[71] The darkness seems to absorb and throw back to him his sense of foreboding about the coming collapse of the relationship. The surrounding world participates in his love affair, absorbing Nabokov's feeling that it cannot last long, but the natural world also shares in his happier moments. When he manages to free himself from all responsibilities and sets off to hunt butterflies, he writes that 'the animation and luster of the day seemed like a tremor of sympathy around me'.[72] Images of trembling, rippling and glowing recur throughout Nabokov's descriptions of his home, contributing to an impression of pre-revolutionary Russia as bursting with febrile energy.

For Nabokov, home is a place where connections are readily established between self and world. The mental life of the young Nabokov melts into his parents' world, the natural world, and the world of books. Each of these is so vivid to him that it absorbs him completely. Figures in the natural world have a life similar to his. He speaks of a boulder where 'a little mountain ash and a still smaller aspen had climbed, holding hands, like two clumsy, shy children', establishing a parallel between the trees and his encounters with seaside playmates.[73] Adventures he reads about in Mayne Reid novels are re-enacted in play with his cousin, creating a continuity between the worlds he enters through reading and his own world.[74] The self at home becomes part of beings and worlds larger than itself, and home is seen as capable of holding many different domains.

In particular, it is portrayed as a link between earthly and heavenly worlds. In the tradition of many Russian aristocratic memoirs and fictional memoirs from the second half of the nineteenth century onwards, Nabokov's home is spoken of in terms of an earthly paradise. The richness, variety and beauty of his home make it a 'veritable Eden'.[75] By speaking of home as a paradise, Nabokov connects his autobiography with Tolstoy's Детство [Childhood], where the evocation of an edenic domestic world also acts as a way into a nostalgic portrayal of a lost world.[76] The depiction of the author's childhood as idyllic acts as an implicit criticism of the present world. Nabokov's portrait of the heavenly world of his childhood, as well as being a personal recollection of happiness, establishes itself in opposition to the Bolshevik idea that the pre-Revolutionary world was wholly bad. Nabokov describes a harmonious world of abundance where servants are well-treated, bonds between parents and children are strong, and there is ample intellectual and sensual stimulation for the sensitive mind of the child. These qualities are all characteristic of childhood narratives written by members of the Russian gentry from the middle of the nineteenth century.[77] By echoing these tropes, Nabokov aligns himself with the pre-Revolutionary literary tradition and goes some way toward continuing its life.

Chamoiseau's depiction of his childhood home as a living space also acts as an implicit (and at times explicit) criticism of the way life is lived in contemporary Martinique. He depicts the house he grows up in as an animate space. The way it lives and shelters many other kinds of life offers a point of contrast with more recent ways of life in Martinique, where cement buildings come to represent the inert relationship between contemporary Martinicans and the surrounding world. The wooden walls of the old house are figured as a living membrane. They quiver and crackle with heat, and when a breeze blows, they begin to sing.[78] The house's walls shift in response to changes in the outside world, taking on a different colour when it rains, and shedding a skin like a snake in long dry spells.[79] The roof and walls of the house are also quite literally porous, as every time it rains, water comes flooding in through leaks. Chamoiseau's mother hangs up an oilskin sheet to catch the water that leaks from the ceiling of one of the bedrooms. The child watches as the sheet gradually curves as it collects more water. His fascination with the sheet and the way it is referred to as a chalice lend this scene connotations of the mysterious and the sacred.[80] Though we might question this romanticizing of what is, after all, a dangerous and unpleasant effect of poverty, this scene encapsulates the way the porous boundaries of the house allow the child contact with extended interstitial spaces between inside and outside.

The way the house makes possible this contact with the transitional space between inside and outside is depicted as a specific attribute of Creole culture. Chamoiseau draws the reader's attention to the connections between Creole culture and the physical form of the house. The house's form is figured as an expression of a Creole practice of architecture and construction which has now been lost.[81] The way it creates transitional spaces between inside and outside can be connected to the value the créolistes place on the interstitial nature of Caribbean culture, which draws upon and exists in between European, Asian and African influences.[82] The balconies where plants are grown are one kind of transitional space associated with the Creole house and the remnants of outdoor kitchens are another.[83] The kitchens are no longer used by the time Chamoiseau is a child but they still speak of porosity between different kinds of spaces because the child's mother uses them as chicken coops, so that the yard is somewhere in between an urban and a rural space. There are recurrent references to the increasing rarity of such houses, which are replaced by more European buildings as the child enters adolescence. The autobiographical text then becomes a way of recording the collective past of Fort-de-France, as Chamoiseau moves from remarks on his own house to general comments about homes in Fort-de-France, using his home as a synecdoche for changing collective experiences of dwelling in Martinique. Chamoiseau's evocation of his childhood experience of domestic space thus functions as a way of recording aspects of a collective cultural past.

The positive aspects of Nabokov and Chamoiseau's portrayals of the child's experience of the domestic interior are in strong contrast with those found in *W ou le souvenir d'enfance,* where there are very few evocations of the child within the house. Perec's childhood differs from that of Nabokov and Chamoiseau in that it is not spent in any one house, nor in a set of family houses; rather, after the move from the rue Vilin, he moves between different schools, *pensions* and relatives' houses in Villard-de-Lans. As with other members of the 1.5 generation, living with another family leads to a level of confusion and falseness about the child's position within it, as we see when Perec begins the chapter about his time living with relatives in Villard-de-Lans with a convoluted sentence pointing out the inaccuracy of some of his habitual ways of referring to members of his extended family: 'Henri, le fils de la sœur du mari de la sœur de mon père, que j'ai, depuis, pris l'habitude d'appeler mon cousin bien qu'il ne le soit pas...' [Henri, my father's sister's husband's sister's son whom I have since become accustomed to calling my cousin although he is not...].[84] Henri's family live in Villard-de-Lans because of his asthma, and it was because of this that Perec's aunt took refuge there during the war.[85] The house where he lives with her is called Les Frimas, and the house where Henri lives with his family is called the Igloo.[86] Already these names suggest cold rather than domestic warmth, and the fact that 'Frimas' means freezing fog sets up an echo with the Nazi policy 'Nacht und Nebel' [night and fog] of suppressing all information about their treatment of camp inmates, which gives its name to Alain Resnais's 1955 film on the camps, present obliquely throughout Perec's text. This association of the family home with the actions that would lead to Perec's mother's death continues with a reference to his aunt making soap with baking soda, beef fat and ashes.[87] There is an echo between this mention of soap and the final line of the W story, which signals its connection to the camps by referring to 'des stocks de savon de mauvaise qualité' [stocks of poor quality soap].[88] These hints at the presence of violent history in the domestic space are echoed by the absence of any image which would suggest that the home protects the child from the outside world. Rather, his memories of it are based on photographs which recall its exterior.[89]

Perec does not spend long in Les Frimas and will move on to various schools and 'homes d'enfants'.[90] These are homes in the French rather than the English sense, public institutions rather than protected, private spaces. Like Les Frimas, they have echoes with aspects of the fictional strand of the autobiography and with elements of wartime history. The Collège Turenne, where Perec spends most time, is described in terms which echo the camps as 'un lieu terriblement éloigné, où nul ne venait jamais, où les nouvelles n'arrivaient pas, où celui qui en avait passé le seuil ne le repassait plus' [a dreadfully far off place where no one ever went, a place which news didn't reach, where those who crossed its threshold never crossed it again].[91] This school is the scene of one of the very few memories in the text of the child in an interior space. He is the only child left in the school on Christmas Eve and he gets out of bed to see if he has received any presents. The cold physical contact between the child and the building is in striking contrast with the evocations of continuity between child and world found in *Speak, Memory* and *Une enfance créole*:

> Je crois que la scène tout entière s'est fixée, s'est figée dans mon esprit: image pétrifiée, immuable, dont je garde le souvenir physique, jusqu'à la sensation de mes mains agrippant les barreaux, jusqu'à l'impression du métal froid contre mon front quand il se posa sur la barre d'appui de la balustrade. J'ai regardé en bas: il n'y avait pas beaucoup de lumière mais au bout d'un instant je suis arrivé à voir le grand arbre décoré, l'amoncellement de chaussures tout autour et, débordant d'une des miennes, une grande boîte rectangulaire.
>
> C'était un cadeau que m'envoyait ma tante Esther: deux chemises à carreaux, genre cowboy. Elles piquaient. Je ne les aimais pas.[92]
>
> [I think the whole scene has lodged and been frozen in my mind; a petrified image, unchangeable, which I can recall physically, down to the feeling of my hands clenched around the uprights, down to the cold metal pressing on my forehead when I leaned against the handrail. I looked down: there wasn't much light, but after a minute I could make out the great decorated tree, the mound of shoes all around, and, sticking out of one of mine, a big rectangular box.
>
> It was a present my aunt Esther had sent for me: two check shirts, cowboy style. They made me itch. I did not like them.]

Here, the discontinuity between child and world evoked by the physical sensation of the cold metal on his forehead is mirrored by the disappointment of the unwanted gift, which itself suggests an uncomfortable bristling between the child's body and the material that surrounds it. All these elements of uncomfortable insertion in the world gesture towards the absence of his parents and perhaps especially of his mother, whom Esther cannot replace.

Relationships of Symbiosis between Mother and Child

As this exploration of childhood animism has begun to make clear, the child's ability to soak in the surrounding world within the home is dependent to a large extent on his relationship with his mother. He absorbs her memories so that he experiences the home both as it is during his childhood and as she remembers it in previous times. His relationship with his mother thus shapes his experience of time, and the interaction between separate eras, as well as introducing him to sensory and aesthetic pleasure. Nabokov's interaction with his parents within the home is associated with a striking softening of his ego boundaries. Communication between parent and child continues within the home even when the two individuals are not physically present in the same place.⁹³ The text also hints that the shared mental world established within the home is connected to other kinds of dissolution of the self achieved through creativity, love and immortality. The loss of home is significant, then, not because it is a stable place, but rather because it is an unstable place, where borders between various selves and worlds are fluid. What T. I. Radomskaya writes of the way home works in Pushkin's poetry is also true of its role in Nabokov's autobiography: 'Дом — это такая граница земного пространства, через которую уже "просвечивают" черты небесного мира. Дом — *это не застывшая статика, а переход, преображение временного Вечным* [Home is a kind of border of earthly space, through which glow aspects of the heavenly world. Home *is neither static nor frozen, but is a kind of crossing, a place where the transfiguration of the temporal into the eternal takes place*].'⁹⁴ The idea that home might be a place where the wall between the phenomenal and the noumenal starts to crumble fits in with the blurring of boundaries that occurs between past and present, self and other, human world and natural world, physical reality and imagined realities in the text. This blurring of boundaries between self and other, and between the phenomenal and noumenal realms, is particularly evident in the portrayal of his relationship with his parents.

In scenes such as Nabokov's walks with his mother around their country estates, where she points out details of the natural world, and instructs him to remember them clearly, and when his father ritually goes over the story of how he caught a certain butterfly at a certain spot, we see Nabokov absorbing memories of scenes he himself never witnessed.⁹⁵ Such interactions also involve the transmission of a certain practice of memory. From such moments, Nabokov learns, and subsequently conveys to the reader, that good practice of memory is dialogic, involves some element of performance, and a level of awareness that one is creating or renewing a memory. Equally as importantly, through the young Nabokov's absorption of his parents' memories, people and events he never knew or experienced become real to him.

This is particularly the case with Nabokov's mother's memories. His mother's relationship to her past prefigures his adult relationship to the world of his childhood and youth. As in Nabokov's life, there is a painful split between the world of her childhood and youth, and the world of her early adulthood. Six of her seven siblings had died by the time she was married and her parents died shortly afterwards.⁹⁶ Nabokov's mother shares her memories of her lost family with her son, so that certain places within the family estates become connected with these dead relatives for him, like the room his maternal grandmother had used as a chemical laboratory, or the old tennis court where his maternal grandfather would play.⁹⁷ The child absorbs his mother's memories and her attitudes toward them.⁹⁸ The extent to which his mother's family life was real to Nabokov becomes clear in his embarrassment over the magic lantern afternoons his tutor hosts.⁹⁹ The tutor, Lenski, invites classmates and friends of his charges to the Nabokov home to listen to works of literature accompanied by magic lantern slides. It bores many of the children, who are only there out of politeness. This reminds Nabokov of his maternal grandfather, who decided to set up his own school for his sons, and asked his acquaintances to send their sons there too, even paying the parents of poorer children, so that his sons would have some classmates.[100] Nabokov's embarrassment over Lenski's enterprise is heightened by his absorption of his mother's memory of an event that happened long before he was born.

The author's connection to his mother's mind is strongly associated with his initiation into aesthetic pleasure. There are many images from his depiction of his childhood which suggest that the absorption of beauty was its defining feature. This absorption is sometimes almost literal, as when he wraps a ruby-coloured ornamental egg up in a sheet and then sucks on the sheet until the red glow of the gem shines through it. This softening of the boundary between the ruby egg and the child is linked to the way the child's mind and that of his mother come to overlap. This scene is connected with the jewels that Nabokov's mother would take out for her son to play with. Her jewels remind him of the coloured lights which decorate the city.[101] They offer him a smaller version of the world's beauties, miniatures which he can play with and so come to know in an intimate, tactile way. This play readies him for the beauty of the outside world, making it knowable. As well as the child licking the ruby egg, other images of oral absorption of beauty are associated with Nabokov's relationship with his mother, as when he would put his lips to her bedroom window through a gauze curtain, which recalls his description of 'the reticulated tenderness' of kissing his mother's cheek through her veil.[102]

Nabokov's playful interaction with his mother stimulates his sense for visual beauty. She also nurtures this sense by painting pictures for him: 'My mother did everything to encourage the general sensitiveness I had to visual stimulation. How many were the aquarelles she painted for me; what a revelation it was when she showed me the lilac tree that grows out of mixed blue and red!'[103] Nabokov's mother's paintings reveal to him the joys of colour and form. As well as a shared pleasure in visual beauty, mother and son also have in common several quirks of perception. They are both synaesthetes, and both suffer from mild hallucinations.[104] On one occasion narrated in the text, Nabokov has a vivid hallucination where he sees his mother shopping for a present for him on the streets of St Petersburg while he is ill in bed.[105] This vision later turns out to have been accurate. It provides a striking illustration of the degree of communication possible between the two minds.

Chamoiseau's mother also plays an important role in mediating her son's experience of domestic space. The way she moves through the home conveys something of her view of it, and she passes this on to the young Chamoiseau. An example of this is her refusal to allow cold air to enter the house when she is doing the ironing. She shuts up doors and windows to prevent draughts as she completes the task out of the Creole belief that experiencing heat and cold at the same time will lead to illness. The child-self in the text might not have a verbal understanding of this belief but because he likes to be in his mother's presence at all times, he also participates in her refusal to move from the hot room.[106] This fits in with Paul Connerton's concept of memory being transmitted from generation to generation via bodily actions, learned and practiced through habit.[107] Chamoiseau also absorbs a sense of the changing seasons in Martinique through observing and absorbing aspects of his mother's interaction with the natural world. Her daily routine and mood change depending on the kinds of fish, fruit and vegetables in season. These changes in mood and routine become connected with the tastes of the seasonal food for Chamoiseau, and so he has a connection to the passage of time through his relationship with his mother and his sense of taste. Chamoiseau compares his mother's sensitivity to seasonal changes to that of a jellyfish who moves with the slightest lapping of the tide and writes that his mother's body was 'branché aux saisons de la lune' [plugged into the seasons of the moon].[108] The child absorbs his sense of the passage of time in the outside world through his mother's life, which functions as a kind of umbilical cord tying his own life to wider kinds of immersion, fluid movement, and cycles of ebb and flow.

As we have seen, a parallel is established between the space of the house and the space of Creole culture. The child is initiated into Creole culture through his experience of the house. However, a further parallel is set up between the space of the maternal body and the domestic space. The house possesses certain womb-like qualities; it is protective, it is associated with shadowy, sheltered spaces, it nurtures an abundance of life and its walls are porous. Conversely, the mother's body is spoken of in terms of a containing space. It is repeatedly characterized as possessing vast capacities and is once referred to as the child's 'racine-case' [root-hut].[109] This mapping of the internal space of his mother's body on to wider dwelling places recurs when Chamoiseau speaks of family illnesses. He writes that his mother would use conventional medicine to treat her children when they were sick, but would only take Creole, herbal medicine for herself. Chamoiseau writes: 'Pour son corps n'avait droit de cité que les médicaments créoles' [When it came to her own body, only Creole medications had right of passage].[110] Here the mother's body is figured as a Creole civic space. The children's bodies, by contrast, are not mapped on to the space of Creole culture. They are depicted as containing new kinds of spaces and are treated with Western medicines. Writing of this generational change of approach to illness and healing, Chamoiseau relates it to a broader distancing from the Creole past: 'La médecine créole perdait ainsi ses voies de transmission' [Thus Creole medicine was losing its paths of transmission].[111] The collective move away from Creole culture is thus associated with the child's body being thought of and treated differently from the mother's body. This different treatment can be seen as a kind of move away from the child's previous fusional relationship with his mother and with the domestic interior. It is associated with cultural loss and distance from the child's early experience of the world, throwing into relief the role of the relationship with the mother in integrating the child's life within temporal and cultural continuities.

As touched on in the previous section, a distanced, uncomfortable relationship between child and world, arising in part from an absence of a mediating maternal presence, is present throughout the evocation of the child's perception of the world in *W ou le souvenir d'enfance*. Other female relatives are referred to anonymously and interchangeably as 'une tante', 'une cousine', 'une grand-mère' and their contact with the child is transitory and unpredictable.[112] Rather than filtering the world for him, their comings and goings give a concrete form to the unstable, distrustful relationship between child and world.[113] The presence of the mother within the domestic space is not remembered and has to be imagined, based on representation of such experiences in children's literature: 'Moi, j'aurais aimé aider ma mère à débarrasser la table de la cuisine après le dîner. Sur la table, il y aurait eu une toile cirée à petits carreaux bleus [...] C'est comme ça que ça se passait dans mes livres de classe' [As for me, I would have liked to help my mother clear the dinner from the kitchen table. There would have been a blue, small-checked oilcloth on the table [...] That's what happened in the books I read at school].[114] The reader can see that such images exerted a powerful pull on Perec because the blue squares of this passage also appear in a description of a kitchen in his first published novel, *Les Choses,* which came out in 1965, a full decade before his autobiography.[115] The focus on the detail of this imagined kitchen, and its source in books the child reads at school, only emphasizes his distance from the experience of inhabiting a home made safe by a mother's protective presence.

The distance suggested by these devices also evokes a kind of crumbling in the processes of finding and creating meaning in the experience of space. Modes of making space meaningful are called into question throughout Perec's work. One system for ordering space which recurs repeatedly across Perec's non-fictional essays is latitude and longitude. In 'Quelques-unes des choses qu'il faudrait tout de même que je fasse avant de mourir' [Some Things which I Really Should Do All the Same Before I Die], Perec lists travelling through the 0.0 point where the equator meets the Greenwich Meridian. In *Espèces d'espaces,* he devotes one of the essays to such points of origin, like sea-level, or the point which marks the very centre of France, and writes of his fascination with 'les points zéro, ces axes et ces points de référence à partir desquels peuvent être déterminés les positions et les distances de n'importe quel objet de l'univers' [those points of origin, those axes and points of reference in relation to which one can determine the position and distance of any object in the universe].[116] In 'De quelques emplois du verbe habiter' [Some Uses of the Verb 'To Live'], Perec notes the strangeness of the system of latitude and longitude to everyday life, remarking that he would not be understood if he gave his flat's latitude and longitude in reply to a question about where he lives.[117] Similarly, *Espèces d'espaces* contains an anecdote about the British Postmaster-General forbidding the use of poetry, riddles or references to latitude and longitude in addresses.[118] Here, the geographical system, like poetry and riddles, becomes a means of estranging an individual (in this case, the postman) from his or her usual perception. Situating a place through latitude and longitude is then associated both with utter mastery of the spatial world and with a degree of exteriority to everyday human experience, where space is made sense of in different ways.

These references to geographical techniques might seem irrelevant to Perec's autobiographical work, but in fact the image of an origin appears very early in the autobiography, when he refers to childhood as 'coordonnées à partir desquelles les axes de ma vie pourront trouver leur sens' [a set of co-ordinates from which the axes of my life may draw their meaning].[119] Childhood is here situated as a point of origin in a personal and mathematical sense, which would allow Perec to make sense of the rest of his life. The pun on 'sens' (direction and meaning) indicates the importance of spatial orientation in this attempt to understand the past. This image foregrounds the central role of childhood and spatial orientation in self-understanding, but it also associates them with absence, most obviously by connecting childhood with the 0.0 point, but also because the image of axes forms an X, which Perec connects elsewhere in the text with the imbrication of his own history with the history of Nazism.[120] This image of spinning axes also suggests a need to resort to external, theoretical systems to make sense of the connection between childhood and adulthood, which gestures toward the problematized, questioning relationship the author has with his past and with the question of space.

The tension between control over space and distance from the everyday, embodied relationship to it suggested by the exploration of longitude and latitude in *Espèces d'espaces* and elsewhere is also apparent in the autobiography. The images of precise grid-like structures alongside references to disordered, or overwhelming space evoke two extremes of a relationship to the surrounding world, one characterized by a high level of human control over the world, the other by utter disorientation. This is apparent in the quotation above in the image of the orderly kitchen, with its checked blue table cloth and elaborately balanced lamp, which contrasts sharply with the upheaval that characterized Perec's actual childhood experience of domestic space. Another instance of such contrast is the juxtaposition of the demolished houses on the rue Vilin and the domestic appliances strewn across the street with the author's vague memory of playing as a child with paving stones on the street. The stones are described as 'joliment cubiques'.[121] These movements between descriptions of space where there are no bearings and grids which divide it up neatly point to the effect of his mother's absence. Without a maternal figure filtering and making sense of the surrounding world, it is experienced as simultaneously distant and overwhelming.

As we saw in the examination of *Speak, Memory* and *Une enfance créole*, the mother influences the child's apprehension of time and memory, as well as filtering the spatial world. The domestic space then becomes the scene of a transmission of a practice of memory which goes on to inform the autobiographical text. The handing on of practices of memory that occurs in domestic spaces in the work of Chamoiseau and Nabokov is notably absent in Perec's text. If Perec's text suggests the difficulties of entering into a generational continuity in the absence of a stable domestic space, it is largely because the boundaries of the places he lives are not secure. As Lisa Villeneuve notes, 'the idea of dwelling implies a form of privacy or separateness', both of which are absent in Perec's experience of home.[122] As we saw in both the description of the rue Vilin as seen by the adult and the evocation of the child's experience of the interior of the school, marks of the history which would disrupt Perec's family life are not confined to the exterior world, but are present in the very shape of the street where he was born and within the school where he is seeking refuge from Nazi violence. The walls of the various places Perec lives do not then function to create a barrier between the life of the self and the family and a broader history of violence. Rather, the evocation of dwelling-places brings out the imbrication of the two.

Stephen Kern, writing of Frank Lloyd Wright's architectural practice, highlights the importance of the walls of the home. Kern describes how Wright sought to build homes where all elements of the building organically blended into the whole, which in turn flowed into the landscape around it. This was designed to allow its inhabitants' lives to blend harmoniously with their surroundings, both interior and exterior. Yet, as Kern notes, this sense of fusion between the individual and his or her surroundings paradoxically depends on a degree of separation from them. Kern writes that although Wright sought to build walls which created a continuity between inside and outside, these porous boundaries were themselves encased within thick stone walls.[123] These ensured the degree of privacy necessary for the individual to integrate his or her own life with that of the environment while still feeling safe. Kern's insights into Wright's architectural practice can be applied to the ways in which domestic spaces function in the texts under discussion. While they do indeed enable fusion between the child and the mother, and between the child and the world in the case of Chamoiseau and Nabokov, it is the walls of the home which create the conditions for this fusion. As we saw at the beginning of this chapter, there are parallels between the way the author depicts the childhood home(s) and the portrait of his own mind that emerges from the text. Damage to the walls of the home, or a breakdown in their role as a filter or protective barrier, thus takes on much weight within the text. It becomes a way into the depiction of wounds to the self, to parental relationships and to a given cultural milieu. Looking at the kinds of damage the walls of the childhood home suffer in each of these texts thus brings out the specificities of the historical violence which places distance between the author's present life and his childhood.

Damaged or Destroyed Boundaries of the Childhood Home

Though the walls of the home have the function of creating a safe space and so allowing the child to absorb beauty and enchantment in *Une enfance créole* and *Speak, Memory*, there are more ambivalent sides to their role within the text. As we have seen, in Perec's text, there are very few narrations of the child's experience of the home from within. Rather, depictions of the damaged or destroyed walls of the former childhood home make present the difficulty of maintaining a protected world for the family and the self in the face of historical violence of a vast scale. Though less obvious, the borders of the home in Nabokov and Chamoiseau's text also play this role. Damage to the walls' protective function allows the passage of historical violence into the protected world of the self, the family and the first language. Though Nabokov and Chamoiseau use depictions of the child's perception of the world as animate to build an image of early experiences of the world as benevolent, in contrast to an adulthood shadowed by a legacy of historical violence, they simultaneously complicate this opposition, pointing toward the permeable boundaries between the periods before and after contact with violent histories. In an essay on the significance of damage to a home's walls, Beatriz Colomina draws out the subtleties in the relationship between public and private spaces and areas of safety and danger. She refers to an aphorism which says that you make a cannon by taking an empty hole and twisting some steel wire around it and draws a parallel between public space and the empty space at the centre of the cannon. Colomina compares the steel wire to private spaces which make public space visible and possible, destabilizing the concept of the interior as a safe, protected space and the exterior world as threatening.[124] Colomina's insights are relevant to the other side of the portrayal of the home's boundaries in *Speak, Memory* and *Une enfance créole*. As well as creating a safer world which the child can absorb into himself, the walls of the home also make visible the violence and oppression that shape the exterior world.

The dual nature of the boundaries of the home is particularly evident in *Speak, Memory*. As we have seen, the idea of the home as a place of softened boundaries between different temporal periods, self and other and the earthly and the supernatural or heavenly is central to the idyllic qualities Nabokov lends his early life. The home is the place where the child's mind is enriched by its easy absorption of elements of the surrounding world. Yet, this porosity between the mind and physical world can become double-edged. The windows of the home at times act as a charged barrier, which excludes violence on the street while allowing images of it to enter into the home. Because of the parallel drawn between the interior of the home and the inner world of the child, this crossing of the boundary of the home also suggests the entry of violence into the self. The use of windows to portray the entry of violent images into the child's mind becomes particularly significant in the light of Nabokov's depiction of glass, crystal and other reflective surfaces as images for artistic consciousness, which makes possible creativity, imaginative movement between different periods and loving relationships. As mentioned before, the child's absorption of beauty is strongly connected with his play with jewels and coloured glass. Imagery of windows as the means of transmission of scenes of violence thus interweaves the aesthetic with the historical.

Richard Terdiman identifies such interweavings recurring across a range of French modernist texts through the imagery of windows. He finds examples of protagonists contemplating a menacing social reality beyond a windowpane in Gautier's preface to *Albertus ou L'Âme et le péché*, whose protagonist is devoted to art and indifferent to politics. He confines himself to a room to write, but his haven is disturbed when bullets shatter the windows during revolutions.[125] In Baudelaire's 'Les Yeux des pauvres', the speaker and his mistress are disturbed by a family of beggars peering through the windows of the café where they are sitting.[126] There is an echo of this, whether intentional or not, in *A l'ombre des jeunes filles en fleur*, where the narrator writes that the upper classes dining in a room with large windows are like exotic fish to the working people who observe them from the outside, and run the risk of one day being eaten by them.[127] Mallarmé's 'Le Conflit', a prose poem which is in part a meditation on similar themes, opens with an image of a window.[128] Terdiman argues that such images are a way of lending a concrete form to the tensions inherent in the modernist project of sealing off the aesthetic from the historical and the social. Images of violence or the threat of violence crossing over or smashing these windows embody an uneasy awareness of the potential return of the historical into the realm of the aesthetic, or even a sense that the two can never be fully separated. Terdiman writes of the window that 'its very brittleness is an acute reminder of the sort of menace it frames and simultaneously seeks to forestall'.[129] Such crossings are also present in Nabokov's text, and they nuance the depiction of the home and the world of early childhood as an idyllic time of emotional and aesthetic enrichment.

This interweaving of the historical and the aesthetic occurs in a particularly striking way when Nabokov describes looking through a window in his mother's bedroom while waiting for his English teacher. This is the same window which Nabokov kisses through a gauze curtain, and just after he mentions this, he says that it was through this window that he saw a murdered man for the first time. He writes that as the corpse was being carried away, another man was trying to rip its boot off, even though the men carrying the body were punching him and pushing him away.[130] Nabokov does not dwell on this image but moves on smoothly to write that when he sat looking through this window before his art lessons, there was nothing to see on the quiet street. The early memories of putting his lips to his mother's window, the much later one of seeing the corpse, and the intermediate one of waiting on his English teacher are all contained within one passage. The later and more violent memory cannot be separated from the earlier, more peaceful recollections. This effect is repeated later in the autobiography when Nabokov remembers the trees lining the streets near his house, and writes that the ear and finger of a terrorist who had been blown up by his own bomb had once been found in one of them.[131] He also says that during the revolution of 1905, children had climbed into the trees to escape the violence, but had been shot down at random by mounted police.[132] As before, the trees are connected both with violence and beauty. Nabokov writes of how they create 'a pattern of silver filigree in a mother-of-pearl mist' before relating the violence that took place in and around them.[133] The connection between artistic consciousness and violence is reinforced when Nabokov refers to one of their servants leading Bolshevik soldiers through the house to the room where he was born and where his mother kept the jewels Nabokov would play with as a child.[134] The image of Bolshevik soldiers in the room where Nabokov was born and where the jewels are kept speaks of an interweaving of the safety, love and beauty of the domestic sphere and the violence of public history.

This connection between domestic spaces and violent histories is also made in Nina Berberova's 1972 *Курсив мой*.[135] Berberova mentions that she was born on the same street as Nabokov, two years and four months after him.[136] She shares Nabokov's clear visual memories of the house where she was born, though she dwells much less on its description.[137] She also moves between descriptions of the domestic space which emphasize its safety to references to the violence which took place within it after the October Revolution and during the Civil War.[138] In one particularly striking episode, the young Berberova stands looking at the full moon through a window of her house. Her father approaches and says that soon the elephants and tortoises will be coming to reclaim their ivory and combs. Here, objects associated with the bourgeois interior are resituated as the bodily exterior of exotic animals. Berberova's father's comments play with ideas about inside and outside, suggesting the presence of an untamed exterior presence within the home that will soon overwhelm its boundaries both from within and without. Both *Курсив мой* and *Speak, Memory* complicate the idea of the domestic sphere as protected from a hostile exterior world, calling attention to the permeability of the boundaries of the home. Because there is a continuity between the domestic interior and Nabokov's inner world, the permeability of the boundaries of the house also suggests the passage of images of violence into the artist's mind. A close reading of Nabokov's portrayal of domestic spaces then brings out the presence of traces of violence within the intimate world of the self and the family, and the interpenetration of the child's absorption of beauty and the pain of others.

In Nabokov's text it is the permeable boundary between the world of the self and the exterior world which is portrayed as the sign of the self's vulnerability to historical violence. In Chamoiseau's text, it is the closing up of the borders between self and world that suggests the encroachment of the legacies of violent histories on the protected world of the self. The author draws a parallel between his own transition from childhood to adulthood and Martinique's transition to new economic structures which lead to greater dependence on France. He conveys both kinds of transition through metaphors of hardening boundaries. The author's move from the creative perception of childhood to the more conventional perception of adulthood is suggested through images of husks or crusts forming around labile material.[139] Similarly, Martinique's economic transformation is encapsulated by the move from wooden to concrete houses. Both kinds of transition are figured as a kind of loss and are associated with blindness to the outside world and diminished life. Rigid boundaries as a metaphor for impoverished perception appear especially prominently in this passage, where Chamoiseau meditates on the difference between childhood and adult perception, and their relationship to reality:

> On ne quitte pas l'enfance, on la serre au fond de soi. On ne s'en détache pas, on la refoule. Ce n'est pas un processus d'amélioration qui achemine vers l'adulte, mais la lente sédimentation d'une croûte autour d'un état sensible qui posera toujours le principe de ce que l'on est. On ne quitte pas l'enfance, on se met à croire à la réalité, à ce que l'on dit être le réel. La réalité est ferme, stable, tracée bien souvent à l'équerre — et confortable. Le réel (que l'enfant perçoit en ample proximité) est une déflagration complexe, inconfortable, de possibles et d'impossibles. Grandir, c'est ne plus avoir la force d'en assumer la perception. Ou alors c'est dresser entre cette perception et soi le bouclier d'une enveloppe mentale. Le poète — c'est pourquoi — ne grandit jamais ou si peu.[140]

> [You never leave childhood, you hold it tight inside. You never detach from it, you repress it. It's not a process of improvement that leads to adulthood, but the slow sedimentation of a crust around a sensitive state that will be the core of what you are. You never leave childhood, you begin to believe in reality, what is said to be real. Reality is firm, stable, often drawn at right angles — and comfortable. What is real (which the child perceives in close proximity) is a complex, uncomfortable deflagration of possibilities and impossibilities. To grow up is to cease to have the strength to perceive it. Or else to erect a mental shield between this perception and the self. That's why poets never grow up, or so little.]

Here, rigid boundaries around the self prevent true perception, which is replaced by a simplified, conventional view of the world. The attributes of 'la réalité' — 'ferme, stable, tracée bien souvent à l'équerre' [firm, stable, often drawn at right angles] — echo those of concrete homes, while the reference to the set square suggests the uniformity and univocal meaning of technical drawings as opposed to the co-existence of opposite states found in the poetic 'réel' experienced by the child. This co-existence of opposite states is reminiscent of the old wooden house where 'les lumières et les ombres, les mystères et les évidences' [light and shadow, mystery and truth] intermingle.[141] Given the repeated association of the wooden houses with fire, 'déflagration' also connects perception of 'le réel' with older modes of dwelling.

The parallel between the loss of childhood perception and the movement from wooden to concrete houses becomes more significant when one recalls the mapping of the domestic interior on to the maternal body, and the intertwined roles of mother and house as transmitters of Creole culture and filters of the world. Movement away from childhood perception also entails greater distance from the mother and the culture she represents. There is a parallel between this process and the way the concrete walls exclude the life which used to flourish in the transitional space between the house and the outside world. The Creole plants which would bloom on balconies during the author's childhood disappear with the coming of air-conditioning, which creates a sharp contrast between indoors and outdoors.[142] Transitional spaces are further dismantled by the narrowing of the yard which used to contain the kitchens and Man Ninotte's chicken coops.[143] The reduction of such in-between areas where private life and public life blend is echoed by a more general retreat to the indoors, as for example in the move from public water fountains to a supply piped to individual homes.[144]

Like a cell membrane or the passable boundary of an eye, the wooden walls filter the child's experience of the world. This idea is made explicit in its closing passages, where Chamoiseau contrasts the shabby look of the house with its powerful role in his life and the collective life of his family and generation: 'Elle signifiait la misère grise du bois dans un Fort-de-France qui commençait à se bétonner les paupières' [It represented the gray misery of wood in a Fort-de-France that was beginning to cement its eyes shut].[145] This metaphor situates the house as a kind of organ of perception. According to this image, the walls of the house are not just an ordinary boundary, but a sense-making boundary. The movement to concrete walls thus blocks perception of the outside world just as the child's acquisition of adult perception prevents him from seeing 'le réel'. These metaphors have implications for the relationship the text suggests between the life of the self and the legacy of colonialism. The painful image of concrete eyelids and the idea of an opaque and rigid boundary preventing vision conveys Chamoiseau's conception of neo-colonial 'domination insidieuse'.[146] Under this dispensation, the very sense-making capacities of the individual are damaged, so that it becomes difficult or impossible to see beyond the self or to perceive one's own alienation. The metaphor suggests that neo-colonial economic structures both define the limits of the self and prevent perception of the way it defines those limits.

Though it might seem that this is a process imposed only from without, elements of the text suggest complicity in it on the part of the child, the house and the town. The opening page of the main body of the trilogy connects the child's growth in rational knowledge with a more distanced relationship to the world around him. The author speaks of childhood as a kind of lost knowledge, and questions his ability to recover it:

> Peux-tu dire de l'enfance ce que l'on n'en sait plus? Peux-tu, non la décrire, mais l'arpenter dans ses états magiques, retrouver son arcane d'argile et de nuages, d'ombres d'escalier et de vent fol, et témoigner de cette enveloppe construite à mesure qu'effeuillant le rêve et le mystère, tu inventoriais le monde?[147]
>
> [Can you tell of childhood what is no longer known? Can you not describe it but survey it in its magical states, recover its mystery of clay and clouds, of stairway shadows and mad wind, and bear witness to the enclosure constructed while, plucking off petals of mystery and dream, you were taking inventory of the world?]

This passage suggests childhood is a gradual process where growing knowledge of the world is intertwined with a less imaginative relationship to it. Here, childhood is a process whose natural unfolding will lead to its own destruction. This suggestion that destruction is embedded within the qualities that make a certain state most valuable is also present in the description of childhood perception more broadly and in the evocations of the wooden house and the town. As noted earlier, childhood perception is spoken of as a 'déflagration' which links it with the wooden houses and Creole culture. This image suggests the explosive energy of childhood and the way it creates the conditions for opposite states to spark off each other. Yet it also hints that it will inevitably burn itself out. This suggestion that a capacity for self-destruction could be an integral part of valuable ways of being in the world is also present in the author's speculation in the preface that his house might have willingly abandoned itself to the flames which destroy it.[148] On a broader level, the town which is built of such houses also possesses this ambivalent quality of openness to change which includes an openness to its own destruction. Chamoiseau draws out the dual nature of its openness in this passage, which comes shortly after a lament over the replacement of wood by cement:

> ... Cette ville n'a jamais été lourde, ni monumentale, ni en pierre éternelle, juste en bois offert à la dent des cyclones et des embrasements ... maintenant, elle vit l'aventure de ce monde, en fluidité extrême, l'urbain se développe sans faire ville, effaçant des souvenirs, n'accordant qu'une écaille mémorielle dénuée des forces pérennes qu'élevaient les villes de pierre ...[149]
>
> [... This city has never been ponderous nor monumental nor carved in eternal stone, just wood offered to the bite of hurricanes and blazes ... now, it's experiencing the adventure of this world, living in extreme fluidity, urban areas are developing without creating a town, erasing memories, granting only a shell of memories stripped of the perennial might which the cities of stone built up ...]

Here the familiar imagery of a surface layer associated with diminished engagement with the world is complicated by the idea that impermanence and vulnerability to destruction are some of the qualities which make the Creole modes of dwelling valuable to the author. The idea that the hardening or complete disappearance of such permeable boundaries is in some way a natural process, like the end of an explosion or the washing away of fragile buildings, stands in tension with the idea that such loss is caused by contact between the child, house or town with the neo-colonial economic structures and modes of thought. This tension between damage to the self occurring as part of a natural process and being imposed by contact with history will be further explored in the third chapter, but for now I will note that the boundaries of the home in Chamoiseau's work, as in that of Nabokov, both create a world where the child is sheltered, and hold within them the outside forces which make this world vulnerable to destruction.

These nuances in the portrayal of the home's boundaries bring out the different points at which painful histories make themselves felt in the author's life. Perec, unlike Nabokov and Chamoiseau, does not suggest there was a time in his life 'before' contact with 'l'histoire avec sa grande hache'.[150] Indeed his image of history as an axe is evocative of its power to curtail the temporal continuities which would make concepts of before and after meaningful. His text suggests that his experiences of the domestic interior and of the other places he lived were always inflected by traces and anticipatory signs of the violence which would fracture his family life. Nabokov and Chamoiseau take a more ambivalent approach to this question of the time before contact with history. On the one hand, each connects his own most vivid experience of violent histories with places that are quite distinct from the home. As I will go on to explore, school is the most prominent place where the young Chamoiseau will come into contact with the painful legacy of colonialism and Nabokov's vulnerability to historical violence begins in earnest once he has left Petrograd for the Crimea, then Cambridge, Berlin and Paris. The child's experience of the domestic interior is largely opposed to later, painful events which take place in the outside world. Yet even as the two authors construct such an opposition between a benevolent domestic world and a dangerous public sphere, they work to undermine it, drawing attention to the ways in which the boundaries of the home both exclude the violence without and make it present within the intimate world of the family, the self and the first language. Their portrait of the domestic interior is an ambivalent one, which suggests that safety and danger, the intimate and the strange are intertwined at the roots of the self.

An examination of these authors' portrayals of childhood dwelling-places brings out their engagement with a set of concerns common to all three. Each author seeks to narrate the interaction between an individual life and a larger history which has triggered inter-generational changes in language, greater distance from the previous generation and a problematized relationship to the spaces inhabited by the child-self. The portrayal of home in these texts brings out the challenges involved in depicting damage done to the self by historical events, when those events have also been instrumental in forming the self. This becomes visible in particular in the image of the author on the threshold of his former home. In these texts, such images lend a political edge to the sense of exclusion from the past common to many autobiographies, as each author draws attention to the role of the state in widening the gap between past and present. The portrayal of the child's experience of the home emphasizes the importance of close contact with the previous generation and the first language and culture in allowing the child to grow into an imaginative, nourishing relationship with the surrounding world, an importance which is thrown into relief by Perec's text, where their absence is associated with difficulty in establishing a positive relationship with others and the world. Though Perec's portrayal of the presence of traces and anticipatory signs of historical violence within the domestic space at first seems quite distant from the more celebratory accounts of early childhood found in *Speak, Memory* and *Une enfance créole*, closer examination reveals that these texts, too, locate elements of violent histories even within the space of the home.

The violent histories whose resonances each author traces are fundamentally histories of mobility. Nabokov's exile from Russia for Europe and then America means his evocation of childhood home as it currently stands is entirely imagined. His physical distance is reinforced by a linguistic distance suggested by the insertion of translated Russian words into his discarded foreword. The clear physical and linguistic distance shaping Nabokov's recollections of his childhood home are in contrast to the muted portrayal of a local journey in a familiar city through which Perec depicts his return to the rue Vilin. The short distance from Perec's adult home to the rue Vilin belies the unbridgeable distance separating Perec from the former home. His sense of distance from it is in fact greater than that found in Nabokov's autobiography, as Perec's memories of the place and the traces of his parents' lives there have been much more effectively erased. Though Perec lives almost all of his adult life in Paris, returning to his earliest childhood home involves addressing a family history of oppression and multiple migrations which open gaps between his adult life and his early years with his parents. Chamoiseau, like Perec, writes in the city he was born in. In his case, the return to childhood spaces must be made through the imagination rather than physical space because of the destruction of the old house and the economic and social changes in Martinique in the last fifty years. Changes in the physical surroundings of Martinique are accompanied by the creation of a linguistic and cultural gulf between child and adult-selves which further deepens the gap between adult-self and childhood home. This gulf is portrayed as the result of neo-colonial French policy in Martinique, and consequently can be seen as part of the ongoing legacy of French colonial movements into Martinican spaces. For all three authors, the relationship to geographical points of origin is tied up with the question of linguistic and cultural change, which will be examined in the next chapter.

Notes to Chapter 1

1. The '1.5 generation' is a term for people who were children during the Second World War and Holocaust, and who are therefore in between the first and second generation of those affected. It first appears in Susan Rubin Suleiman, 'The 1.5 Generation: Thinking About Child Survivors and the Holocaust', *American Imago*, 59 (2002), 277–95 (p. 277).
2. *La Poétique de l'espace* (Paris: Presses universitaires de France, 1957), p. 24.
3. Georges Perec, *Ellis Island* (Paris: P.O.L., 1995), p. 56.
4. *Chemin*, 69.
5. Vladislav Khodasevich, Некрополь (Moscow: Vagrius, 2001 [1939]), p. 186; Iurii Terapiano, Встречи (New York: Izdatel'stvo imeni Chekhova, 1953), p. 153.
6. Said, p. 50.
7. Suleiman, p. 292.
8. See, for example, Claudine Vegh, *Je ne lui ai pas dit au revoir: Des enfants de déportés parlent* (Paris: Gallimard, 1979), pp. 26–27, Sarah Kofman, *Rue Ordener, rue Labat* (Paris: Galilée, 1994), p. 57 and Lore Groszmann Segal, *Other People's Houses* (London: Victor Gollancz, 1965), p. 165.

9. There is a depiction of such a moment in a fictional text by one of the members of the 1.5 generation: Élisabeth Gille, *Un paysage de cendres* (Paris: Seuil, 1996), pp. 88–89.
10. Vegh, p. 113.
11. McCusker, *Recovering Memory*, p. 47; Hardwick, *Childhood, Autobiography and the Francophone Caribbean* (Oxford: Oxford University Press, 2013), pp. 2–4.
12. Maeve McCusker, ' "Troubler l'ordre de l'oubli": Memory and Forgetting in French Caribbean Autobiography of the 1990s', *Forum for Modern Language Studies*, 40 (2004), 438–50 (pp. 440–41).
13. Jean Bernabé, Raphaël Confiant and Patrick Chamoiseau, *Éloge de la créolité/In Praise of Creoleness (bilingual edition)*, trans. by M.B. Taleb-Khyar, 2nd edn (Paris: Gallimard, 1993); *Childhood, Autobiography and the Francophone Caribbean*, p. 56; McCusker, *Recovering Memory*, p. 73.
14. Bachelard, p. 24.
15. *SM*, 17.
16. Washington, D.C., Library of Congress, Manuscript Division, Vladimir Vladimirovich Nabokov Papers, Box 9.
17. *DB* 30.
18. *SM*, 17.
19. 'Speak, Photographs?: Visual Transparency and Verbal Opacity in Nabokov's *Speak, Memory*', *NOJ/НОЖ: Nabokov Online Journal*, 3 (2009).
20. *La Chambre claire: note sur la photographie* (Paris: Gallimard 1980), pp. 23–24.
21. *SM*, 17.
22. Kaplan, pp. 3–4.
23. *W*, 68–69.
24. *Espèces d'espaces* (Paris: Galilée, 1974), pp. 122–23.
25. *Ellis Island*, p. 56.
26. *Ellis Island*, p. 57.
27. Geoffrey Hartman, *The Longest Shadow: In the Aftermath of the Holocaust* (Basingstoke: Palgrave Macmillan, 1996), p. 19, quoted in Anne Whitehead, *Trauma Fiction* (Edinburgh: Edinburgh University Press, 2004), p. 10.
28. *Fear and Hope: Three Generations of the Holocaust* (Cambridge, MA: Harvard University Press, 1995), p. 1.
29. *Espèces d'espaces*, p. 86.
30. *Espèces d'espaces*, p. 86.
31. *W*, 68.
32. *Espèces d'espaces*, p. 86.
33. *W*, 212.
34. *W*, 76.
35. *Espèces d'espaces*, pp. 76–77.
36. *W*, 68.
37. *SM*, 17. I am grateful to Muireann Maguire for drawing my attention to this point.
38. *W*, 67.
39. Bachelard, p. 48.
40. *W*, 57.
41. *W*, 68.
42. *L'Infra-ordinaire* (Paris: Seuil, 1989), pp. 20–21.
43. *W*, 67.
44. *W*, 57–58.
45. 'Dwelling Space in Post-war French Fiction: Camus, Sollers, Perec' (unpublished doctoral thesis, University of Oxford, 2008), p. 8.
46. Villeneuve, p. 213.
47. *La Vie mode d'emploi: romans* (Paris: Poche, 2002), p. 818; cited in Villeneuve, p. 218.
48. *La Vie mode d'emploi*, p. 660, cited in Villeneuve, p. 196.
49. Villeneuve, p. 214.
50. *L'Infa-ordinaire*, pp. 20–21.
51. *Antan*, 10–11.
52. *Antan*, 11.

53. *Antan*, 11.
54. *Antan*, 9.
55. *Antan*, 9.
56. *Antan*, 10.
57. Patrick Chamoiseau and Raphaël Confiant, *Lettres créoles: Tracées antillaises et continentales de la littérature: Haïti, Guadeloupe, Martinique, Guyane 1635–1975* (Paris: Gallimard, 1999), pp. 33–34.
58. *Antan*, 9.
59. *Antan*, 11.
60. Richard Price, *The Convict and the Colonel: A Story of Colonialism and Resistance in the Caribbean* (Durham, NC: Duke University Press, 2006), p. xiii.
61. Price, p. xi.
62. *Childhood, Autobiography and the Francophone Caribbean*, p. 13.
63. Jean Piaget, *The Child's Conception of the World*, trans. by Joan and Andrew Tomlinson (London: Routledge & Kegan Paul, 1971), p. 169.
64. Piaget, p. 170.
65. *The Child in the House: An Imaginary Portrait* (Boston: Everett, 1895), p. 5.
66. *The Mill on the Floss* (London: Vintage, 2010), pp. 169–70, quoted in Said, p. 49.
67. *SM*, 72.
68. Suleiman, p. 277.
69. Laci Mattison uses the term 'temporally layered' in 'Nabokov's Aesthetic Bergsonism: An Intuitive, Reperceptualized Time', *Mosaic*, 46 (2013), 37–52 (p. 40).
70. *SM*, 182.
71. *SM*, 187. 'Tamara' is a pseudonym; the real name of the person she represents is Valentina Shulgina.
72. *SM*, 100.
73. *SM*, 104.
74. *SM*, 152.
75. *SM*, 13.
76. Andrew Baruch Wachtel, *The Battle for Childhood* (Stanford: Stanford University Press, 1990), p. 54.
77. Wachtel, pp. 83–131.
78. *Antan*, 46.
79. *Antan*, 42; 47.
80. *Antan*, 38.
81. *Antan*, 43–44.
82. Bernabé, Confiant and Chamoiseau, p. 13.
83. *Chemin*, 77; *Antan*, 51–52.
84. *W*, 103.
85. *W*, 103.
86. *W*, 103–04.
87. *W*, 108.
88. *W*, 218.
89. *W*, 104–08.
90. *W*, 103.
91. *W*, 125.
92. *W*, 154.
93. *DB*, 171.
94. T. I. Radomskaya, *Дом и отечество в русской классической литературе первой трети XIX в.* (Moscow: Sovpadenie, 2006), p. 235, italics in the original.
95. *SM*, 25.
96. *SM*, 47.
97. *SM*, 25–26.
98. *SM*, 26.
99. *SM*, 124–28.
100. *SM*, 127–28.
101. *SM*, 91.

102. *SM*, 65; 24.
103. *SM*, 22.
104. *SM*, 20–22.
105. *SM*, 23–24.
106. *Antan*, 103–04.
107. *How Societies Remember* (Cambridge: Cambridge University Press, 1989), pp. 72–105.
108. *Antan*, 180.
109. *A bout*, 47.
110. *Antan*, 104.
111. *Antan*, 105.
112. *W*, 94–95.
113. *W*, 136–37.
114. *W*, 95.
115. *Les Choses: une histoire des années soixante* (Paris: Poche, 2002), p. 54.
116. *Espèces d'espaces*, p. 111.
117. *Penser/Classer* (Paris: Hachette, 1985), p. 14.
118. *Espèces d'espaces*, p. 112.
119. *W*, 21.
120. *W*, 105–06.
121. *W*, 68.
122. Villeneuve, p. v.
123. *The Culture of Time and Space* (Cambridge, MA: Harvard University Press, 2003), p. 187.
124. Beatriz Colomina, 'Battle Lines', in *Rethinking Borders*, ed. by John C. Welchman (Basingstoke: Macmillan, 1996), pp. 51–64 (p. 53).
125. *Poésies complètes,* ed. by René Jasinski, 3 vols (Paris: Nizet, 1970), I, 81, quoted in Richard Terdiman, *Present Past: Modernity and the Memory Crisis* (Ithaca, NY: Cornell University Press, 1993), pp. 159–60.
126. *Oeuvres complètes,* ed. by Claude Pichois, 2 vols (Paris: Gallimard, 1976), I, 317–19, quoted in Terdiman, p. 164.
127. *A la recherche du temps perdu*, ed. by Jean-Ives Tadié, 4 vols (Paris: Gallimard, 1987–89), II (1988), 41–42, quoted in Terdiman, pp. 161.
128. *Oeuvres complètes,* ed. by Henri Mondor and G. Jean-Aubry (Paris: Gallimard, 1945), pp. 355–60, quoted in Terdiman, p. 164.
129. Terdiman, p. 165.
130. *SM*, 65.
131. *SM*, 142.
132. *SM*, 142.
133. *SM*, 142.
134. *SM*, 145.
135. Berberova's autobiography appeared in 1969 in an English translation before being published in its original Russian version in 1972.
136. Nina Berberova, *Курсив мой* (Munich: Fink, 1972), p. 36.
137. *Курсив мой*, p. 36.
138. *Курсив мой*, pp. 38–39.
139. *Antan*, 21.
140. *Antan*, 93–94.
141. *Antan*, 185.
142. *A bout*, 186.
143. *Antan*, 186.
144. *Antan*, 94.
145. *Antan*, 185.
146. *Ecrire en pays dominé* (Paris: Gallimard, 2002), pp. 17–18.
147. *Antan*, 21.
148. *Antan*, 111.
149. *A bout*, 186–87, italics in original.
150. *W*, 13.

CHAPTER 2

Writing Between Languages

Writing in the light of histories of mobility involves addressing shifts in linguistic and cultural expression as well as changing relationships to childhood dwelling-places. In the previous chapter we saw how each author explores the resonances of histories which create an ambivalent mix of connection and distance in his relationship to childhood homes. Ambivalence is present to an even greater degree in each author's attitude towards the language he writes in. Each seeks to evoke a family history and childhood world in a language which is the most visible and enduring sign of his distance from it. Nabokov published the first and final full-length versions of his autobiography in English, though he grew up speaking Russian, French and English. Perec sets out to recover memories of his early childhood with his parents and extended family in a French-language text, though his family spoke French as a second language. Chamoiseau evokes in French the trauma of the forced acquisition of French. For each author, representing his childhood self and family history involves representing one language in a text written in another. Their autobiographical practice triggers reflection on what it means for different languages to come into contact.

Reviewing the history of translation in Canada, Vanamala Viswanatha and Sherry Simon write: 'it becomes clear that translation practice has been shaped by dramatic changes in conceptualizations of cultural difference'.[1] Their remark points to the way translation is 'always grounded in a set of assumptions about ways in which linguistic forms carry cultural meanings — in short, in an implicit theory of culture'.[2] The purpose of this chapter is to study the kind of cultural meaning carried by these authors' use of linguistic forms, focusing particularly on those moments where there is a tension between the linguistic forms used and the cultural meanings they carry. All three authors are at pains to have the languages of the family past resonate within the chosen idiom of the autobiographical text. How do they go about this, and what are the implications of their style for the idea of a French-language author?

The First Language: Home or Passage?

To study these authors' movements between languages, we need a working answer to the question of what it means to speak a first language, and what it means to leave it behind. But what is a first language? For Nabokov, Perec and Chamoiseau, this simple question proves difficult to answer. Is it the first language heard, spoken, written, or read? What if one's mother's tongue is not one's mother tongue? Because of the movements between languages in each author's individual and family history, their autobiographical writing engages closely with ideas about where the borders of a given language lie in an individual life and within cultural communities. For each author, to recall the past means considering what it means to have crossed linguistic borders. In Bassnett and Trivedi's terms, he must create links between the linguistic forms of French and English and cultural meanings more often connected to Russian, Creole, Hebrew or Yiddish. Nabokov and Chamoiseau must express the meanings associated with a first language in another language, while Perec searches for a way to have other languages echo through his first language. Creating this kind of link poses a significant challenge to author and reader alike.

Dante, in one of the earliest arguments for writing in a European vernacular, distinguishes between the first language and those learned later by the degree of effort necessary to acquire fluency. He suggests that the difference between a first and second language is that the first language is learned through imitating people without learning any rules, while the acquisition of a second language is necessarily more deliberate, involving careful study of the language's grammar.[3] In this view, the move from first to second language is a move from intimacy to formality. This distinction is at play in views of language change which see a shift into another language as a diminishment of the potential for self-expression, a loss of meaning which is also a personal loss. Sherry Simon sums up this view of selfhood and language when she speaks of the 'pathos of dislocation, the loss of spontaneous contact with one's inner self, of emotional immediacy and wholeness, which is so often associated with translation'.[4] Simon is sceptical as to whether such a view of translation is the only possible one. These authors too present the idea of the first language as a home, a linguistic space allowing a peculiar freedom and intimacy of expression not found in other languages, only to complicate any simple division between first and second languages. In what follows, I look first at the points in each text where the idea of the first language as a home emerges, before studying how each author questions and complicates this concept.

Nabokov speaks of his transition from Russian to English as a difficult metamorphosis. In the foreword to *Другие берега* [Other Shores], he writes that in leaving Russian behind he was abandoning a medium he had made his own. He speaks of Russian as a living being he has come to know and tame, and then writes: 'чудовищные трудности предстоявшего перевоплощения, и ужас расставанья с живым, ручным существом ввергли меня сначала в состояние, о котором нет надобности распространяться; скажу только, что ни один стоящий на определенном уровне писатель его не испытывал до меня' [the monstrous difficulties of the coming reincarnation and the horror of the separation with the living, docile being put me in a state there is no need to dwell upon; I will say only that no writer above a certain level had experienced it before me].[5] The characterization of Russian as a living language and the efforts needed to leave it as monstrous situate Nabokov's move into the English language as unnatural. The foreword suggests that Russian offers a fuller mode of self-expression than English, as Nabokov writes that the first English version is to the Russian text what a stylized profile is to looking into a real face.[6]

Comparison of the different versions offers some support for the view that Russian is connected with intimate sensory experience that could only be expressed with difficulty in another language. Nabokov writes that the Russian root for the verb to feed, 'корм', is associated for him with the feel of warm, sweet porridge in his mouth, and surmises that this association must go back to his earliest childhood.[7] His synaesthesia connects Russian letters with different colours from their English counterparts, even when both letters represent the same sound.[8] When he remembers the special projector one of his tutors brought to organize magic lantern afternoons, a snatch of his tutor's speech comes back to him. This is recalled in the Russian-language text, but not in the English one.[9] The speech is ascribed to Mnemosyne, making Memory a Russian speaker. Together such moments situate Russian as a linguistic home which leaves possibilities open to the author which are lost when he crosses its threshold.

Chamoiseau's text, too, suggests that certain emotions and sensations can be expressed more easily in Creole than in French. Creole often signals an upsurge of (remembered) emotion in the text. We see this when the child learns how to manipulate a piece of chalk so he can write with it:

> Découverte: il tenait la craie à pleine main (n'importe quelle main) comme un poignard. Puis, une main fut repérée comme plus habile qu'une autre. Puis, il fut clair qu'en tenant la craie au bout de certains doigts la souplesse était reine. *Manman-manman-manman!...*[10]
>
> [Discovery: he held the chalk with his entire hand (either one), like a dagger. Then, one hand turned out to be more skillful than the other. Then, it became clear that holding the chalk with the tips of certain fingers was easiest of all. *Mama-Mama-Mama!*]

The italicized Creole words at the end of this passage evoke a sudden burst of excitement as the child has a breakthrough in his writing technique. Instances like these reinforce a point Chamoiseau makes explicitly when he writes that although he always knew some French, Creole was the language he would use with most ease, especially when he spoke to other children or spoke to express an emotion.[11] Like Nabokov, Chamoiseau both presents the intimate, spontaneous quality of his childhood language and laments the move away from it. He quotes his schoolteacher's criticisms of the children's speech to show how the move away from Creole replaces one cultural universe with another. The teacher rolls his r's, over-correcting his local accent: 'Quoi, quoi, quoi, un "zombi"? N'avez-vous jamais entendu parrler des elfes, des gnomes, des fées et feux follets?! Éparrgnez-moi vos "soucougnan" et vos "cheval-trois-pattes"!' [Here now, what's this about a zombie?! Haven't you ever hearrd of elves, gnomes, fairries, and will-o-the-wisps? Spare me your *soucougnans* and three-leg-horses!'] [12] When the author remembers the games of marbles he would play as a child, he refers to the marbles as 'billes', the standard French term. He then has the chorus of *Répondeurs* or 'backtalkers' reproach him by saying:

> J'ai dit 'bille'.
> En fait, on disait 'mab'.
> C'est ça l'ennui.[13]
>
> [Problem is,
> I said marble,
> But we really used *mab*.]

The way the chorus takes up the author's words to correct them speaks of the doubled allegiances and heightened level of linguistic self-consciousness brought about by the shift in language between childhood and adulthood. The self-consciousness at play even within the author's introduction of Creole words into the French text suggests that it no longer fits the definition of a first language as one that is used freely and spontaneously.

Chamoiseau's childhood transition from Creole to French so that both languages are used self-consciously in his autobiographical writing suggests one way in which his text begins to undermine the clear distinction between first and second language. In Perec's text, the idea of a first language as a linguistic home is undermined as soon as it is raised. We saw in the previous chapter how the idea of home which is present though complex in the autobiographies of Nabokov and Chamoiseau is absent in Perec's text, as there is no time he can remember before wartime history disrupts his family life. His early memories of learning to speak and read are similarly shadowed by 'l'histoire avec sa grande hache'. The first childhood memory Perec relates involves Yiddish, Hebrew and his place within a family. He remembers sitting amongst scattered Yiddish newspapers and drawing a Hebrew letter to the delight of his assembled family.[14] The scene is initially one of family togetherness: 'toute la famille, la totalité, l'intégralité de la famille est là, réunie autour de l'enfant qui vient de naître (n'ai-je pourtant pas dit il y a un instant que j'avais trois ans?), comme un rempart infranchissable' [the entirety, the totality of the family is there, gathered like an impregnable battlement around the child who has just been born (but didn't I say a moment ago that I was three?)].[15] The certainty of this memory is undermined first by the anxious accumulation of words for wholeness and secondly by the parenthetical questioning of the accuracy of the memory which ironically distances the word 'enfant' from 'rempart infranchissable'. Even as it is narrated, this memory is questioned. A footnote to a slightly later part of the passage reveals that the letter he remembers writing does not exist: 'Il existe en effet une lettre nommée "Gimmel" dont je me plais à croire qu'elle pourrait être l'initiale de mon prénom; elle ne ressemble absolument pas au signe que j'ai tracé' [There is in fact a letter called "Gimmel" which I like to think could be the initial of my first name; it looks absolutely nothing like the sign I have drawn].[16] The transition from the main text to the footnote marks a shift from identity within a group setting to individual identity. The author's inability to make a link between the letter he might have drawn and his own name speaks of a broader difficulty in situating his own life in relation to a family or linguistic community.

These hints that the memory is fabricated are given further support when Perec writes that his aunt has told him how he used to play at making out letters in newspapers, but that the newspapers were French rather than Yiddish.[17] Because he was tracing the letters in the newspapers in the late 1930s and early 1940s, he was likely to have been deciphering articles reporting at least partly on the war and its build-up. His first contact with language was then not with an ancestral language, but rather with language referring to the very histories which would distance him from Hebrew and Yiddish. Though this point is left implicit in the autobiographical chapter, one of the early fictional chapters draws out the idea that contact with the French language is something to be feared. The fictional narrator, who has taken up a false identity after deserting from the French Army, receives a letter. It panics him because it is written in French. He worries that the letter is from the authorities who are tracking him down, or from someone who wishes to blackmail him. He then reassures himself by reflecting on the extra-national character of the French language: 'le fait que cette lettre fût écrite en français ne signifiait pas qu'elle s'adressait à moi, à celui que j'avais été, au soldat déserteur; mon actuelle identité faisait de moi un Suisse romand et ma francophonie ne surprenait personne' [that the letter was written in French did not mean that it was intended for me, for the man I had been, for the deserter; my current identity established me as a French-speaking Swiss, so my command of the language was not likely to surprise anyone].[18] The French language first appears in the text as a kind of accusation which triggers fear, and Gaspard Winckler's reassurances to himself that the French language is not necessarily associated with a vengeful French state ring hollow.

Perec's narration of his false memory of drawing the Hebrew letter amongst his extended family grants the idea of a linguistic and familial home a kind of ghostly reality in the text. Although he cannot write of his parents' languages as his lost linguistic homes, French retains some of the characteristics of a second language. Arrived at through a family history of migration, it is not portrayed as the intimate language of spontaneous expression but is rather associated with newspapers and unwanted detection, with violence and fear. French is Perec's first language in the sense that it is the first language he learned to read and write and the language he is most comfortable speaking. But his relationship to it contests the idea of the first language as the language of 'spontaneous contact with one's inner self, of emotional immediacy and wholeness' identified by Simon. We have already seen how the self-consciousness that enters Chamoiseau's use of Creole also begins to contest this concept of the first language in his text. A closer look at the portrayal of Russian by Nabokov and Creole by Chamoiseau suggest that the division between first and second language is further complicated in each author's work.

There are moments in *Une enfance créole* and *Speak, Memory* when the house of language seems less a dwelling-place than a passage. At these moments, the author's first language acts as more of a bridge than a home, connecting his early linguistic life with the languages he will later go on to learn and write. Nabokov's narration of his childhood and youth lays emphasis on its cosmopolitan qualities. He embeds French and English words in the Russian version of his autobiography, and Russian words in its French and English versions. The particular way he does this challenges the division between Russian as an intimate language of sensory experience and English as a language he is forced into by circumstance. It situates his earliest experience of language as one of sensory absorption of several languages, interwoven. Nabokov creates continuities between the different periods in his life by pointing to the presence of English, American, French, and Russian cultures within each other. Though in the full-length version of the autobiography none of the chapters have titles, when they were published as individual sketches, they did, and one chapter was called 'My English Childhood'. It puts forward the idea that the author's childhood, though spent in Russia and interspersed with holidays in France and Germany, was in fact strongly inflected by English culture. The opening sentence of this chapter, in a feat of syntax, situates the Anglophilia of the author's childhood as an expression of his family's rootedness in a peculiarly Russian time and place. The chapter opens: 'The kind of Russian family to which I belonged — a kind now extinct — had, among other virtues, a traditional leaning toward the comfortable products of Anglo-Saxon civilization.'[19] Later, Nabokov will remember his father's concern at his children's ability to read in English but not in Russian. To remedy this, his father invites the village schoolmaster to come and teach his sons the Cyrillic alphabet.[20] Here Russian occupies the place Dante assigns to the second language as a set of rules deliberately acquired. By contrast, the child's first contact with the English alphabet is never narrated, so that it seems to the reader to have been simply absorbed rather than learned. The entry of the Russian alphabet into the home is an occasion of excitement. The child is fascinated with the coloured alphabet blocks the schoolmaster brings to teach the children. We read: 'these cubes he would manipulate as if they were infinitely precious things, which for that matter, they were (besides forming splendid tunnels for toy trains)'.[21] Here the blocks of language do not form a dwelling-place, but rather a passage enabling travel. Like all boundaries, the walls of the trains and its tunnels make present what lies beyond them. Trains and railway tunnels are consistently associated with emerging into a new world in *Speak, Memory*.[22] By situating the Russian alphabet as a tunnel for toy trains, Nabokov portrays his first literary language as a passage which brings him to consciousness of the unknown worlds beyond it.

Throughout the autobiography, Russian cultural expression comes into being through travel. Of a travelling case his mother bought in Florence for her honeymoon, took from Russia into emigration and passed on to her son, who carried it through the United States, Nabokov writes: 'The fact that of our Russian heritage the hardiest survivor proved to be a traveling bag is both logical and emblematic.'[23] In his treatment of foreign influences on his life, Nabokov anticipates his Russian critics, who had long claimed that he was 'un-Russian', that his writing had suffered from his immersion in European literary culture and long exile from Russia. One way of fending off such criticisms about a French strain in his Russian writing is to point it out himself. He brings French echoes in his Russian text to the attention of the reader, as for example when he writes, 'Восемнадцати лет покинув Петербург, я (вот пример галлицизма) был слишком молод в России, чтобы проявить какое-либо любопытсво к моей родословной' [Having left St Petersburg at the age of eighteen I (and here is an example of a Gallicism) was too young in Russia to take any interest at all in my family history].[24] At another point he asks in parenthesis 'Интересно, кто заметит, что этот параграф построен на интонациях Флобера' [I wonder who will notice that this paragraph has been constructed according to Flaubert's intonations].²⁵ But he also defends himself against criticisms that he is not a true Russian writer by celebrating Franco-Russian contact as part of his family's history in Russia and as foundational to modern Russian literary culture. He recalls a walk on the family estates named 'Le Chemin du Pendu' after an aristocrat who had been hanged for rebellion. The walk was named in French, Nabokov writes, because generations of Nabokov children had been shown the estate's many paths by their French-speaking governesses.²⁶ Here the Francophone resonances of his Russian writings come to seem part of his roots in Russia rather than a product of exile.

Pushkin is a recurring figure in the autobiography, and through the several versions of the autobiography he becomes more and more closely linked with the Nabokov family tree. In his writing on Pushkin's poetry, Nabokov brings out the way Pushkin's art was strongly influenced by the French language.²⁷ Pushkin is written into the autobiography as both a literary forefather and an almost-literal forefather, because he offers a model of a writer who is at once both deeply Russian and entirely open to literary cultures and languages from elsewhere. Seen in the light of Pushkin's art, Nabokov's work comes to seem part of a rich Russian tradition of writing arising out of exposure to foreign ideas and literature. We find this in the Russian text when Nabokov recalls his first love affair. He meets a young woman called Tamara while he is staying at his family's country estates for the summer. They pass a blissful summer together in the country and a forlorn winter back in Petrograd. Both are nostalgic for the freedom afforded by the vast Nabokov family grounds with their forests and groves of trees. In *Другие берега* Nabokov writes that Pushkin's Gallicisms, his allusions to the solitude of the country or whisperings of trees, were more than poetic clichés to him and Tamara.²⁸ Here the incorporation of French phrases and ways of thinking is rooted in Russian literature rather than being an individual aberration of Nabokov's. French influences also lose their connotations of artifice and superficiality by being intertwined with the experience of nature and love.

The portrayal of Russian linguistic and cultural life as constantly absorbing influences from without contests those strands of the autobiography which see the Russian language as a fixed home whose boundaries Nabokov has crossed to enter into French and then English. Rather, multiple crossings of national borders by people, texts, words and ideas are shown to form Nabokov's experience of Russian life. A similar tension between language as home and language as travel is at play in Chamoiseau's treatment of Creole in his autobiography. Though, as we have seen, he situates Creole as naming a cultural universe which does not exist within the French language, at other points in the text he creates a fluid continuum between standard French, local French and Creole words. Aural effects bind words of different origins together, as when he writes of 'gros bondas qui brimbalaient dans le chemin' [big butts sashaying along the street], where 'bondas' is a local word and 'brimbaler' is a standard French word.²⁹ His syntax also creates echoes and overlappings between words of different origins. Free indirect discourse allows the mainly French narrative voice to merge with the imagined Creole voices of the people who figure in the author's memories, as in the following example: 'Telle marchande bousculée, dressée au même endroit, tentait de reconnaître l'isalop qui lui avait ranimé une vieille inflammation [Over here, a rudely jostled shopkeeper still craned her neck to find that little bugger who'd stirred up her rheumatics].'[30] The boundaries of the author's voice, like the boundaries of French and Creole, are open and in flux. By bringing standard French and Creole into a text together, Chamoiseau goes back into the history of each language. He uses Old French forms which are no longer used in standard French but which are the roots of contemporary Creole forms. The word 'bailler' (an Old French word meaning 'to give') is an example of this. It is no longer used in standard French, but it gave rise to the Creole word 'bay'.[31] By employing the word 'baille', Chamoiseau is writing neither Creole nor standard French, but is rather going back to a time when the two languages were one. Celia Britton writes that Édouard Glissant's theoretical explorations of what it means to mix languages lead him away from a view of a given language as a specific system, distinct from the structures which create every other language-system.[32] Chamoiseau's writing, which plays on the possibilities of mixing French and Creole, also discourages this perspective on differentiation between languages.

Chamoiseau goes back to the common history of French and Creole but he also writes each language into the future by creating new words. His neologisms undermine the idea that either language is a concrete given. Marie-José N'zengou-Tayo has brought out the various ways Chamoiseau creates new linguistic forms in *Texaco,* and he employs the same techniques in *Une enfance créole*. He forms new words through employing Creole grammatical structures in French, as when he creates hyphenated verbs or doubles adjectives as a form of superlative.[33] By forming new words that are not already part of French or Creole, Chamoiseau gestures towards the potentiality of language, creating 'a new language strange but familiar at the same time for both Creolophone and non-Creolophone readers'.[34] Because the new words Chamoiseau coins draw on both French and Creole grammar and lexis, the reader is hard pressed to decide which language they belong to. For a reader from outside the French-speaking Caribbean, the doubt about where such words belong goes hand in hand with an uncertainty about whether they are in fact coinages or part of a collective idiom the reader simply does not know.[35] Reading Chamoiseau's language is an experience of fluidity. As the reader moves through the text she moves more or less smoothly between standard French, high literary French, Martinican French, Creole, Old French and neologisms. As this chapter will go on to examine, Chamoiseau deploys a range of strategies to ensure he can use an unusually broad range of grammar and vocabulary while maintaining the engagement and comprehension of the reader. Though the reader is conscious as she reads that certain words are outside her usual linguistic experience, if she sets out to categorize the different varieties of language encountered, she will find herself confused. Chamoiseau's language both broadens the reader's sense of the words she can comprehend and challenges her confidence that she can situate those words with certainty within a given language or register.

If Chamoiseau releases the poetic potential of the French language by creating new forms from it, Perec does so by looking back to the transformations words make as they enter into his literary French. His description of the history of his surname is one example of this. For Perec to remember the names of his parents and to read or write his own, he must cross the boundaries of multiple languages and cultures. In the absence of a tangible inheritance from his parents or a shared language, the family name is one of the sole connections between the author and the previous generation, and it takes on a charged role in the autobiography.[36] The name changes as it crosses the borders of Hebrew, Russian, Polish, and French. The combination of its movement between alphabets and countries means that Perec's name is pronounced differently in France from in Lubartów, the town where his grandparents lived and where his father was born. The 'ts' sound at the end of the name was represented through 'c' in its Polish spelling, but when Perec's father came to French, this meant the 'ts' sound was pronounced as a 'k'.[37] Another layer of linguistic confusion is brought about by the fact that the –ec ending is associated with Breton names in France. As Perec's biographer writes:

> Nobody distorted Georges Perec's family name. Nobody mangled it on purpose. It just changed, automatically, through the introduction of a Polish spelling into French [...] He was the French son of Jewish immigrants from Poland, and it was his bizarre fortune to be called by a Hebrew word spelt in Polish, which, when pronounced in French, sounds Breton.'[38]

The name accrues even more linguistic resonances when Perec tells the reader what it means in Hebrew (hole or gap), Russian (pepper) and Hungarian (pretzel).[39] The French word for pretzel, 'bretzel' has in fact occurred in the text by the time the reader reaches this explanation of the multiple meanings of the Perec family name. It is first introduced in a fictional chapter, when the barman offers pretzels to Gaspard Winckler. Attention is drawn to it through the narrator's initial misunderstanding of the offer and through the repetition of the word three times.[40] The new mention of pretzels activates the reader's memory, sending her mind back to the disquieting scene in the bar. Triggering these kinds of backward looks is Perec's way of drawing attention to the presence of multiple languages within his written French.

An examination of the verbal texture of these books brings up some of the difficulties of defining what it means to be a French-language writer, as each author's language leaves open the question of where exactly the borders of the French language lie. Is Perec a French name? Is the 'Chemin du Pendu' Nabokov recalls a Russian place name or a French one? Is 'bailler' as it appears in Chamoiseau's writing a French or Creole verb? Turning to these texts leads this reader to say that each of these words is French, but saying this draws attention to the stretch in the boundaries of the French language. The particular historical circumstances which situate these authors at an angle to the French language and the possibility of comparing them will be explored in the next chapter, but for now, I will note that each writer's work brings out the possibility of the French language echoing through other languages and making present the resonances of other tongues within itself.

Translating for the Reader?

In the last section we saw how the style of each author calls into question the idea that French has firm boundaries demarcating it from other languages. These common-sense boundaries seem to grow faint and disappear as the critic zooms in to consider the origins of a particular word or phrase. As elusive as they may be when examined up close, however, they nonetheless hold significant meaning at a broader level. Importantly, many of these authors' readers are likely to experience French and English as separate from Creole, Russian, Hebrew and Yiddish. The echoing of other languages through the author's autobiographical writings raises the question of his situation within a literary community. Two kinds of relationship are fundamental to the creation of literary community: those between authors and readers and those between writers. What is the nature of the relationship between author and reader when the author connects linguistic forms familiar to the reader with cultural meanings likely to be distant from her? As explored in the last chapter, each author portrays the spaces inhabited by the child-self as distant from his adult life, a distance created or complicated by linguistic change. This creates difficulties in narrating childhood, difficulties which are heightened by the fact that the reader, too, is likely to be geographically, linguistically or culturally distant from many of the scenes and experiences the author seeks to evoke. That both Nabokov and Chamoiseau address a far-off reader is evident from the distance between the childhood home each recalls and the address of his publisher, which is just over four thousand miles for each author. Perec spends most of his life in Paris where his books are also published, but as we have seen, he charts a resonating family history of migration and oppression, and the scope of his autobiography extends from pre-war Russia and Poland to wartime Germany to contemporary Chile, all places and contexts unlikely to be wholly familiar to his reader.

This poses a dilemma: to what extent should the author explain words, phrases and ideas that might cause difficulties of comprehension to the reader? The task of cultural explanation raises worries that the object of explanation will become just that, an object. André Lefevere speaks of this as 'the most important problem in all translating and in all attempts at cross-cultural understanding: can culture A ever really understand culture B on that culture's (i.e. B's) own terms?'[41] The work of Lawrence Venuti is helpful in understanding the dynamics at play in these authors' approach to translating for the reader. Venuti distinguishes between visible translation, where the translator foregrounds the cultural mediation involved in the creation of the new text, and invisible translation, where the work of cultural mediation is obscured and the new text is written as if it had been conceived in the target language.[42] Invisible translation creates a clear target-language text which implicitly emphasizes the translatability of the source language. Visible translation allows certain obscurities to persist in the translated text as an expression of the belief that no language is entirely translatable. Each of these authors is on one level committed to visible forms of translation. They stage the impossibility of speaking the past in the language of the present. Each text resists full understanding, as the author at times refuses to explain fully linguistic and cultural specificities likely to be unfamiliar to the reader. Yet there is fine line between creating a resistant text and alienating the reader. Each of these authors tussles with the dilemmas involved in exploring the impossibility of translation, even as he relies on it to narrate a life-history to the reader.

Let us look first at those moments where each author stages untranslatability. An instance of this arises in Nabokov's English text when he employs the Russian adjective *брезгливый* ('squeamish' or 'fastidious') to describe the habits of one his tutors. He gives the word in its transliterated form but does not translate it, stating simply that its meaning cannot be conveyed in English. The word does not appear in the equivalent passage of the Russian version of the autobiography. It seems that Nabokov employs it in the English text not so much because it is an essential feature of this particular memory, but rather to signal to the English-language reader that he is translating his memories and that the match between his medium and his memory is not always a perfect one. The memory of the place where his father proposed to his mother offers another instance of untranslated Russian in the English text which does not appear in the Russian text. Nabokov writes that there was a steep hill leading up to this place, and that his father would joke that it was a place to take one's bike by the horns.[43] Because the word bike sounds similar to the Russian word for ox, *бык*, this is a bilingual pun on the English phrase for taking the bull by the horns. The linguistic pun finds a visual parallel in the similarity between the shape of a bicycle's handlebars and a bull's horns. This instance fuses both aspects of the author's approach to the translatability of experience and memory. On the one hand, like the reference to the Russian word for squeamish or fastidious, it embeds an untranslated Russian word in the English text, even though this pun is not present in the Russian text. In this way it underlines the distinction between the language of his childhood and the one in which he writes. On the other hand, by making a pun that works through criss-crossing the two languages, he points to their commensurability. This duality is also present in his pronunciation instructions for the place name Gryazno, 'accented on the ultima', which come just before this pun.[44] Such instructions both bring the reader into the Nabokovian world by offering her guidance on proper speech, and exclude her through emphasizing that she is in need of such guidance.

If Nabokov pedantically explains exactly how the reader is to understand Russian words to emphasize the reader's need of a mediator, Chamoiseau parodies such explanations. He employs the traditional apparatus of the translator's footnote only to undermine it. The first time an explanatory footnote occurs is when the teacher asks the children what to call someone who takes apples that do not belong to him. This is the answer he receives:

— C'est un volêr-dê-poule, mêssié...
— Vo...*leurr*, pas *volêr*! Voleurr de pommes, pas de poules![45]

['He's a chicken t'ief, *mêssié*... 'Th... ief, not t'ief! Apple thief, not chicken thief!]

The child's answer has a footnote, which reads: 'En langue créole, le chapardeur est appelé "voleur-de-poule", quel que soit l'objet de son délit' [In Creole, a pilferer is called a chicken thief, no matter what has been stolen].[46] Though at first glance this is a straightforwardly explanatory footnote, the formal tone of the last phrase begins to hint that it may in fact be a parody of the authoritative style of such textual guidance. Subsequent footnotes, labelled 'Note de l'Omniscient', are more explicitly satirical.[47] Chamoiseau also explains without fully explaining, as he does when he describes what the children would do when two of them were fighting: 'Les petites-personnes se rassemblèrent pour psalmodier de concert les traditionnels *iii salé iii salé iii salé iii sicré iii sicré* qui se devaient d'accompagner les coups [All recess activity ceased instantly while kids gathered around to chant in unison the traditional cries of encouragement which had to accompany the blows].'[48] The phrase in italics has a footnote, which reads: 'C'est salé, c'est salé, c'est sucré, c'est sucré! (Traduction de l'Omniscient)' [It's salty, it's salty, it's salty, it's sweet, it's sweet! (Translation courtesy of the Omniscient One.)].'[49] This is a translation which resists attempts to map it on to the original, as *salé* is repeated three times in the original but only twice in the translation. As well as this, the translation does not make the meaning of the chant any clearer than the main text. This non-explanatory footnote further heightens the irony of its source in 'l'Omniscient'. At one point a footnote is written in Creole rather than French so that it offers supplementary information to the Creolophone reader but not to a French metropolitan reader.[50] This part of the text plays on the non-Creolophone reader's desire for clarity only to disappoint her, by beginning the footnote in formal French 'Permettez-moi de préciser' [Allow me to be more specific] before beginning a long list of Creole nouns.[51] Together these strategies create a text which resists the total comprehension of a non-Creolophone reader.

In interviews about his work, Chamoiseau locates his reluctance to offer translations as part of a commitment to 'opacité', Édouard Glissant's term for ethically productive gaps in comprehension in the relationship between self and other. In the spirit of this commitment, Chamoiseau portrays himself as committed to writing passages whose meaning might not be clear to all readers:

> People don't accept the fact that a narration may have opaque, unintelligible, untranslatable zones which are maybe true for me and do correspond to realities which mean nothing to them, which are opaque to them. And so I had to impose certain things. In that spirit, I don't put glossaries in my books, there is no glossary at the end. I include the Creole words such as they are. I don't translate them, etc.... Those are some of the things I stand by.'[52]

This refusal to take up the role of translator works to discourage the foreign reader from seeing his texts as source-texts in need of explanation by a higher authority. It places value on the moments of incomprehension the reader might experience as a result of this refusal to translate. Underlying this commitment is the idea that ethical encounters between self and other depend on an openness to the strangeness of the other.

The stagings of untranslatability examined here serve to delineate spots of opacity in these authors' lives. They lead the reader to focus her curious attention on an aspect of the text which challenges her usual way of perceiving linguistic meaning. Yet, as any translator knows, all attempts at 'bringing the audience to the text' raise the question of 'information load'. Where the reader's usual cultural and linguistic ways of perceiving meaning are too consistently challenged, there is a risk that she will disengage. In this case, the translator will not achieve the aim of creating an encounter between the reader and the resisting opacities of another cultural community. Close examination of these texts suggests that Nabokov and Chamoiseau are all too aware that moments of opacity can only emerge where the reader has a sense that meaning is possible if not always present. In spite of Chamoiseau's public declarations that he is content to create texts which are not wholly comprehensible to every reader, when we look at his writing we find a range of strategies which allow him to write Creole words while maintaining the understanding and engagement of a non-Creolophone reader. Both Nabokov and Chamoiseau explore ways of naming and explaining people, places and things in new ways to address a reader from elsewhere. Crucially, more often than not they do this without seeming to explain anything. In this way, though they are doing the work of cultural translation, they avoid the pose of cultural translator. This allows each author to avoid the impression that the world he describes will hold still to have its portrait taken, which would reduce the reader's sense of the complexity of that world. Teaching the reader new cultural and linguistic meanings without seeming to do so also allows the author to depict himself as part of the canvas, where more obvious explanation would situate him outside the world he describes.

Comparison of the Russian and English versions of Nabokov's text illuminates the efforts he makes to accommodate an English-language reader. So we read in the English versions of the autobiography: 'The oilcloth that covered the round table smelled of glue. Miss Clayton smelled of Miss Clayton.' But in the Russian version we find 'Клетчатая клеенка на круглом столе пахнет клеем. Чернила пахнут черносливом. Виктория Артуровна пахнет Викторией Артуровной [The check oilcloth that covers the round table smells of glue. The ink smells of prunes. Victoriya Arturovna smells of Victoriya Arturovna].'[53] Here we have a translation of a name which makes it fit comfortably within the language the author writes in. Elsewhere Nabokov takes into account the likely cultural knowledge of his reader. When he remembers figures from a children's book he read who wore dresses made from the American flag, in the English version he writes that they made the dresses 'by the illegal method of cutting themselves frocks out of the American flag'.[54] In the Russian version there is no reference to illegality.[55] In another instance there is a wholesale cultural transposition of an anecdote to make the sense clear to the reader. Nabokov is describing the lack of education of his last home tutor. In the Russian version he illustrates this point by saying that the tutor did not know how Tatiana's letter began in *Evgenii Onegin*, but in the English version he writes that the tutor thought Charles Dickens had written *Uncle Tom's Cabin*.[56] Given Nabokov's whole-hearted commitment to autobiographical accuracy, this willingness to change the details of the conversation to maintain the reader's engagement and understanding speaks of a determination to 'bring the text to the reader' as well as the other way round.

Chamoiseau's text also reveals such a determination. He 'walks the tightrope of cultural specificity between the transmission of otherness and a perplexing *opacité*'.[57] As we have seen, he refuses to incorporate a glossary and parodies the cumbersome apparatus of translator's footnotes. Yet though there is no extra-textual explanation of words or ideas likely to be unfamiliar to a foreign reader, such explanation is to a large extent woven into the verbal fabric. At times Chamoiseau incorporates Creole words but ensures the meaning they convey is present elsewhere in the sentence through a French word.[58] We see this here, where he mocks the self-importance of his toddler-self beginning nursery school: 'Il charroyait un bidime cartable sur sa hanche, et semblait être de ces importants qui hantaient le lycée Schoelcher [He carried along an enormous schoolbag on his hip and seemed to be one of those influential people who haunted the lycée Schoelcher]'.[59] 'Bidime' is a Martinican Creole word for 'enormous', so it qualifies the noun 'cartable'. The Creole word here adds an element of opacity but the meaning of the sentence as a whole is perfectly clear to a monolingual Francophone reader, because the idea of the weight of the schoolbag is also carried by the French verb 'charroyer' (to carry along or cart around). The meaning would not have been so clear if, for example, 'cartable' had been given in Creole. Another way of making Creole intelligible to a non-Creolophone reader is to translate a phrase within the text. We see this when the child's mother scolds him for writing on the walls when he has a small blackboard he could write on: '*Ou pa ni an ti tablo?!... Tu as ton ardoise, non!?...*' [*Ou pa an ti tablo* — You've got your slate, haven't you?!]*[60] Here the translation seems unlikely to have been part of the actual conversation, but by raising the explanation from the footnotes to the main text, Chamoiseau sets the two languages echoing off each other and makes his role as an intercultural mediator a little less obtrusive.[61] Sometimes Creole appears as the transcription of a non-verbal sound, rather than a word from another language. We see this when the child runs to find his brother Paul in the playground but ends up bumping into him: 'Paul, lui-même en pleine zouelle, se tourna malencontreusement quand le négrillon parvint à sa hauteur ... Bok! ... La collision fut inévitable' [Paul, completely absorbed in his game, turned — unfortunately — just as his brother ran up to him. Bonk! The collision was inevitable.][62] Raphaël Confiant's dictionary of Martinican Creole gives 'Bok' as 'rebuffade', a rebuff or a put-down.[63] But to the non-Creolophone reader, the word might seem to be the transcription of the sound of the two children's heads knocking together (and, indeed, this is how Linda Coverdale has rendered it, translating 'Bok!' as 'Bonk!'). Here Chamoiseau has arranged the sentence so that it can be read on two levels, as sound by the non-Creolophone reader and as language by the reader who understands Creole.

Such strategies allow Chamoiseau to weave Creole into his text while making it comprehensible to a wide international readership. Chamoiseau's intra-textual translations also have a didactic purpose. He introduces Creole words along with French translations the first time he uses them and then later uses the Creole word by itself, so his text allows the reader to learn some Creole words. We see this particularly when Chamoiseau remembers the games of marbles he played as a child. He introduces the word for a throw of the marble in this way: 'Ses tirs (ou zigues, si tu préfères) ne s'échouaient jamais dans les rainures qui faisaient perdre' [His shots (or his zigs if you prefer) never got sidetracked into the grooves that spelled disaster].[64] The parenthesis belies the importance of the introduction of the word 'zigues' which Chamoiseau will later use without translating it.[65] Even as the author laments leaving the childhood language behind, he is passing it on to the reader. Another instance of such irony is the way Chamoiseau's quotation of his teacher scolding the children educates the foreign reader in Creole. The fragments of dialogue where the teacher corrects a Creole word for a French one allow the author to offer a translation without taking an exterior point of view on the child's world: ' — Dieux du ciel! on ne dit pas: *C'est ma manman-doudou nian nian nian*, on dit: *C'est ma grand'mère...* ! ou bien: *C'est ma mamie...* !' ['Ye gods in heaven! You shouldn't say, *She's my grammy-nana-nyah-nyah-nyah*! You say, *She's my grandmother!* Or else, *She's my grranny!*]'[66] By embedding translations within snatches of remembered speech, Chamoiseau can make local linguistic specificities comprehensible to readers from elsewhere without relegating such explanations to footnotes or glossaries. Such memories also situate the author's childhood and youth within a context of ongoing translation.

The kind of reading I have been doing of these authors' strategies for addressing both a local and a foreign reader depends on the idea of a clear distinction between the two. Insofar as both Chamoiseau and Nabokov at certain points address a foreign reader who cannot understand the narration without some help, such a distinction is at work in these texts, but at times it starts to falter. The assumption that a shared language or a shared locality would make for shared cultural understanding is undermined at a few key points in each text. We see this in a playful mode in Nabokov's text in the narration of an episode of mushroom-hunting. In *Другие берега*, Nabokov writes that he had assumed that an understanding of mushroom-hunting, though obviously not available to Americans, would be shared by his fellow Russians. Yet upon conversation 'с москвичами и другими русскими провинциалами' [with Muscovites and other Russian provincials] he found that this was not the case.[67] Though the coupling of Muscovites with other Russian provincials is obviously a joke, there is an underlying anxiety here about the limits of shared cultural understanding among speakers of Russian, an anxiety which emerges with greater force later in the text. Here again Nabokov is speaking of an issue he expects to be opaque to Americans but perfectly clear to Russians, but this time the issue in question is weightier than mushroom-hunting. It concerns the understanding of the politics of the Russian revolution. Nabokov writes that Bolshevik propaganda had been so effective that people in the English-speaking world failed to understand that there had been a broad opposition to autocracy at all levels of Russian society, an opposition the Bolsheviks had ruthlessly destroyed upon coming to power. Nabokov writes that this of course would be perfectly clear to a Russian, but then comes a telling qualification: 'по крайней мере свободному русскому читателю моего поколения' [at least to a free Russian reader of my generation].[68] As in the mushroom-hunting episode, the circle of belonging created by a shared language shrinks suddenly from the whole of Russia to a quite specific social group. And here the stakes are higher because this shared cultural understanding concerns his father's memory and the appreciation of the Russian liberal context in which his life took shape. These rare moments speak of an awareness that the linguistic and cultural migrations of the author's own life have affected the language and culture itself as well as the author's life. Here Nabokov's movement away from Russian literary culture and the environment in which Russian liberalism grew up is paralleled by changes in that literary culture and by the withering of the political liberalism alongside which it existed. Explanations of aspects of both literary and political Russian culture then become necessary not only for an English-language reader but for a Russian-language reader of the generation following the migrations that shaped Nabokov's youth. This ambivalence about the necessity of cultural explanation is present in the way Nabokov writes in the Russian text that he is sure no such explanations are needed there, and then goes on to give them anyway.[69]

A comparable ambivalence is present in Chamoiseau's conception of his local reader. We have examined the devices which create a text that can be read by a reader from elsewhere while still evoking a local reality on its own terms. But when challenged about the choices he makes to explain elements of the local reality to a foreign reader, Chamoiseau indicates that the zones of opacity in his writing are present for a local reader as much as for the reader from elsewhere. As noted previously, his 1992 novel *Texaco* is written using many of the same translation strategies which help make his autobiographical writing comprehensible to a foreign reader. Rose-Myriam Réjouis writes: 'when I read *Texaco*, I hear a friend telling me a story in the presence of a stranger. In order to include the stranger, my friend is forced to explain certain allusions, to translate inside jokes'.[70] Chamoiseau says that such explanations are also necessary for a Martinican audience.[71] The distinction between the local reader and the foreign reader which lies behind my own approach to understanding the language of *Une enfance créole* here breaks down. As in the case of Nabokov, the linguistic and cultural changes lived through by Chamoiseau are not unique to him but rather signal broader changes in the language and culture itself. Chamoiseau's move away from Creole is part of a broader generational move, which complicates the idea that the author and his local reader share an understanding of Creole language and culture. In fact, both local author and local reader are at some distance from what are presented in *Une enfance créole* as local cultural practices. This has been pointed out by critics of the *créolité* movement, which see its nostalgia for the Martinique of the past as complicit in the production of images of Martinique which avoid the complexities of contemporary Martinican life, now very distant from the way of life evoked in *créoliste* work.[72] Chamoiseau acknowledges to Réjouis that familiarity and strangeness cannot be mapped easily on to local realities and distant realities but are interwoven within him: 'The stranger is in me [...] Although I have my very own opacity, I still possess references and frames that are outside of me and which I inherit from the dominant culture'.[73]

For both Nabokov and Chamoiseau, then, an effort of cultural explanation is necessary, even for readers who share the author's linguistic background and birthplace. Each writes on the cusp of the disappearance of the particular kind of community in which his life took shape. For each, to remember is always to translate. This in turn involves mediating between the disappearing linguistic community who shared his childhood experiences and the readership the author addresses as a result of his weakened ties to the language and culture of his past.

Where integration within a linguistic community is becoming more fragile for Nabokov and Chamoiseau as each moves from childhood to adulthood, for Perec such integration never existed. His life marks the point in family history where Polish, Yiddish and Hebrew become a haunting presence rather than spoken or remembered languages. When Nabokov and Chamoiseau stage the untranslatability of Russian or Creole, they lament their inability to name the cultural universe in which their lives took shape in French or English, the second language and written idiom of the autobiography. Perec similarly laments his inability to name his family past, but in his case he does not speak or understand the languages on the other side of the linguistic gap. He thinks through the dilemmas of remembering and evoking family histories lived in other languages within one language. Like Nabokov and Chamoiseau, he tussles with the dilemmas of (un)translatability, but he does so using only French. His writing consistently stages failures to refer, moments when the word and the thing it is supposed to name do not quite match up. He draws attention to the way the person, place or object named always exists before the moment of naming, so that to name something is to reach back in time from the moment of speech. In Perec's writing this temporal gap between the coming into being of the named entity and the moment of naming is a place where meaning gets lost. This is foregrounded through apparently trivial examples, such as the difference between pine trees and fir trees:

> C'est à cette occasion que j'appris que les pins et les sapins étaient des arbres tout à fait différents, que ce que j'appelais sapin était en réalité un pin, que les vrais arbres de Noël étaient des sapins, mais qu'il n'y avait pas de sapins à Villard-de-Lans ni même dans tout le Dauphiné.[74]
>
> [This was when I learnt that pines and firs were quite different trees, that what I called a fir was really a pine, that real Christmas trees were firs but that there were no firs at Villard-de-Lans or anywhere in Dauphiné.]

In this passage, there is a gap between the name Perec has been using and the plant he has been trying to name. The attention given here to an apparently insignificant point of detail creates a confused unease in the reader. The reason for this attention becomes clearer when we consider that the child's disorientation after his flight from Paris is experienced largely as a confusion about how to name people and things: 'Les choses et les lieux n'avaient pas de noms ou en avaient plusieurs; les gens n'avaient pas de visage' [Things and places had no name, or several; the people had no faces].[75] Difficulties in naming are connected with the disintegration of the family. In Villard-de-Lans Perec is looked after by various relations, who are presented anonymously as 'tantes'.[76] Most unbearably, Perec is literally unable to name his parents. He misspells his mother's name, and for most of his childhood and youth misremembered his father's.[77] His mother's death is misnamed in the official language of the French state, as it assigns the day of her deportation as the day of her death, even though no one is certain when or how she died.[78] Perec's mother's death is impossible to articulate for many reasons, including the author's lack of memory of the event, its absence in official record and the enormity of the loss, and the question of language change only deepens this impossibility. Shifting linguistic and cultural expression and wartime attempts to hide Jewishness mean that even aspects of his parents' lives which should be easily known and spoken, such as his father's name, also become associated with impossible or inaccurate reference.

In a posthumously published essay entitled 'Douze regards obliques', Perec uses the concept of fashion to think through a case of a failure of reference: 'L'objet de mode, en l'occurrence, importe peu. Ce qui compte, c'est le nom, la griffe, la signature. On peut même dire que si l'objet n'était pas nommé et signé, il n'existerait pas. Il n'est rien d'autre que son signe.' [The fashionable object is of little consequence here. What matters is the name, the brand, the signature. One could even say that if the object were not named and signed it would not exist. It is nothing except its own sign.][79] In Perec's view, fashionable clothes are a kind of circular sign which only refer back to their own status as fashion. They create a kind of meaning where the focus is on a present moment unconnected or only falsely connected with what has gone before. Perec sees this kind of meaning as a hollow version of human communication: 'Connivence factice, absence de dialogue: on partage la misère d'un code sans substance: le dernier cri... [Even the connivance is artificial, for there is no dialogue: what you share is the poverty of a code without substance: the last word...]'[80] Fashion, as a 'code sans substance', is the epitome of a language which fails to refer properly to the surrounding world, and so hampers the possibility of community through communication. This description of fashion provokes a dream of its opposite: 'Le contraire de la mode, ce n'est évidemment pas le démodé; ce ne peut être que le présent: ce qui est là, ce qui est ancré, permanent, résistant, habité: l'objet et son souvenir, l'être et son histoire.' [The opposite of fashion is obviously not the unfashionable. It can only be the present — what is here, what is rooted, permanent, resistant, lived-in: an object and the memory of it, a being and its history.][81] Perec's vision of fashion's opposite shows how high the stakes are in his evocations of meaning-making. The image of 'l'être et son histoire' is the opposite of the broken connections between the life of the child and the life of the parents which become visible in Perec's failure to spell his parents' names. It is his very being which is at stake in his exploration of meaning-making, the idea of continuity of life as opposed to a confused relationship to the past.

Perhaps because of the inevitability of translation and its failures in the author's work of memory, the idea of an untranslatable language fascinates him. He recalls seeing a man sawing using a tool which is called an X, because it is in the shape of an X. This fusion between the word and the thing creates a kind of original and untranslatable language.[82] There is no gap between the named thing and the naming word because both share the same form. This means that the naming word cannot be exchanged for another and so there is no longer a risk of misnaming the object. An untranslatable language is one where meaning is stable; it allows the author to name things in the world. Naming losses allows them to be mourned, and because of this, the idea of an untranslatable language is closely linked to the scene where Perec's bereavement can be articulated and mourned. The X tool is in the shape of a St Andrew's cross, which connects it with Perec's father. Though Perec's father's legal name was Icek Judko, he sometimes used the name André and Perec misremembers this as his real name. Perec does not mention this in the autobiography, but his father wrote his name as André on his son's birth certificate.[83]

Like the X, the father's name is connected with an untranslatable anchoring in the world through Perec's narration of his visit to his father's grave, where he sees his father's name written on a wooden cross. Seeing his father's grave is a relief, as it lends the bereavement a concrete form.[84] The materiality of the wooden cross is in liberating contrast to the abstract quality of the death that occurred before Perec could fully understand what it meant. The tool in the shape of the cross, the letter X and his father's grave come together to gesture towards the fragile possibility of naming loss.

This untranslatable word acts as a fixed site of meaning in a life marked by shifting signs. But the same sentence which introduces the untranslatable X also draws attention to the way this letter and the shapes derived from it can refer to a whole host of opposites.[85] The X is both a sign of absence in technical scientific writing and a sign of multiplication, a way of orientating information through the creation of axes and a sign of an unknown quantity in an equation. The basic elements of the X can be rearranged to form a Star of David or a swastika. Even the letter that embodies the possibility of an untranslatable language can refer to a wide range of different ideas. The instances of untranslatable words which are fused with the object they represent remain rare in *W ou le souvenir d'enfance*, whose very title foregrounds the way a single letter can represent a range of experiences: a wartime childhood, a fantastic island, an oblique approach to an unspeakable history. For all three authors, the idea of the untranslatable remains a kind of dream of rootedness, while in practice they live and write in the aftermath of ongoing histories of translation.

Nabokov, Perec, and Chamoiseau all hover between writing in a way which celebrates untranslatability and creating texts which are legible to readers requiring some degree of translation. In this way, each author's work itself partakes in the flows of translation and cultural change which he laments. By having his linguistic forms carry cultural meanings unlikely to be familiar to the reader, each author creates a text which can be read on multiple levels. It is likely to mean more to a reader conversant with the languages of the author's past, or at least attentive to the resonances of other languages within the main language of the text. Yet it remains legible, if opaque in places, to a monolingual reader. This kind of author-reader relationship gestures towards a variegated literary community where readers have varying levels of competency in the languages present within each text and the author writes for readers situated in a wide range of local, national and international places. The extensive efforts made by Nabokov and Chamoiseau to translate for readers from elsewhere, and the ambivalence in their writing about whether the reader from elsewhere might also be a local reader, point towards the necessity of such cultural translation even to address one's compatriots. All three texts present the idea of closed cultural and linguistic communities only to illustrate how the author's own life has been lived within a context of linguistic communities in flux. Each of these texts is a product of lives lived at the interstices of national languages. Together they demonstrate the wide variety of ways in which writers can create contact zones between languages within the narration of an individual life.

For these authors, articulating a life-history involves exploring how the spaces between languages in which each author's life takes shape can be spoken within a French-language literary space. Looking at the place of the French canon within each text tells us more about the second kind of relationship through which literary communities are created: the relationship between writers. Nabokov and Chamoiseau each rewrites a canonical poem by Baudelaire, while Perec revives the literary practice of listing which he associates with Jules Verne and Rabelais. Each of these rewritings serves to create continuities between French literary space and lives and histories lived outside the French language. They situate literary language as a search for a kind of speech which will always remain out of reach, inscribing the author's literary practice within a tradition of French writing which arises from and engages with histories of travel whose articulation is never quite possible.

Chamoiseau embeds a fragment of 'L'Albatros' in his memory of playing marbles as a kind of experiment with what can be said within the language of the French canon. It relocates Baudelaire's poem so that it comes to articulate Chamoiseau's everyday experience as a child in Martinique. In Chamoiseau's narration of his memories of playing marbles, he speaks of children known as 'bawoufeurs'. The *bawoufeurs* approach others playing a game of marbles, shout 'Bawouf' and then take the other children's marbles. In retaliation, the other children set a trap to attract the *bawoufeurs* and then thwart them at the last minute. This is the passage in question:

> Et voici la foudre du piège:
> Leurs griffes s'étant refermés sur un rien de poussières, les bawoufeurs demeuraient échoués, lamentables parmi nous, un peu comme les princes des nuées qui hantent les tempêtes et se rient des archers: exilés sur le sol au milieu des huées, leurs ailes de rafleur les empêchent..[86]
>
> [And here is the thunderbolt of the trap:
> When their claws close on barren dust, the *bawoufeurs* are ignominiously stranded among us, a bit like albatrosses — those princes of the clouds who haunt the tempest and laugh at the archer: exiled on the earth amid shouting people, their thieving wings prevent them from...]

The last word of this passage has a footnote which reads 'Que Charles-Pierre me pardonne' [May Baudelaire forgive me], a playful reference to Chamoiseau's rewriting of the last verse of Baudelaire's 'L'Albatros':

> Le Poète est semblable au prince des nuées
> Qui hante la tempête et se rit de l'archer;
> Exilé sur le sol au milieu des huées,
> Ses ailes de géant l'empêchent de marcher.[87]
>
> [The Poet is like the prince of the clouds,
> Haunting the tempest and laughing at the archer;
> Exiled on earth amongst the shouting people,
> His giant's wings prevent him from walking.]

In Chamoiseau's rewriting of 'L'Albatros', the lonely albatross is replaced by a whole flock. The author plays on the sounds of French which allow his writing to make present a number of 'princes' without changing the syllabification of the lines. The words 'princes des nuées qui hantent les tempêtes et se rient des archers' are spoken almost exactly as Baudelaire's original lines, though in Baudelaire's version every noun is singular while in Chamoiseau's they are all plural. This pluralization of the birds who represent the poet gestures towards the multiple voices present in Chamoiseau's rewriting of the poem: his own, Baudelaire's, the remembered voices of the *bawoufeurs*. By erasing or blurring the beginning and ending of the poem, Chamoiseau opens it out so that careful checking is needed to see where his text ends and Baudelaire's begins. The omission of the last two words of the line, 'de marcher', activates the reader's literary memory. If the reader fills in the last two words of the line, she becomes one of the author's 'Répondeurs' and the dialogue between author and reader takes on something of the antiphonal quality of Creole folk-tales. In this way the reader becomes a collaborator in Chamoiseau's construction of continuities between his Martinican memories, his text and French literary space.

By embedding Baudelaire's lines within the writing of a memory, Chamoiseau connects his work to the French canon, but also to a local literary tradition. The Martinican poet Aimé Césaire also embeds a line from 'L'Albatros' within a narration of a memory in his foundational poem *Cahier d'un retour au pays natal*. The speaker recalls seeing another black man on a tram in Paris. He evokes the man's clumsiness, the way his large limbs fit uncomfortably on the small tram seat. Labour has damaged the man's body so that he offers a perfect image of 'un nègre hideux' and the women around him on the train are laughing at him.[88] The speaker describes him as 'COMIQUE ET LAID' repeating this phrase from 'L'Albatros' twice.[89] There is a complex layering of points of view in the use of this phrase, as it holds at once a racist, denigrating perspective and a respectful one which sees that, like the albatross, the man has dignity outside the particular situation in which he finds himself. Just as the albatross becomes majestic when it takes to the skies, Césaire's allusion to Baudelaire suggests the man's large limbs could become a source of power if freed from the constraints which make him appear clumsy. The poem both situates the man as a kind of exile in urban Paris and draws on a metropolitan French tradition to combat the racist view of him ascribed to local Parisian women. Césaire quotes from the third stanza of 'L'Albatros' to achieve this intertwining of perspectives; Chamoiseau draws on the fourth, carrying the Martinican tradition of engagements with Baudelaire forward.

By creating these kinds of continuities between his text, Baudelaire's poem and Césaire's *Cahier d'un retour au pays natal*, Chamoiseau situates his writing within a lineage which sees the poet as clumsy in certain contexts. The double allusion to Baudelaire and Césaire gestures towards an aesthetics of failure. The connection with Césaire suggests the ethical failures of vision of the poet, while the link to Baudelaire situates the poet as someone who is awkward outside the realm of art. The particular way in which Chamoiseau employs the Baudelairean allusion also suggests that the quest for a fruitful aesthetic language also triggers certain clumsy failures on the part of the poet. Like the *bawoufeurs* who fall into the children's trap, the poet is someone whose bold dives for beauty leave him empty-handed. Chamoiseau aligns himself with a modernist aesthetics of failure elsewhere when he speaks of Faulkner: 'literature (or Art in general) remains unattainable because the solitary wayfaring that leads towards it can only remove it still further into the distance'.[90] Such a view is also present in *Chemin-d'école*, the text most explicitly concerned with the question of reading, writing and developing a literary voice. The epigraph reads: 'Quand tu es poète, oh quel fer...!' [When you're a poet, is it ever tough!...].[91] The refrain 'quel fer', a phrase which denotes difficulty, recurs throughout the text and is present at the beginning and end of the paragraph where he speaks of his pain at realizing he did not speak French well.[92] Together, these elements of the text suggest that the quest for a poetic language is the subject of the book just as much as the movement from childhood Creole to adult French and that the two are linked. Both the quest for a literary language and the moment on the threshold of the French language are connected with failures of articulation. Literary speech fails in that there are elements of the self which are beyond the understanding of the speaker and so cannot be transmitted with clarity to the listener. Chamoiseau brings out the specificities of this kind of failing speech through the example of the Creole storyteller:

> When a Creole storyteller tells a story, there is always a moment when his voice becomes utterly incomprehensible, it becomes a humming, and then [clearer speech] comes back. At a given moment [the storyteller] has had to confront an unsayable part of the story, an unsayable part of himself; but he goes on feeding [the story] with a kind of verbal vibration that lingers behind, sustaining the hypnosis.[93]

Sustaining language which speaks through the unsayable is the role of the storyteller and writer. In this perspective, those parts of Chamoiseau's writing which resist comprehension do not create, suppose or confuse cultural and linguistic insiders and outsiders, but rather speak of a commitment to modes of speech oriented towards the imagination rather than logic. The difficulties of achieving a satisfactory mode of literary speech are connected both to the challenge of creating a language that can be understood by local and international readers while remaining faithful to a past which is rapidly becoming strange even to local readers and to finding a way to write where a connection with the reader is retained even through passages which elude the comprehension of both author and reader. Chamoiseau's stylistic practice is then motivated by situated concerns of translation between varieties of French and Creole and by a wish to articulate the incommunicable elements of the self and the world.

Like Chamoiseau, Nabokov draws on a poem by Baudelaire to gesture towards what will remain outside the text, despite the writer's best efforts. He does this in the first autobiographical piece he wrote, the 1936 sketch which recalls the Swiss governess who would read to him in French. This sketch, originally written in French, becomes the fifth chapter of the final version of *Speak, Memory*. When published individually, its title was 'Mademoiselle O', but it could have been called 'My French Childhood'. Just as Nabokov, when he writes in English, creates an English past for himself, so the chapter which began life in French traces a French literary genealogy for the Russian author. The chapter speaks of the fluid movements between French and Russian speech, syntax and grammar that the author heard as he was growing up.[94] As well as the French he learned from his governess, there was 'une sorte de tradition française, un français usuel, que l'on se passait directement de père en fils'.⁹⁵ The sketch is scattered with the names of the French writers beloved in Russia during Nabokov's adolescence (Sully Prudhomme, Alfred de Musset, Coppée), and those Nabokov himself preferred, Verlaine and Mallarmé. He recalls Maeterlinck's *L'Oiseau bleu* finding a congenial home in the Moscow Art Theatre, and remembers his dislike of the drama of Corneille and Racine read to him by Mademoiselle.⁹⁶ Images of Nabokov reading Racine aloud as a child, hearing Russian words and syntax casually blended with French speech, and of the performance of French-language plays in Russian theatres create continuities between French literary space and Nabokov's Russian past. At the end of the piece Nabokov will go on to show how his present artistic practice both draws on and moves beyond that of a foundational French predecessor, Baudelaire. The sketch's ending narrates a visit the adult Nabokov makes to his old governess in Switzerland, where she is now living in retirement. This part of the French sketch is retained and even slightly expanded in the Russian and English versions of the autobiography, and I will examine it here as it occurs in *Speak, Memory*. The visit comes about because he happens to be in Lausanne with a friend and looks her up. They go to see her twice. The first time the visit is unsuccessful because she has become completely deaf, so they come back again, bringing a hearing-aid. Mademoiselle expresses delight at being able to hear her former charge's voice, but he knows she must be lying, as the machine has not yet been switched on.

Mademoiselle offers the author a way of thinking through what it means to remember a country one has left. She is a kind of double exile, as she left Switzerland to take up residence with the Nabokov family, then left Russia after many years there. Like the author and his family, she lives among a community of people who had to leave Russia because of the October Revolution, though in her case these are fellow French-speaking governesses, rather than Russians.⁹⁷ In many ways, she is a model of how not to be an exile. Her memory of the past is self-deceptive; she has rewritten her often difficult relationship to Russia and the people she knew there.⁹⁸ She dwells on the idea that she enjoyed her time in Russia as a way of underlining how miserable she is in her current home in Switzerland, forgetting she was also miserable in Russia. At Nabokov's visit, it is apparent that she continues to suffer from the faults she always had: a sensitive ego; physical and social clumsiness; a misunderstanding of her surroundings which is partly willed and partly due to intellectual weakness. These flaws make her ridiculous. Her main role in the text is to create comedy, or to act as a foil for the author's more aesthetically and ethically valuable approach to memory and exile. Yet in the closing passages of the chapter, the text questions its mobilization of Mademoiselle as a figure of fun. She is compared to a swan that Nabokov sees in the lake as he is leaving her home:

> Below, a wide ripple, almost a wave, and something vaguely white attracted my eye. As I came quite close to the lapping water, I saw what it was — an aged swan, a large, uncouth, dodo-like creature, making ridiculous efforts to hoist himself into a moored boat. He could not do it. The heavy, impotent flapping of his wings, their slippery sound against the rocking and plashing boat, the gluey glistening of the dark swell where it caught the light — all seemed for a moment laden with that strange significance which sometimes in dreams is

> attached to a finger pressed to mute lips and then pointed at something the dreamer has no time to distinguish before waking with a start. But although I soon forgot that dismal night, it was, oddly enough, that night, that compound image — shudder and swan and swell — which first came to mind when a couple of years later I learned that Mademoiselle had died.[99]

Here clumsiness, ego and self-deception, the qualities that make Mademoiselle a comic figure, take on a kind of dignity through their association with the swan. Like Mademoiselle, the swan misunderstands its surroundings, and is struggling into a role it cannot play. Even though the word 'ridiculous' is used of the swan's efforts, it still possesses a kind of nobility through the emphasis on the weight and power of its movements, an effect heightened by the general cultural resonances of the swan as a graceful bird. More specific cultural resonances are at play too through its connection to Baudelaire's poem, 'Le Cygne'.[100] Both Nabokov's passage and Baudelaire's poem use the figure of a swan to think through the questions of exile, memory and ethical perception of another's suffering. The Baudelairean allusion further points up the dignity of the swan and by implication Mademoiselle, as it associates both figures with the creative artist. The relationship of contrast between Nabokov and Mademoiselle here becomes a relationship of analogy. A parallel is set up in this passage between Mademoiselle, the swan, the poet and the dreamer. Each of these figures is engaged in a failed attempt to seek meaning; what each attempts to establish is elusive. Nabokov too cannot articulate except through the 'alliterative unity' of 'shudder and swan and swell' what it is that this scene means.[101] Yet though he cannot make sense of the 'strange significance' of the scene at the time and quickly forgets it, its obscure and difficult meaning is more valuable and expressive than all the remembered anecdotes he has narrated in the chapter.

Nabokov goes on to make explicit the idea of the inexpressible being more valuable than what can be expressed in language a few lines later, where he questions the value of his recreation of Mademoiselle and gestures towards something about her that lies beyond articulation:

> Just before the rhythm I hear falters and fades, I catch myself wondering whether, during the years I knew her, I had not kept utterly missing something in her that was far more she than her chins or her ways or even her French — something perhaps akin to that last glimpse of her, to the radiant deceit she had used in order to have me depart pleased with my own kindness, or to that swan whose agony was so much closer to artistic truth than a drooping dancer's pale arms; something, in short, that I could appreciate only after the things and beings that I had most loved in the security of my childhood had been turned to ashes or shot through the heart.[102]

Here, the analogy set up between Mademoiselle O and the author becomes even closer. Earlier in the chapter, her perception is shown to be faulty and incomplete; here the author's perception is lacking. The style of the passage reinforces the point. The recurrence of the language of approximation ('something in her', 'something perhaps akin', 'something, in short') underlines the author's inability to articulate what it is he has missed. He is not thinking in language but is listening to a rhythm which is escaping him. His failure is both ethical in that he has never noticed Mademoiselle's generosity, and aesthetic in that his writing distorts her image.

It is only once Nabokov becomes an exile like Mademoiselle that he comes closer to perceiving her dignity. Both Baudelaire and Nabokov link the exiled state of an outsider with an ethically and aesthetically productive vision. Yet though both Baudelaire and Nabokov use the image of a struggling swan to evoke the pain of exile, they do so in different ways. Baudelaire's swan is lost in urban Paris, searching in the dust for its native lake. Nabokov's swan is in its native lake, struggling to get into a moored boat. Where the Baudelaire poem establishes a clear contrast between native and distant places, Nabokov's passage complicates the idea that a return to the native place is desirable. As John Burt Foster Junior points out, both Mademoiselle and the swan in the lake are technically already at home, but they are not comfortable there.[103] This prepares the reader for the final line of the passage and the chapter which speak of the destruction of the world of Nabokov's youth; even if he could return to the place where he grew up, in an important sense it would not be there. Nabokov, like the swan, is struggling to root himself in a vehicle of travel, a new language. The Baudelairean allusion is an example of the paradoxical dynamics at play in such an enterprise. On the one hand, it creates links between Nabokov's writing and the French poetic tradition. In the French-language version of the sketch, it points to a literary ancestor as part of the attempt to create an artistic home within the new language. But the particular way in which he sets himself up in a new linguistic home is to create links between a French exploration of exile, memory and the failures of literary speech and his own experience of linguistic and artistic marginality. The allusion then has two roles: it creates a new literary home for the author and calls into question whether a stable home in language is possible or desirable. The dual role of the allusion helps account for its retention in the English-language translation of the sketch, even when the references to other French writers mentioned above are deleted or severely reduced. Because those passages are solely designed to create a French literary genealogy for the author, they are not as relevant in a context where he is becoming an American author. But he keeps the closing passage's allusions to Baudelaire and even makes them more detailed, because the idea of a literary home shaped by experiences of exile and change becomes even more fitting as he remembers his past through the prism of two major moves, the first from Russia and the second from Europe. Here Nabokov establishes a conflictual relationship to the French literary tradition where, like the swan in the boat, he is half-in and half-out.

Like Nabokov, Perec draws on the French literary tradition to gesture towards what cannot be spoken. He experiments with modes of speech that can never quite articulate what they wish to articulate through playing with lists. Lists run through *W ou le souvenir d'enfance* in both its autobiographical and fictional strands. The autobiographical chapters are often laid out in loose list form, with several memories described in separate paragraphs without any explicit connection being made between them. Numbered lists occur in the long series of footnotes Perec appends to an earlier piece of writing on his parents' lives embedded within the autobiography. Perec also creates a list of headlines from newspapers published at the time of his birth and incorporates that into an autobiographical chapter.[104] The fictional chapters include fewer formal lists, but their sentences often become enumerations, as they do when Perec describes the names Athletes can be given, their sporting achievements or the numbers of competitors in each event.[105] In an interview Perec spoke of the pleasure of coming across long lists within literary texts: 'Quand on poursuit une énumération jusqu'au bout, on en arrive à une valse de mots qui se mettent à tourbillonner entre eux. Ce plaisir de l'accumulation était en acte chez Rabelais et chez Jules Verne.' [When one continues a list to the end, one reaches a point where words waltz and begin to whirl. This pleasure in accumulation was at work in Rabelais and Jules Verne][106] Perec goes on to lament the disappearance of such practices in contemporary writing outside his own work and that of Michel Butor. Perec's use of this device then takes on the role of continuing a lost tradition from the French canon. This is somewhat paradoxical, given that Perec's lists partly serve to gesture towards what he cannot say in the French language.

Lists exert appeal for two reasons: they engender a different kind of meaning-making, and they draw attention to what is left out of the list. The meaning of a list is different from that of a sentence. Though a list is based on the assumption that there is something which links its items, the list itself does not make explicit what it is that joins them. Instead, its words accumulate without creating a meaning that can be paraphrased, jostling with other words to which they remain unlinked by any grammar. The element of discontinuity in listing makes it an apt device for the narration of memories which do not form a coherent whole. Gaspard Turin writes: 'en exprimant par la liste des événements autobiographiques, Perec construit une sorte d'anti-histoire, faite de blancs et de vide' [by expressing autobiographical events through lists, Perec creates a kind of anti-history, composed of gaps and emptiness].[107] Perec's lists also have a child-like quality about them which arises from 'la jubilation de la concordance des mots et des choses pour celui qui est à peine sorti de son état d'*infans*, étranger à la parole' [the exultation of seeing words and things come together felt by someone who has barely emerged from the state of *infans*, where he is a foreigner to speech].[108] Several pairs of opposites are at play when a reader encounters a list or an author makes one: boredom and fascination; tidiness and untidiness; completeness and incompleteness. To list is to create an ordered relationship between different elements, but the creation of order always sharpens awareness of what cannot be ordered, what does not fit within the list. Writing of Jules Verne, whose practice inspires Perec's lists, Timothy Unwin remarks:

> The process of mimesis, in which the world is represented figuratively, is replaced by that of mathesis, which attempts to use language as a perfect descriptor and in doing so gets caught in futile, endless accumulation. The result is not coherence but proliferation, indeed potential chaos, in which description and representation no longer have any clear boundaries or function.[109]

Perec's adoption of Verne's device of accumulation extends to a direct rewriting of Verne's description of the eponymous island in his adventure story, *L'Île mystérieuse*. The Vernian tension between coherence and proliferation is at play in Perec's portrayal of W. He draws on the paradoxes which emerge in Verne's project of describing the world in a period of high colonialism in order to make present his own difficulties in articulating the twentieth-century histories which led to the death of his mother. In what follows I examine the implications of Perec's literary relationship to Verne for the idea of a French-language canon.

The description of the W island given in chapter X is strongly reminiscent of the island in Verne's work. One end of Verne's island is described as having the shape of 'une mâchoire ouverte' [an open jaw] and the castaways christen it 'golfe du Requin' [Shark-gulf].[110] The fourth sentence describing Perec's W reads: 'Sa configuration générale affecte la forme d'un crâne de mouton dont la mâchoire aurait été passablement disloquée' [Its overall shape is something like a sheep's head with its lower jaw distinctly out of joint].[111] Both islands possess swamps at one end and are characterized by sharp contrasts between fertile and barren areas of land.[112] Perec also scatters words through this chapter with strong Vernian resonances. The word 'colons' occurs at an important juncture in the chapter of Verne's *L'Île mystérieuse* where he describes the island. The castaways who have been washed up there declare that they will not think of themselves as shipwrecked; instead they will see themselves as 'colons'.[113] In *W ou le souvenir d'enfance*, Perec refers to 'le groupe de colons dont les descendants forment aujourd'hui la population entière de l'île s'y établit à la fin du XIX siècle' [it was colonized, at the end of nineteenth century, by the group whose descendants constitute the entire current population of the island].[114] Three of the possible explanations for the foundation of the society devoted to sport on W connect the island to Verne's work. Perec lists the possible explanations:

> Dans l'une, par exemple, Wilson est un gardien de phare dont la négligence aurait été responsable d'une effroyable catastrophe; dans une autre, c'est le chef d'un groupe de convicts qui se seraient mutinés lors d'un transport en Australie; dans une autre encore, c'est un Nemo dégoûté du monde et rêvant de bâtir une Cité idéale.[115]
>
> [In one version, for instance, Wilson was a lighthouse keeper whose negligence is supposed to have caused a frightful disaster; another version has him as the leader of a group of convicts who mutinied during transportation to Australia; and in yet another, he was a disenchanted Captain Nemo who dreamt of building an Ideal City.]

'Phare' occurs in the title of a Jules Verne novel, *Le Phare au bout du monde*, whose story is echoed elsewhere in *W ou le souvenir d'enfance*.[116] The scattering of the English words 'convicts' and 'transport' in the second explanation echoes Verne's use of this stylistic trait and also calls up the nineteenth-century context of imperial expansion in which he wrote. These subtle but self-reinforcing Vernian resonances then culminate in an explicit reference to the protagonist of *Vingt mille lieues sous les mers*.

Both Perec's lists and his creation of the W island are inspired by Verne's literary practice. The lists and geographical writing found in both authors' work point towards the failure of literary language to map the world. Verne's project was global in scope and ambition; he set out to write a series of novels which would describe every country in the world and encompass the latest advances in technology of all kinds. The chapter of *L'Île mystérieuse* that Perec draws upon to describe his own island offers a synecdoche of Verne's literary project as a whole. In this chapter, the characters set about giving each part of the island a name. Like many characters in Verne's novels, they, like the author, go about exploring the world and making it knowable through language. Yet in the attempt to name the world and make it knowable to French readers, Verne constantly comes up against the power of language to make the world strange as well as known. As Timothy Unwin points out above, the attempt to contain the whole world in writing leads to proliferation and chaos rather than control. It is this idea of a project which is global in scope and also inevitably a failure which allows Perec to draw on Verne's writing as a way of simultaneously inscribing himself within the French literary tradition and pointing to the difficulty of articulating his life and family history within French literature. By aligning himself with Verne, Perec roots his writing in a tradition that simultaneously looks towards global horizons and registers its failures to articulate the world it explores.

Perec's suggestion that in some way the W island arises in part from Verne's literary world raises questions about the relationship between colonial histories and European wartime history, the Holocaust and imperial violence, Europe at home and Europe abroad. In fact, all three authors' engagements with the French canon cross and complicate the boundaries between Europe and the Americas, as Baudelaire's albatross comes to stand for a child playing marbles in Martinique and, through the translation of 'Mademoiselle O' into *Speak, Memory*, his swan comes to represent a Russian-American author. These authors' rewritings of Baudelaire and Verne demonstrate their ability to make other lives and histories speak through the French literary tradition, but they also point to the formative presence of non-French lives, histories and spaces within these nineteenth-century texts even before they are rewritten. In this view, the writing of Nabokov, Perec and Chamoiseau continues a literary tradition that precedes them as well as challenging it. Reading Baudelaire and Verne through Nabokov, Perec and Chamoiseau brings into being a constellatory French literary space, where writers in the metropolitan centre (Perec, Baudelaire, Verne), on its imperially-constructed peripheries (Chamoiseau), and outside both (Nabokov) engage with and rewrite a common set of images as they grapple with the failures of literary speech to articulate the perplexed encounter with otherness in a global world.

These authors' literary practice complicates the idea of a French or French-language author from various directions. The words and syntax each author uses at times hover between French and other idioms; at certain points the texts seem to address readers who speak French as one among several languages; the French language is both a kind of dwelling-place each comes to inhabit and a passage connecting the author's life to lives and histories elsewhere. The ambivalent relationships to the French language explored in this chapter, and the first chapter's examination of the common concern with writing the spaces of the past in the light of violent, transnational histories, gesture towards a particular kind of literary space, one where the relationship to language emerges in the context of the migrations of modernity. How should a literary critic move within this space, created and riven as it is by histories of oppression? The next chapter considers the dilemmas involved in bringing these authors together when each writer's particular relationship to language arises out of such varying historical circumstances, from Perec's loss of his parents in the Second World War, to Nabokov's youthful flight from post-revolutionary Russia and time in inter-war Berlin and wartime Paris, to Chamoiseau's much less direct contact with the violence of French imperialism, which echoes down to his generation though not experienced by him. The concept of trauma has the potential to sharpen an exploration of the dilemmas of such comparative readings, as well as opening up a closer examination of the links between personal bereavement and cultural loss, questions that are explored in the next chapter.

Notes to Chapter 2

1. 'Shifting Grounds of Exchange: B. M. Srikantaiah and Kannada Translation', in *Postcolonial Translation: Theory and Practice*, ed. by Susan Bassnett and Harish Trivedi (London: Routledge, 1999), pp. 162–82 (p. 175).
2. Susan Bassnett and Harish Trivedi, 'Introduction: Of Colonies, Cannibals and Vernaculars', in *Postcolonial Translation: Theory and Practice*, pp. 1–19 (p. 16).
3. Dante Alighieri, *De vulgari eloquentia*, trans. and ed. by Steven Botterill (Cambridge: Cambridge University Press, 1996), p. 3.
4. 'Translating and Interlingual Creation in the Contact zone: Border Writing in Quebec', in *Postcolonial Translation: Theory and Practice*, ed. by Susan Bassnett and Harish Trivedi (London: Routledge, 1999), pp. 58–75 (pp. 67–68).
5. DB, 7–8.
6. DB, 8.
7. DB, 76.
8. DB, 26–27.
9. DB, 153.
10. Chemin, 31.
11. Chemin, 69.
12. Chemin, 93.
13. Chemin, 139.
14. W, 22.
15. W, 22.
16. W, 23.
17. W, 24.
18. W, 16–17.
19. SM, 57.
20. SM, 16.
21. SM, 16–17.
22. SM, 13–14; 107–11.
23. SM, 108.
24. DB, 43.
25. DB, 103.
26. SM, 44.
27. SM, 36; 44; 48; 199. Aleksandr Pushkin, *Eugene Onegin: A Novel in Verse*, trans. by Vladimir Nabokov, 4 vols (London: Routledge & Kegan Paul, 1964), I, p. x.
28. DB, 202.
29. Chemin, 18.
30. Chemin, 18.
31. 'Literature and Diglossia: The Poetics of French and Creole "Interlect" in Patrick Chamoiseau's *Texaco*', *Caribbean Quarterly*, 43 (1997), 81–101.
32. *Language and Literary Form in French Caribbean Writing*, p. 147.
33. Chemin, 111; 19.

34. N'zengou-Tayo, p. 91.
35. N'zengou-Tayo, p. 94.
36. Manet van Montfrans, *Georges Perec: la contrainte du réel* (Amsterdam: Rodopi, 1999), p. 186.
37. *W*, 52.
38. David Bellos, *Georges Perec: A Life in Words* (Boston, MA: David R. Godine, 1993), pp. 4–5.
39. *W*, 51.
40. *W*, 26.
41. 'Composing the Other', in *Postcolonial Translation: Theory and Practice*, ed. by Susan Bassnett and Harish Trivedi (London: Routledge, 1999), pp. 75–95 (p. 77).
42. *The Translator's Invisibility* (London: Routledge, 1995), p. 1.
43. See *SM*, 123 for брезгливый and *SM*, 26 for the pun on 'bike'.
44. *SM*, 26.
45. *Chemin*, 79.
46. *Chemin*, 79.
47. *Chemin*, 185.
48. *Chemin*, 121.
49. *Chemin*, 121.
50. *Chemin*, 127.
51. *Chemin*, 127.
52. Rose-Myriam Réjouis, 'A Reader in the Room: Rose-Myriam Réjouis Meets Patrick Chamoiseau', *Callaloo*, 22 (1999), 346–50 (p. 347).
53. There is a pun in the second sentence, as the Russian word for 'ink' and 'prunes' have a similar sound and spelling.
54. *SM*, 59.
55. *DB*, 71.
56. *SM*, 130; *DB*, 160.
57. Hardwick, *Childhood, Autobiography and the Francophone Caribbean*, pp. 65–66.
58. *Chemin*, 21.
59. *Chemin*, 145.
60. *Chemin*, 27.
61. N'zengou-Tayo, 'Literature and Diglossia', p. 87.
62. *Chemin*, 61.
63. <http://www.potomitan.info/dictionnaire/b.pdf>, consulted 21 November 2015.
64. *Chemin*, 136.
65. *Chemin*, 140.
66. *Chemin*, 95.
67. *DB*, 35.
68. *DB*, 61.
69. *DB*, 61.
70. Réjouis, p. 349.
71. Réjouis, p. 350.
72. Richard Price and Sally Price, 'Shadowboxing in the Mangrove', *Cultural Anthropology*, 12 (1997), 3–36 (p. 15).
73. Réjouis, p. 349.
74. *W*, 152.
75. *W*, 94.
76. *W*, 95.
77. *W*, 45; 51.
78. *W*, 57–58.
79. *Penser/Classer*, p. 46.
80. *Penser/Classer*, p. 55.
81. *Penser/Classer*, p. 55.
82. van Montfrans, p. 193.
83. van Montfrans, p. 193.
84. *W*, 54.

85. *W*, 105–06.
86. *Chemin*, 146.
87. *Les Fleurs du mal*, ed. by Jacques Dupont (Paris: Flammarion, 1999), pp. 61–62.
88. *Cahier du retour au pays natal*, ed. by Abiola Irele (Ibadan: New Horn, 1994), pp. 19–20.
89. Césaire, p. 19, capitals in original.
90. Patrick Chamoiseau, 'Mondialisation, mondialité, pierre-monde', trans. by Chris Miller, *Caribbean Globalizations, 1492 to the Present Day*, ed. by Eva Sansavior and Richard Scholar (Liverpool: Liverpool University Press, 2015), pp. 1–14 (pp. 1–2).
91. *Chemin*, 11.
92. *Chemin*, 69.
93. Réjouis, pp. 349–50.
94. 'Mademoiselle O', p. 167.
95. 'Mademoiselle O', p. 167.
96. 'Mademoiselle O', p. 167.
97. 'Mademoiselle O', p. 171.
98. *SM*, 87.
99. *SM*, 88.
100. This connection is pointed out by John Burt Foster, *Nabokov's Art of Memory and European Modernism* (Princeton: Princeton University Press, 1993), p. 42.
101. Foster, p. 39.
102. *SM*, 88.
103. Foster, pp. 42–43.
104. *W*, 32–34.
105. *W*, 132.
106. *Entretiens et conférences*, ed. by Dominique Bertelli and Mireille Ribière, 2 vols (Nantes: Joseph K., 2003), I, p. 76.
107. Gaspard Turin, 'Listes perecquiennes et filiation contemporaine: entre hybris et mélancolie', *Cahiers Georges Perec*, 11 (2011), 43–59 (p. 45).
108. Maryline Heck, *Georges Perec: le corps à la lettre* (Paris: Corti, 2012), p. 69.
109. Timothy A. Unwin, *Jules Verne: Journeys in Writing* (Liverpool: Liverpool University Press, 2005), pp. 200–01.
110. Jules Verne, *L'Île mystérieuse*, 3 vols (Paris: Hachette, 1918–1919), I (1918), p. 149.
111. *W*, 89.
112. *W*, 89–90, Verne, p. 144.
113. Verne, p. 146.
114. *W*, 90.
115. *W*, 91.
116. Vincent Bouchot, 'L'intertextualité vernienne dans *W ou le souvenir d'enfance*', *Études littéraires*, 23 (1990), 111–20 (p. 117).

CHAPTER 3

Traces of Trauma

This chapter tests the value of the concept of trauma in reading these texts' responses to the violent histories lying behind each author's experience of language change. Reading these texts through the concept of trauma shows them to be comparable, even when a close focus is maintained on the very different histories which have brought them into being. It offers a way of moving between different points within a literary space emerging from the migrations of modernity without flattening the differences between them. Such a comparative exploration also offers theoretical insights. By examining what is lost and gained by bringing together the wide range of historical and personal experiences explored in these texts, this chapter engages with recent debates on the widening use of the term 'trauma' and the literary and ethical implications of this. These texts have been read as expressions of traumatic memory before,[1] but I want to test here what is to be gained by looking at these works as narrations of trauma in a specifically comparative perspective. There are two ways in which a comparison of these texts as narrations of trauma offers new insights: it suggests that different models of inter-generational transmission of memory can be usefully brought into dialogue, and it offers new ways of thinking about the relationship of the experience of trauma to the everyday.

Each of these texts addresses both the personal pain of losing a parent and grief over a move away from insertion within a language and culture that form a collective identity. To various degrees, the loss of the parent comes to stand for distance from the language and culture of the family past. In the interwoven memorials to the parent and the culture they come to represent, these texts offer fruitful points of entry to questions about the connections or absence of connections between personal and collective experience of loss. Because each of these authors has a different generational relationship to the historical trauma he addresses in his autobiography, a comparison of the texts is one way towards an answer to questions about the transmission of trauma between generations. Looking at these texts side by side suggests there are points of convergence between the conscious experience of scenes of violence (Nabokov), living in the direct aftermath of genocide (Perec), and living in the long aftermath of histories of colonial violence (Chamoiseau), and that each author's mode of relation to the personal and collective past is strongly inflected by his parents' experience.

Key Concepts in Trauma Theory

Cathy Caruth was one of the first theorists to bring the concept of trauma to the attention of literary scholars in her 1996 book *Unclaimed Experience: Memory, Trauma and History*. Caruth defines trauma as an event which is so overwhelming that it is not understood as it happens and can only be processed belatedly 'in connection with another time and in another place'.[2] Because the event is not understood as it happens, it returns to haunt the individual in the form of flashbacks, nightmares, or unwitting re-enactments of the painful event. Drawing on Freud's description of the latency of traumatic memories, which lie dormant in the individual's mind only to return at unpredictable moments, Caruth's conceptualization of trauma places disrupted temporal experience at the heart of trauma. This obsessive return of the past is often spoken of in terms of possession or haunting.[3] Though less often remarked upon, trauma also has an impact on an individual's experience of space. Because it is processed after the fact, if at all, places very distant from the scene of the trauma can become the scene of its return. Caruth's definition of trauma depends then, not on the content of the traumatic event, but rather on the way it is received by the mind. The event bypasses the individual's usual perceptual filters, and as a result cannot be fully processed by the traumatized individual.

Both the memory of a traumatic event, and its narration, are therefore impossible, strictly speaking. What textual approaches to trauma can do is to illustrate or stage the impossibility of narrating the trauma. They bear witness to the damage the event has done to the individual's usual powers of perception and narration, rather than to the event itself. This emphasis on the mind's reception of the event, rather than its content, means a wide range of experiences can be defined as traumatic. Nevertheless, there is an implicit understanding that in order to trigger such a response, an event must shock the sufferer in some way. Trauma, then, hovers somewhere between form and content.[4] According to Dori Laub and Shoshana Felman, it also lies somewhere between the speaker or writer and listener or reader. Because traumatic events are too painful and overwhelming for those who experience them to comprehend or articulate, it is the listener who witnesses to trauma by piecing together the pain alluded to in oblique ways by the traumatized individual.[5]

Caruth's theory of trauma, with its emphasis on non-linear narrative forms, and its concept of painful events being processed in a different place from their origin, offers a helpful theoretical model for understanding the significance of the silences in each of these texts, and the links found in each between different times and places. Because it can describe such a wide range of experiences, it also offers a way of accounting for echoes in each author's approach to personal and collective loss, though the particular mode of his loss varies so greatly. It thus offers a way of bringing together authors who are using their autobiographical work in part to address the troubling of personal and collective identity produced by the state-sponsored violence and mass migrations of modernity.

Textual Tropes of Trauma

Though each author's position in relation to the histories which have brought about linguistic and cultural change in his family history is different, there are some striking points of convergence in the way they articulate this position. In each text, to varying degrees, the reader finds silence where she might expect an articulation of personal or collective loss. This absence of articulation is paired with multiple, oblique references to the silenced subject-matter. At times the text will come close to articulation of a painful episode of the past, only to veer off on to another subject. This interweaving of silence and multiple, repetitive returns to a moment of loss that cannot be articulated echoes the dynamic described in trauma theory. Silences and the development of a fragmentary narrative are both part of what Roger Luckhurst has called the 'trauma aesthetic'.[6] This is characterized by a degree of tension between narrative form and the experience to be recounted, leading to gaps in the narrative structure and a turning away from description of the traumatic event. Rather than describing the traumatic scene, the author arranges a collection of fragmentary memories related to it. The reader must then deduce the origin of the trauma by reflecting on the links between the fragments and paying close attention to narrative gaps.[7] Meaning is not encoded in the text alone, but also in its blank spaces, which are signs of events so painful that they cannot be narrated.

In Nabokov's text, meaning is encoded in the blank spaces of the text, most clearly in the narration of his father's death. Though I refer to a narration, it is really more an assembly of scattered fragments of the text which point to this central loss. Brian Boyd articulates this dynamic using the metaphor of the wound. He writes: 'Again and again throughout his autobiography Nabokov returns obliquely to his father's murder as if it were a wound he cannot leave alone but can hardly bear to touch.'[8] This is also the case to a lesser extent for other painful episodes in Nabokov's past, including grief over the loss of his mother and brother, and worry over his wife and son in 1930s Berlin and wartime Paris. The text also takes a laconic approach to the societal turmoil that must have accompanied Nabokov's time in late imperial Russia, inter-war Berlin and wartime Paris. As with more personal episodes of violence or loss, Nabokov's text evokes such scenes momentarily, only to pass on rapidly to an entirely different time or place.

The communicative role of silence in gesturing toward Nabokov's father's death becomes most marked in the final version of the autobiography. In this version, Nabokov for the first time narrates his memory of the telephone call which brings news of his father's fatal wound, received as he tried to protect a friend and colleague from two assassins.[9] Crucially, Nabokov does not tell the reader about the news the telephone call brings. Instead, he breaks off the sentence mid-phrase, and then moves to another paragraph where his father's death is implicitly acknowledged. The reader then has to deduce the reason for the broken-off sentence by bringing together two separate parts of the text, which locate this phone call on the same night as Nabokov's father's death. The very active role the reader has to take on to draw meaning from this silence resonates with Felman and Laub's argument that, in the case of trauma, both listener and speaker share the responsibility of witness. It is significant that the reader can only understand this passage if she has been reading attentively enough to remember its details; Nabokov here rewards memory and a willingness to cast one's mind retrospectively over the text. He thus encourages the reader to become, to a limited extent, a collaborator in the enterprise of mentally preserving the details of his past.

Though language seems to fail Nabokov when it comes to the details of his father's death, these details surface in other, seemingly unrelated, parts of the text, leading Michael Wood to write that '*Speak, Memory* is strongly organized around the father's death'.[10] When Nabokov is still in secondary school, he hears that his father has challenged another man to a duel. This belatedly makes sense of the extra boxing lessons his father had had recently and of the changed atmosphere in his house.[11] On the journey home from school, he worries about his father's fate and his mind drifts to the choice of weapons. The text refers to various weapons, but when it comes to pistols, Nabokov's train of thought suddenly swerves away.[12] Because Nabokov's father did eventually die from a gunshot wound, we can read this swerving away from the idea of the pistols as a result of the same inability to articulate the details of his father's death that causes him to break off the sentence about the telephone call. In both cases, it is the text's sudden silence and movement away from the subject under discussion that suggest the presence of remembered pain.

As Brian Boyd brings out in his reading of the end of Chapter One, similarly oblique hints at Nabokov's father's eventual death are present when he describes his memory of the way the peasants on the estates would throw his father up into the air.[13] Sitting in a first-floor dining room, Nabokov and his family would see his father appear at intervals on the level of the window. Nabokov compares his father's body floating in the air to the figures painted on ceilings in churches, which one sees at funerals, where the deceased's face is always hidden by candles and flowers.[14] Boyd convincingly reads this as a reference to Nabokov's father's funeral, which is never described directly in the text. The masking of the face in the coffin can be read as the result of an inability to articulate the fact of his father's death, while simultaneously wishing to present it to the reader. As before, the reader can identify the deceased's face as belonging to Nabokov's father if she brings two separate parts of the text together by mapping the image of his horizontal body in the air on to the horizontal body in the coffin.

As Barbara Straumann notes, a comparable silence surrounds Nabokov's relationship to his younger brother, Sergey. Like the father's death, Sergey's life and death appear to be too troubling to be addressed directly.[15] As in the case of the father, Nabokov does not write of his grief over his brother's death, but rather draws the reader's attention to his inability to voice it, writing that he finds it 'inordinately hard' to write about Sergey.[16] This difficulty is perhaps at the source of the pared-down language of his narration of his brother's death: 'He was arrested, accused of being "a British spy", was sent to a Hamburg concentration camp, where he died of inanition, on 10 January 1945.'[17] Will Norman speaks of 'the strange precision of the date of death' and we might add that the high level of precision about this one detail finds its counterpart in the general paucity of detail around Sergey Nabokov's life and Nabokov's reaction to his death.[18] The avoidance of detail along with the striking level of detail about the date and the use of the technical term 'inanition' can be read as the combination of obsessive focus and avoidance characteristic of a traumatic response. Further evidence of an oblique approach to Sergey's life is the link Nabokov makes between his Uncle Ruka and Sergey. Nabokov joins the two when he speaks of his uncle's stammer and then refers to Sergey, 'who also stammered, and who is also now dead'.[19] As Wood notes, 'Many people stammer and even more are dead.'[20] Wood sees the link which remains unspoken here as the two men's homosexuality, but we might also add that both were neglected younger sons of parents who favoured their eldest. There is a complex interweaving of different traumas here. The link Nabokov establishes between the two men deepens the gravity of his portrait of Sergey's relative neglect, as elsewhere the text says that Uncle Ruka was beaten savagely by his father.[21] Nabokov's guilt over Uncle Ruka's experience of neglect and mockery within the family, as well as his lonely death, are complicated by the suggestion that his uncle might have abused him as a child.[22] Here, Nabokov's guilt over Sergey's unhappy life and tragic death calls up a series of inter-generational patterns of trauma where the categories of perpetrator and victim are blurred.

The presence of traces of trauma in such narrations of personal loss has been noted by Straumann, Boyd and Wood, amongst others. What has less often been noted is that similar devices are used to evoke the deaths or misfortunes of people outside Nabokov's family. References to such deaths evoke the historical conditions which led to the Nabokovs' loss of a home, first in Russia, then in Europe. Thus, after a lengthy and affectionate description of his village schoolmaster, the author notes briefly that he was sentenced to hard labour by the Bolsheviks for belonging to a party on the radical left.[23] Nabokov does not dwell on this fact, and the reader has to surmise from the affectionate tone of the previous description that this would have caused him some pain. Similarly brief comments are made about the killings of other members of the household, as in the case of the usher who is shot for keeping the Nabokov family bicycles rather than turning them over to the state.[24] At times the destruction of his childhood world is evoked, not through the deaths of his family servants, but through a change in their way of life. An example of this occurs when Nabokov remembers girls weeding his family's gardens and then says that later they would dig state canals, connecting the regime change in Russia with a generic move from the pastoral to the political dystopia.[25] Occasionally, the reflections on the eventual fate of people he knew as a child become slightly more explicit. Thus, in recounting the fate of his Jewish tutor Lenski, Nabokov writes that he set up an amusement park in the Crimea, before 'the Bolsheviks came along and turned the lights out'.[26] Lenski moves to France, and Nabokov comments: 'I do not know — and would rather not imagine — what happened to him during the Nazi invasion of France.'[27] In the gap between 'I do not know' and 'I would rather not imagine', the reader must imagine for herself the deportation to the camps that Nabokov probably has in mind.

It could be argued that Nabokov's laconic comments on the violent deaths of various people he knew as a child reflect, not a traumatic response, but rather an aesthetic decision to focus on the development of his individual mind, leaving aside political and historical questions. Alternatively, the brevity of these notes might be seen as a sign that the people involved were simply not very close to Nabokov, and that their deaths therefore do not merit extensive space in the autobiography. Comparisons of the different versions of the text, published and unpublished, Russian and English, suggest, however, that this brevity does elide a degree of pain. When Nabokov speaks of his father's friend, General Kuropatkin, at the beginning of the work, he writes simply, 'I hope old Kuropatkin, in his rustic disguise, managed to evade Soviet imprisonment, but that is not the point.'[28] He then goes on to elaborate on an aesthetic lesson he learned from the old man. The English text, then, does not dwell on the general's later fate and could even be said to pass over it in a somewhat careless fashion. The Russian text nuances this impression slightly with an interpolated comment: 'Дело не в том, удалось ли или нет опростившемуся Куропаткину избежать советского конца (энциклопедия молчит, как будто набрав кровь в рот)' [It is not important whether the disguised Kuropatkin managed to avoid a Soviet end (the encyclopaedia is silent, as if its mouth is full with blood)].[29] This suggestion of an unacknowledged act of violence by the state suggests rather more anxiety than is explicitly present in the English text, as well as an emphasis on the problematic nature of written records of the post-Revolutionary period.

Changes in Nabokov's narrations of his personal losses also suggest that brevity does not indicate a lack of feeling or pain. In the drafts of the manuscript, the text's single sentence on his mother's death is edited to remove any trace of pathos. Referring to the long periods he went without seeing his mother when she lived in Prague and he in Berlin, and his eventual absence at her death, Nabokov changes, 'I was too hard up to visit her,' to 'I could not visit her' (in the final version it becomes 'was unable to visit her').[30] This small change eliminates any hint of self-pity, leaving the reader to imagine for herself the pain Nabokov must have felt at not being present for his mother's death or funeral. In the case of his brother, the laconic references to a certain sense of guilt in earlier versions are magnified in the final text, suggesting that the initially brief references to him were a result of complex feeling, rather than its absence. Nabokov goes so far as to criticize his previous inability to narrate his brother's life, writing of it as a task before which he had 'balked'.[31] Together, such variations in the different versions of the text contribute to a sense of elided pain even in brief and apparently neutral references to loss. The idea of an undercurrent of pain piercing through the surface of the text at certain points fits with Wood's description of the text as 'full of cracks in apparently smooth surfaces'.[32] This image picks up on the idea of the duality inherent in the text's approach to loss, the way it is 'awkwardly caught between time's brilliant but momentary abolition and its imminent and inevitable return', as the author, '[r]ather than possessing the past [...] himself comes to be possessed by the relentless return of reminiscences'.[33]

Such readings go against the grain of the interpretive paradigm the text itself sets up. The concept of trauma draws on Freudian ideas about the repression of painful knowledge and situates the author as unconscious of his own motivations. Nabokov makes very clear in the text that he does not wish it to be read through any kind of

Freudian framework.[34] More generally, he privileges a conscious, active approach to remembering and recording the past. Reading the text as an expression of traumatic memory is in tension with the author's professed commitment to a quite different mode of memory. This objection to reading the text as a narration of trauma is worth considering and I will do so when I treat the limits of the trauma paradigm, but for now I wish to note that, although Nabokov's tone in the autobiography is largely positive, if not triumphant, attention to the text's moments of silence and its swift moves away from more painful topics suggests that these episodes can be read as not fully assimilated into *Speak, Memory*'s broader celebration of the mind's mobility and power to preserve modes of access to an idyllic past world.

In contrast to this approach to *Speak, Memory*, reading Perec's text as a narration of trauma does not involve reading against the grain of the text's own rhetoric quite so clearly. Indeed, *W ou le souvenir d'enfance* has been referred to as a 'too perfect a counterpart to Caruth'.[35] It is connected with two courses of psychoanalysis which Perec underwent and it can be read as a conscious engagement with psychoanalytic discourse on trauma and mourning. Eleanor Kaufman points to three aspects of Perec's text which situate it as a narrative of trauma. The first is Perec's belated knowledge of the significance of his departure from the gare de Lyon.[36] Though he could not know it at the time, this would be the last time he would see his mother. The fact that this moment of leave-taking can only be understood in retrospect connects it with Caruth's argument that trauma, by definition, is never understood as it happens, but only after the fact. Kaufman further argues that the way Perec narrates this moment three times in three different ways reflects the haunting quality of traumatic memories, which keep returning in different forms. This repeated return to the moment of departure could be compared with Nabokov's scattering of references to his father's demise. Caruth argues that memory of the traumatic event returns repeatedly, not only so that the individual can come to terms with the trauma or death that has occurred, but also so that he or she can come to grasp the fact of his or her own survival in the face of the deaths or suffering of other people. Kaufman finds an echo of this simultaneous attempt to come to terms with the death of others and one's own survival in Perec's statement that writing is the sign of his life and of his parents' death.[37]

Lawrence D. Kritzman turns his attention to an aspect of Perec's text that Kaufman passes over, namely the role of silence and the interweaving of the autobiographical and fictional narratives. He draws attention to the way the text 'recognizes the mourning process as an engagement with the aporia created by the inability to bear witness', emphasizing the ways in which Perec's memories of his childhood remain 'cognitively somewhat inaccessible'.[38] This sense of the past as inaccessible is reflected in the opening statement of the first autobiographical chapter, stating that the author has no memories of childhood, a statement which is echoed in the fictional strands of the text, where the child Gaspard Winckler is mute and deaf, and where the adult Gaspard Winckler bears a false name, suggesting a break between his childhood and adult identity in several different ways. This doubling of the figure of Gaspard Winckler is evocative of another trope of narrations of trauma, dissociation, or the splitting of the self.

Splitting of the self can be seen as an extreme version of the way trauma fractures communication between the conscious mind and the past self who experienced the traumatizing event. The way there are literally two Gaspard Wincklers in the text lends this idea an embodied reality. The adult Gaspard Winckler's failed attempt to save the deaf and mute child from dying at sea can be read as a fictionalization of the impossible task facing the traumatized individual of coming to understand a past which is defined by the fact that it resists comprehension according to the ordinary categories of meaning. Kritzman notes that because Perec's memories are out of reach, he has to imagine how things could have been.[39] The fictional strands of the text and the speculative character of some of the autobiographical statements thus become signs of the traumatic destruction of the usual avenues into the past.

Like Nabokov, Perec breaks off his text as a way of signifying the loss of a parent, in this case his mother. Where Nabokov simply breaks off one sentence, Perec places a blank page with an ellipsis in brackets at the centre of his text.[40] The greater space given over to blankness reflects the greater difficulty in processing the loss of a parent whose death was orchestrated by state machinery which consciously prevented any record of the time and place of death from surviving. The movement of textual blankness from the middle of one sentence to the centre of the text can be read as symptomatic of the migration of trauma from the periphery to the centre in post-Holocaust narratives of the 1.5 generation and others. The central blankness which signifies his mother's disappearance is mirrored by multiple smaller blanknesses which draw the reader's attention to the difficulty of writing a personal life-history against the background of collective loss. These range from textual gaps, when place names are given with a first letter followed by a dash, to imagery of blankness, such as the gaps in the ship's log, to narrative gaps, like the unexplained disappearance of the adult Gaspard Winckler.

One kind of blankness especially disruptive to the reader's absorption in the text is the way each chapter ends. In the Denoël edition, at least, there are blank pages between each of the chapters, thus opening up a physical gap between the autobiographical and fictional strands of the narrative. Because the fictional chapters construct an engaging story-world, the physical act of turning the page on to blankness creates a sense of surprise, as if the absorbing fictional world has just disappeared. This is particularly the case at the end of chapters three, five, nine, and eleven, all of which end with an unanswered question or unresolved tension.[41] A comparison is possible here with Nabokov's use of a similar technique. Elizabeth Bruss has written of how Nabokov creates absorbing worlds in each of the chapters of his autobiography, then dissolves each world, or exposes its fragility, at the chapter's end.[42] In this way, both authors lead the reader to contemplate the constructed nature of a textual world she has just experienced vividly.

What differs about the way Nabokov and Perec use this technique is that each of Nabokov's chapters could be read as a stand-alone piece and indeed were published as separate pieces before he assembled them into a full-length work. Because of the stand-alone quality of Nabokov's chapters, when the world each chapter creates disappears, the reader can sometimes feel disoriented, but this sense of disorientation is confined to the moment of dissolution. Once the reader starts a new chapter, she enters into a new, and separate, setting. In contrast to this, once Perec's reader finishes a chapter, she does not begin engaging with material completely new to her. Rather, she re-enters a world she has seen created and erased many times. Whereas Nabokov all but tells the reader in the first chapter that there is a hidden thematic coherence to his work, in Perec's text the reader must keep struggling to make connections through material whose thematic coherence is not obvious on a first (or indeed a subsequent) reading. His reader then shares to a certain extent in the constant return of the traumatized mind to material which resists understanding.

The question of the reader's response to the text leads on to the issue of traces of secondary, attenuated trauma in critical writing on *W ou le souvenir d'enfance*. There are elements of the writing on Perec's autobiography which suggest that his narration of his own trauma triggers a kind of muted echo of a traumatic response in his readers. Philippe Lejeune has spoken of readers skipping over the autobiographical chapters, whose painful subject matter and halting pace makes them difficult to absorb.[43] The reader's difficulty in absorbing the text's meaning can be linked to its memorial function. We see this when Perec explains his reluctance to give information about his parents' lives, because only the blankness of his writing can communicate their absence and its effects on him. Using a restricted lexical range, he articulates this point, and then goes on to emphasize the role of the materiality of writing in manifesting this blankness:

> C'est cela que je dis, c'est cela que j'écris et c'est cela seulement qui se trouve dans les mots que je trace, et dans les lignes que ces mots dessinent, et dans les blancs que laisse apparaître l'intervalle entre ces lignes.[44]
>
> [That is what I am saying, that is what I am writing, and that's all there is in the words I trace and in the lines the words make and in the blanks that the gaps between the lines create]

Here the space between the words on the page is presented as constituting as much a part of the text's memorial project as their verbal meaning. Perec's success in communicating this aspect of his text can be seen in the way that critics often quote excerpts from this chapter with little elaboration, even in otherwise detailed analysis.[45] The critical practice of repeated quotation can be seen as deferring to Perec's statement that the material form of the words on the page communicates as much about his parents as he could with more elaborate statements about their lives. If the meaning of the lines is held as much in the physical gaps they leave on the page, then the practice of re-presenting these lines to the reader makes as much or more sense as a response to the text as drawing out the nuances of the lines' verbal meaning.

An essay by George Steiner in *Language and Silence* provides some insight into the rationale behind this silent transcription of Perec's words in a number of critical texts. Steiner begins the essay by quoting passages from two books on the Holocaust, a diary written by Chaim Kaplan during his time in the Warsaw Ghetto[46] and Jean-François Steiner's study of Treblinka,[47] but it ends in a kind of retreat from engagement with them: 'These books and the documents which have survived are not for "review". Not unless "review" signifies, as perhaps it should in these instances, a "seeing-again", over and over.'[48] The essay goes on to fulfil its own call for repeated return to painful historical facts:

> In the Warsaw ghetto a child wrote in its diary: 'I am hungry, I am cold; when I grow up I want to be a German and then I shall no longer be hungry and no longer cold.' And now I want to write that sentence again: 'I am hungry, I am cold; when I grow up I want to be a German, and then I shall no longer be hungry and no longer cold.'[49]

The repetition Steiner calls for resonates with the responses to overwhelming events analysed in trauma theory and it finds a very faint echo in the rewriting of a few key quotations in analyses of *W ou le souvenir d'enfance*.

Perec's text, then, in its use of the devices of blankness, repetition, dissociation, and interweaving of the factual and the fictional, can be seen as an expression of its author's trauma at the loss of his parents, especially his mother, and more broadly at the painful task of constructing a sense of identity in a context of collective loss. It preserves the fixed quality of his relationship to the past to such an extent that it informs critical responses to the text. A comparison of *W ou le souvenir d'enfance* and *Speak, Memory* as narrations of trauma is suggestive of the changing place of trauma in accounts of twentieth-century childhoods. Attention to the silences of *Speak, Memory* suggests that even a text like this, which has been read as an archetypal celebration of the mind's freedom from the effects of history, contains traces of a traumatic response to the violence of twentieth-century history. In *W ou le souvenir d'enfance*, the silences have moved from a marginal, if troubling position, to become a founding condition of the text. The text is no longer interrupted by moments of inarticulate pain but takes as its central purpose the delineation of the absences left by violent histories.

The position of trauma in Chamoiseau's text differs from its place in *Speak, Memory* and *W ou le souvenir d'enfance*. Trauma is neither a troubling presence undermining an idyllic portrait of his childhood, nor a moment of irreparable rupture from which the text springs. Rather, the sources of trauma in his text are found in everyday life. Looking at the implications of this location of trauma in the everyday, and the way it relates to the other two authors' approach to historical trauma, offers a way of nuancing recent debates on the widening use of the term 'trauma' and the differences between different kinds of trauma. Though Chamoiseau is writing in a very different context, his text also offers examples of dissociation, silence about painful scenes coupled with repeated oblique returns to them, and the articulation of painful autobiographical facts through the medium of fiction. There are marks of trauma in his narration of his parents' deaths, especially that of his mother, and in his record of the psychological pain brought about by his entry into the public education system.

Dominick LaCapra's distinction between 'structural' and 'historical' trauma is useful in distinguishing between these two different kinds of pain. LaCapra uses the term 'structural' or 'transhistorical' trauma to refer to pain which everyone experiences, while historical trauma arises from specific events of extreme violence which most people do not experience. He argues that the idea of structural trauma is present in various philosophical and everyday modes of thought which see human life as imperfect, distanced in some way from a sense of 'at-homeness, unity or community', which might have been experienced in the past, either in the womb, in the very early years of life, or in a mythical, paradisiacal time before imperfection entered the world (though LaCapra finds problematic this conversion of absence into loss, that is, the move from noticing an absence of at-homeness in human life to assuming that there is a home which must have been lost). Notably, many of the ideas which LaCapra cites as examples of structural trauma, including 'the separation from the (m)other', 'the passage from nature to culture', and 'the entry into language', can be connected to growing up.[50] Structural trauma is then construed as part of the process of forming a separate, independent identity which involves some degree of pain on the part of all who pass through it. Historical trauma, by contrast, is an extreme experience of violence which is not usually part of human life. LaCapra gives the experience of the Holocaust or of the atom bomb in Japan as examples.[51]

Such a distinction is valuable in distinguishing between the different kinds of trauma experienced by Nabokov, Perec and Chamoiseau. Chamoiseau's increasing distance from his mother as he grows up, and his eventual loss of his parents in adulthood, can be seen as structural traumas, different in quality from the historical violence which shapes Perec's life and to some extent Nabokov's. Though LaCapra's distinction is useful in bringing out these points of divergence, Chamoiseau's narration of childhood also unsettles its oppositions, which LaCapra acknowledges to be problematic.[52] The child's increasing distance from his mother is indeed partially a result of him growing up, but it is sharpened by the way the school forces him to speak French and not Creole, his 'langue-manman' [Mama-language].[53] Chamoiseau's mother's death from old age can be seen as part of structural trauma, but it also deepens her son's distance from his childhood Creole self, which is part of the legacy of the historical trauma of colonialism and slavery. An examination of the ways in which traces of trauma appear in *Une enfance créole* suggests, then, that the division between structural and historical traumas, while helpful for establishing clarity in the broad use of the term, needs to be nuanced for application in postcolonial contexts.

The third volume of Chamoiseau's trilogy, published after the death of the author's parents, deals most directly with the structural trauma of their loss. As the title indicates, the volume is also a consideration of the question of endings more generally, and of the nature of childhood's end. It charts the young Chamoiseau's move from the world of childhood into the realm of adolescence. There are strong marks of trauma in Chamoiseau's narration of his parents' death. As in the case of Perec and Nabokov, it possesses an elliptical quality. Their deaths are not recounted in a straightforward manner; they are evoked by insistent return to a few key metaphors. Nor is the narration of the parents' deaths integrated into the main body of the narrative, which recounts the child's increasing bonds to his friends and the beginning of his interest in the opposite sex. Rather, it is presented in brief paragraphs in italics interspersed throughout the text.

The interaction between the paragraphs in italics and the main body of the text in Roman sets up a tension between a story of development and one of decline. The use of this device suggests the traumatic quality of his parents' death in several ways. The contrast between the tone of the two narrative strands and their apparent lack of cohesion suggests the difficulty of assimilating traumatic memory into narrative sequence. The metaphorical language of the passages in italics and their frequent evocation of the bodily sensations of shock and fear further reinforces the idea that these memories exceed the mind's grasp. These fragments often approach the subject of parental death only to break off or to switch to another topic through anacoluthon. These swerves away from painful topics and the use of interrupted sentences to indicate grief echo devices used in other narrations of trauma, including Nabokov's depiction of his father's death.

This is the first mention of the day when Chamoiseau, in France at the time, receives news of his father's death from his sister, 'la Baronne':

> *Et je me souviens du télégramme de la Baronne alors que je me trouvais en terre d'exil, auprès de l'Orge, et qui m'informe de ce lit devenu silencieux dans la grande salle commune, du plateau intouché, et des deux pruneaux dont nul n'héritera ce jour-là ... Basile! Basile!...*[54]

> [*And I remember the telegram from the Baroness when I was in the land of exile, near the Orge, and which informs me about the bed which has fallen silent in the big shared room, about the untouched plate, and the two prunes which no one will inherit that day ... Basil! Basil!...*]

Basile, or Basile la Mort, is a character from Creole culture associated with death, whom Chamoiseau will reference throughout this volume when the subject of death arises. Here the interruption of the sentence with his name, the ellipses, and the euphemisms such as 'lit devenu silencieux' suggest the difficulty of articulating the fact of the father's death directly. This difficulty is further evoked by the breaking off of this passage and the return of its subject matter later in the text. Forty pages after the passage quoted above, the reader encounters another passage in italics which takes up the imagery first introduced here:

> *... chère Baronne ... [...] tâche démesurée que ce simple télégramme qui doit porter Basile ... et moi, pétrifié devant cet ivoire froid, ce petit blanc immense, ces lettres majuscules, laconiques, qui dansent encore ... Moi, en vertige au dessus comme au bord du pire...*[55]

> [*... dear Baroness ... [...] such a boundless task, this simple telegram which must carry Basil ... and I, frozen in front of this cold ivory, this small white immensity, these capital letters, terse, still dancing ... I, dizzy above them as if I am on the edge of the worst ...*]

The return to this moment suggests the ruminative quality of the speaker's grief. The relative lack of verbs in this passage, the use of the present tense, and the movements from one thought to another through ellipsis reinforce the reader's sense of this moment as resistant to containment within linear narrative structure. The interplay here between fixity ('pétrifié', 'ivoire froid') and dizzying turbulence ('qui dansent encore', 'en vertige') is concentrated in the oxymoron 'petit blanc immense', suggesting both the slip of paper in the speaker's hand and a vast absence which could engulf him. This co-existence of opposite states is characteristic of the way traumatic events disrupt the usual categories of experience and expression. Further evidence of this disruption is the inability to relate what the telegram contains, while oblique hints to it surface in the language, as in the metaphor of the sheet of ivory which suggests the coolness and hardness of the tomb.

As in the texts of Nabokov and Perec, then, ellipses, blank spaces and silences take on communicative roles, gesturing both toward the absence of the parent and the difficulty in articulating that absence. Such silences are also present in Chamoiseau's narration of the death of his mother. The communicative role of silence is heightened in this case by thematic convergences and tensions set up between the passages in italics where Chamoiseau dwells on his mother's final years and the surrounding passages where he depicts his initiation into the erotic. In particular, it is possible to draw a parallel between Chamoiseau's mother, Man Ninotte, and a young girl with whom he becomes fascinated, referred to in the text as Gabine la Lune. She lives near the building site where the young Chamoiseau goes to play with his friends. He waits outside her home in the hope of seeing her when she comes out on to the balcony. He never knows when she will appear and when she does, they do not speak, he simply stares at her, aware of a seemingly unbridgeable distance between them. As indicated by the name 'Gabine la Lune' her beauty and inaccessibility lend her a certain unreal quality. Toward the end of *A bout d'enfance*, they do communicate via a letter through a mutual friend, but they never meet.

The way the young girl takes on increasing importance in the life of the child creates a shift in the centre of gravity of the text, which moves from Man Ninotte within the domestic space to Gabine la Lune, seen from the street. The interaction between the main body of the text and the passages in italics suggest that depictions of the girl are in part an indirect approach to the subject of distance from a beloved female figure. This passage is a particularly striking example of this. The sentences in italics evoke his mother's increasing mental confusion during her last years. It refers to those moments when his mother's memory would suddenly return, leaving her struggling to make sense of her illness and of changes that had occurred while she had been mentally absent. The passage in Roman ostensibly concerns the young adolescent's vigils outside the home of Gabine la Lune, but it also seems to evoke something of his grief over his mother:

> ... *Qui ne dit rien, qui l'a vue émerger, revenue sans comprendre?...*
> Le rituel s'était installé. Mémoire, cette scène immobile constitue toute l'époque. Un arrêt sur image. Un repeat incessant. Il faudrait l'écrire mille fois à l'identique, avec de subtiles variations pour en sortir l'ampleur. Lui, accoudé à son escalier, et elle en face, dans une distance d'environ huit mètres. Les deux se regardant.[56]

> [... *Who said nothing, who saw her emerge, returned without understanding?...*
> The ritual had been established. Memory, this fixed scene holds the whole era. A freeze frame. An incessant playing-back. I would have to write it out the same way a thousand times, with subtle variations to bring out its scope. He, with his elbows leaning on her stairs, and she opposite him, about eight metres away. The two looking at each other.]

The photographic imagery of stills and repeats suggests the fixed quality of the images which return to the mind of the grief-stricken author. Similarly, the reference to repeated rewriting suggests fixation on this one moment. Though this passage is supposed to be about the young boy watching Gabine la Lune, the absence of her name and the use of the pronoun 'elle' when its previous appearance has been a reference to the child's mother, encourage the reader to interpret this scene as connected both to the figure of Gabine la Lune and to Man Ninotte. This indirect approach suggests the difficulty of articulating the response to the mother's death.

The transition from Man Ninotte to Gabine as the text's centre goes hand in hand with the child's move from speech to writing. Because the child is too overwhelmed to speak to Gabine, he composes a letter which he asks one of her friends to pass on to her. The text underlines the way the absence of the beloved and the child's inability to approach her drives him to take up the pen.[57] The move from an immediate form of communication to a mediated one reflects the child's move from the womb-like domestic space to the street and from the Creole to the French language. Whereas in the previous two volumes, especially the first, the child is immersed in the female domestic space where the mother's voice shapes his experience, in this volume, most of his time is spent outside of the house and his mother's words have a much smaller role in the text. Increasing distance from the mother is then associated with a move from oral to written culture and hence with a more distanced relationship with language and the surrounding world, in a way that is reminiscent of LaCapra's characterization of structural trauma.

In a move which reinforces the portrayal of the child-self and the mother as bound into a symbiotic relationship, the narration of the increasing distance between mother and child and the mother's eventual death is accompanied by a growing sense of concern, even desperation, about the child-self's disappearance. The third volume of the trilogy is peppered with questions and laments such as 'Mon négrillon, où donc t'es-tu serré?' [*My little black boy, where have you hidden yourself away?*] and 'Où défaille l'enfance?' [*Where does childhood falter?*][58] The device of addressing a child-self who will not reply, and the quest to locate the absent child-self in physical space echoes Perec's use of the two Gaspard Wincklers. Both authors' use of the device indicates a degree of splitting of the self which could be caused by trauma, but the ways in which it is used bring out the differences between each author's experience. In Perec's text, the separation between the two Wincklers is definitive, whereas in Chamoiseau's text a kind of underground relationship does continue between 'le négrillon' and 'l'homme d'aujourd'hui'. The distinction between the almost total alienation of child and adult selves in Perec's work and the gradual accretion of a more attenuated split between the two in Chamoiseau's work reflects each author's different position in relation to histories of violence, and can be read through the distinction between structural and historical trauma. Perec's life in the immediate aftermath of genocide triggers a complex shattering of the self; Chamoiseau's life in the long aftermath of colonial violence is much less destructive of the self, but the unresolved traces of the colonial past nonetheless make themselves felt, installing a rift between the early childhood self and the identity forged upon contact with the French state.

School is the environment where the child first comes into sustained contact with the French state. *Chemin-d'école* portrays the child's entry into the public education system as the beginning of a process which will alienate the child from his first language, the enchantment he finds in the world around him, and his mother. The experience of school is depicted as deeply painful, triggering a destruction of the child's inner world.[59] The first sign of the destructive impact school has on the child is the physical response it triggers. On the child's first day he is so frightened that 'ses genoux tremblaient. Ses jambes s'étaient muées en fines herbes grasses incapables de le soutenir' [his knees were knocking. His legs had turned into slender grass blades incapable of supporting them].[60] He has to stand up when his name is called on the register, which triggers the following response: 'Le négrillon à moitié mort dut se lever et se coincer le ventre contre le banc pour demeurer debout, tête pendante, épaules caves, et le souffle abîmé' [Half dead, the little boy rose, pressed his stomach against the desk to steady himself, and stood slump-shouldered, with lolling head and raggedy breath].[61] This weakening of the body evokes the child's inability to cope with the frightening environment of the school, and the hollowness and ruin suggested by 'caves' and 'abîmé' are proleptic of the way the school will empty the imaginative and cultural world the child inhabits by creating a rift between his mental universe and the physical world he inhabits.

One of the main ways in which school damages the child's ability to interact in a fruitful way with the surrounding world is by depriving him of his autonomy. In school, only the teacher can direct the child's physical movements. Chamoiseau uses the children's point of view to illustrate the shock they feel upon learning this:

> Ils apprirent dans la sidération que, capitaine à bord de droit divin, le Maître était le seul à régenter les actes. Se mettre debout, c'était lui-même. S'asseoir, c'était lui-même. Ouvrir sa bouche, c'était lui-même. Quand il parlait, les regards et les oreilles devaient se nouer sur lui-même.[62]
>
> [They were stunned to learn that, captain of his ship by divine right, the Teacher ran absolutely everything. He and he alone gave permission to stand up. To sit down. To open one's mouth. When he spoke, all eyes and ears were to be trained on him.]

The nautical imagery combined with references to the teacher's total control over the children's bodies evoke the history of slavery. The schoolroom is here implicitly compared to the hold of a ship where the children first learn what it means to be controlled by another person. The idea of the schoolroom as a kind of echo of the hold on a slave-ship fits in with Chamoiseau's approach to this charged space elsewhere in his work. Lorna Milne notes that the hold functions as a kind of point of origin of Creole literature for Chamoiseau, as it is the place of 'le cri originel' of transported Africans.[63] The idea of the hold as the source of a sound that denotes both pain as well as self-expression and the beginnings of a collective identity founded in displacement and oppression resonates with *Chemin-d'école*'s portrayal of school as both the place where the child's cultural identity is damaged, and the place where he will acquire the ability to write. The suggestions of the stirrings of a collective identity founded in common pain are certainly present in the passage above in the use of 'ils' and the children's shared horror, and later passages in *Chemin-d'école* will develop the idea of the classroom as an originary space for the author's writing, but first the volume establishes it as a place where linguistic and cultural identity are stripped away.

This stripping away of the children's identity is most apparent when it comes to questions of language. In school, the child learns that there are two languages, Creole and French, and that French must be spoken in school. Chamoiseau once more employs the child's point of view to illustrate the distress this discovery provokes: 'Le négrillon, dérouté, comprit qu'il ignorait cette langue. La tite-voix babilleuse de sa tête maniait une autre langue, sa langue-maison, sa langue-manman, sa langue non-apprise intégrée sans contraintes au fil de ses désirs du monde' [Baffled, the little black boy realized that he did not know this language. The chatty lil' voice in his head used a different language, his home-language, his Mama-language, the language he had not learned but rather absorbed with ease as he eagerly explored his world].[64] School, by imposing French at all times, evicts the child from his 'langue-maison, langue-manman'. Chamoiseau writes of his child-self: 'le Maître l'avait rendu muet' [the Teacher had made him mute].[65] This silence can be read, like the child's physical weakness triggered by the frightening experience of the classroom, as a response to an environment which overwhelms him. This linguistic shift introduces distance between the child and his mother, who looks at him impressed, but uncomprehending, when he begins to use formal French words in the home.[66]

The idea of linguistic change introducing distance into the child's relationship with his mother offers a fitting way into the question of the interweaving of historical and transhistorical trauma in Chamoiseau's text. LaCapra formulated these useful terms as a response to what he felt was worryingly loose use of the term trauma. He argues that it is ethically problematic to use one term for experiences of extreme violence and difficulties which most people experience, as well as to conflate the categories of victim, perpetrator and bystander. Richard McNally, though writing somewhat later than LaCapra, shares his concern about this 'conceptual bracket creep', arguing that trauma stops being a useful category when it can be applied to events as different as military combat and giving birth to a healthy baby.[67] Wulf Kansteiner echoes this critique when he points out the problems involved in applying psychoanalytic language, developed to name supposedly universal internal struggles, to contexts where specific historical harm is at stake.[68] Kansteiner and McNally argue for a return to earlier definitions of trauma which located its source in extreme events.

LaCapra's distinction between transhistorical and historical trauma is, then, part of an attempt to parse the different meanings the word trauma has accrued since it first entered literary and cultural studies, an attempt perceived as necessary by many in the field. Texts like Chamoiseau's, which present starting school as traumatic, are arguably part of the motivation for such distinctions. There does indeed seem to be an ethical issue about situating a frightening first day at school in the same category of experience as the loss of one's mother in the Holocaust. Distinguishing between structural or transhistorical and historical trauma offers one way out of this problem. According to this distinction, Chamoiseau's experience of school, the distance it opens between him and his mother, and his eventual bereavement would all be structural traumas, simply part of the move from childhood to adulthood.

The text does support this reading to a certain extent. As explored at the end of the first chapter, the opening pages of *Antan d'enfance* present childhood as a state whose natural unfolding will lead to its own destruction. It is in the nature of the child to grow away from the mother and to gradually enter into a more distanced, rational, and less imaginative relationship with the surrounding world.[69] Yet, these natural moves toward greater independence and a more conventional perception of the physical world are accompanied by repeated references to fracture within the self and by strong echoes of the oppression experienced by slaves. Situating the text's narration of growing up as the narration of a transhistorical trauma elides the way the unresolved legacy of Martinique's past deepens the impact of the child's growing pains. Though the move from childhood to adulthood, from home to school, from the private world to the public world, could well be seen as inevitably involving transhistorical traumas, such as the realization that one can be punished for breaking rules, or the loss of the especially close infant relationship with the mother, in Chamoiseau's text these experiences are inextricably interwoven with the historical traumas involved in his encounter with the French state. Chamoiseau's text suggests that rather than distinguishing between historical and transhistorical traumas, attention to their overlapping impacts on one individual can help make sense of the conceptual migration of trauma from extreme to everyday contexts. Comparisons between trauma triggered by extreme experiences and that caused by everyday experiences do indeed have to be undertaken with circumspection and should not seek to establish equivalency between the experiences of people at different generational distances from traumatic events. However, they become less jarring when the historical context of the development of everyday experiences is taken into account and when trauma is seen as a concept which can refer to a range of relationships between structural and historical trauma.

Comparison of these texts as narrations of trauma allows such nuancing of concepts outlined in trauma theory, but also raises questions about the means of transmission of traumatic experience between generations. The question of inter-generational transmission of memory (or its failure) is present in some way in all three texts. As we saw in the previous chapter, Nabokov's relationship with his mother involves him absorbing memories of events he never experienced. This transmission is connected with the expansion of consciousness, but has a darker side in its origins in his mother's loss of her parents and most of her siblings.[70] Barbara Straumann suggests that Nabokov's mother passes on to him a practice of memory which has a painful absence at its centre.[71] As we saw in this chapter, Nabokov's absorption of the memory of his grandfather's cruelty to his uncle (cruelty he never witnessed himself) complicates his response to his brother's life and death. Such afterlives of violence and loss present in Nabokov's family history perhaps suggest that transmission of memories, painful and otherwise, always plays a role in the formulation of an approach to history and the self. In *W ou le souvenir d'enfance* and *Une enfance créole*, however, the process of inter-generational transmission of traumatic memory takes on a central role, because these authors did not themselves experience the violence whose after-effects shape their lives. Whereas Nabokov lives through the rise to power of the Bolshevik and Nazi regimes as an adult, Perec grows up in the direct aftermath of the Second World War and Holocaust, and Chamoiseau comes of age in the long aftermath of the French colonization of

Martinique. Because of the intangible, unspoken quality of the interaction between these authors' lives and the legacy of historical violence, images of the wounded body become a way of making present to the reader the reality of the pain it inflicts.

The Wounded Body and the Transmission of Trauma

In *W ou le souvenir d'enfance* and *Une enfance créole*, imagery of scars evokes the simultaneous fixity and mobility of historical trauma. Scar tissue suggests the interplay of death and survival which is central to the experience and narration of trauma. It testifies to damage done to the body which cannot be fully healed, and so speaks of the body's fragility. Yet once created, scar tissue itself is difficult to destroy and so can act as a form of witness to past pain which is not easily forgotten or ignored. Marks on the skin are not so internal to the self that they are subject to the flux that afflicts the mind, nor are they so external to the self that they are subject to the erosion that wears away at the physical world or to projects of demolition initiated by the state. For both Chamoiseau and Perec, scars are traces which inhabit an intermediate space at the borders of the self. Visible because of the interplay of living and dead tissue, they offer a miniature picture of the structure of these texts, where narration of the author's life is interwoven with fragmentary biographies of deceased parents to make visible something of a larger history and its resonances in the author's life and the contemporary world. The scars' position at the borders of the self connects them with the question of transmission of painful memories. They come to act as traces of histories which are experienced neither from the inside nor from the outside, but which fundamentally mark the boundaries of possibility of an individual life.

The scar which receives most attention in *W ou le souvenir d'enfance* is the one on Perec's upper lip which has the form of a short diagonal line, pointing from right to left. Perec writes: 'Pour des raisons mal élucidées, cette cicatrice semble avoir eu pour moi une importance capitale: elle est devenue une marque personnelle, un signe distinctif' [For reasons that have not been properly elucidated, this scar seems to have been of cardinal importance for me: it became a personal mark, a distinguishing feature].[72] Already this connection of the scar with a sense of secure, unique identity is striking in a text where such concepts are so systematically undermined. Such a level of engagement with this small scar suggests that it offers a way into another memory. Warren Motte argues that this scar, which Perec received when one of his classmates hit him with a ski in a fit of anger, is the visible sign of an invisible, but equally unjust, wound — that is, the loss of his parents, and, especially, the loss of his mother.[73] The long passage devoted to the scar will go on to evoke in greater detail the level of Perec's attachment to it. It shapes the way he shaves and his liking for an Antonello da Messina portrait, it features in his first novel and in an important passage in another novel, *Un homme qui dort*, and it influences his choice of actor for the film version of this last work.[74] This short diagonal line is thus present in a variety of contexts: autobiography, fiction, film and visual art.

This migration between different contexts is significant because it is associated with inter-generational transmission of memory and its failure in several ways. The scar goes from right to left and top to bottom, the same movement that Hebrew writing follows, as Bernard Magné points out, and so is associated with the breakdown in linguistic, religious and literary continuities between Perec and the previous generation.[75] It is also connected with the transmission of corporeal traits, as Perec mentions twice that his mother leans her head to the side in photographs he has of her, a trait he also shares. When describing the photographs, Perec draws attention to the reversibility created by the camera's gaze, with three references in three pages to the way right and left are reversed on the photographs described.[76] This reversibility is also connected to the duality of transmission between generations. The scar on Perec's lip has the form of a *bande*, a figure from heraldry that is mentioned several times in the text. The *bande* is the reverse of the *barre* and indicates bastardy. The same kind of reversibility applies in heraldry as causes the confusion when Perec looks at the photograph, because left and right are taken from the point of view of the wearer of a coat-of-arms, and so are reversed for an observer. Both the photograph and the coat-of-arms thus call up ideas about things becoming their own opposites when seen from the point of view of an outside observer, suggesting Perec's painful position outside or beyond his parents' history while he remains marked by it. The reversibility of the scar connects it both to transmission of various kinds of memory (Hebrew writing, bodily gestures, heraldry) and to the historical events which trigger failures in transmission. The question of the author's relationship to the previous generation thus fuses transmission and non-transmission of memory. The way the scar moves between different contexts (fiction, film, visual art, autobiography) while retaining the same form, and its presence just above the author's mouth, indicates the presence of the marks of the previous generation's trauma in the artistic work created and absorbed by the author.

Physical injury in Chamoiseau is not connected with bereavement, but it is connected with painful contact with history. In *Une enfance créole*, scars also serve to make invisible pain visible. Here the marks left by corporal punishment make present the unseen destruction of the children's confidence and autonomy which occurs at school. The author dwells on the specific kinds of marks left on the children's bodies by the different whips used by the teacher.[77] One whip is known as the 'liane-bois-volcan' [volcano-wood switch] by the children and as the 'liane-allemand' [German vine] by the teacher, 'car elle envahissait' [because it was invasive].[78] Both images suggest the breaking of the barrier of the children's skin, a physical manifestation of the damage done to their minds. The reference to the 'liane-allemand' also contributes the way the whips make manifest the presence of echoes of historical violence of a much broader scale in the classroom. The meditation on corporal punishment experienced at school culminates with 'le négrillon' being beaten by the principal. This episode serves to distil all the humiliation the child experiences in school: 'Il se sentait brisé définitif, banni du monde des vivants et voué à traîner ses stupeurs dans un labyrinthe d'escaliers vides' [He felt broken beyond repair, banished from the world of the living and condemned to drag his bewilderment through a labyrinth of deserted stairways].[79] The pain stays with him:

'Rencontrer Monsieur le Directeur, c'était ressentir encore les brûlures du fouet, précises, exactes' [Encountering Monsieur le Directeur was like experiencing the stinging whiplash — so precise, so exact — all over again].[80]

This sense of abiding pain recurs in a reference to the 'registres de cicatrices' [scrolls of scars] created by the marks of whippings on skin. Because these words figure in one of the stanzas of verse which are scattered through the text and typographically separated from the main narrative, this image of a wounded body is not rooted in any one context and could refer to the skin of the schoolchildren or to the skin of slaves.[81] As in Perec's text, the bodily marks are a kind of floating signifier which can appear in various contexts and on different bodies. Here the piece of verse directs the reader's mind simultaneously to the children's bodies in mid-century Martinique and to the bodies of slaves in previous centuries. The marks on the children's bodies then make present to the reader the physical and mental damage the children experience in school, and also the place of this suffering in a long history of painful contact between the French state and people living in Martinique.

If bodily injury is present as a mark of psychic pain and its survival in the work of Chamoiseau and Perec, but not that of Nabokov, it is perhaps because the first two authors are at a greater distance from the cause of trauma than Nabokov is. Bodily markers of trauma become necessary in their texts as a way of lending substance to psychic pain because it would not be immediately apparent otherwise. The mobility of the scars depicted in each of their texts evokes the way traces of traumas experienced by previous generations can move between different contexts, taking on a persistent presence within the lives of later generations. Such comparisons inevitably raise fraught questions of the equivalency of different experiences of pain. Noting that Perec and Chamoiseau are at a greater distance from the source of trauma in their texts than Nabokov is not to say that they face lesser challenges in confronting it; as theorists of second-generation memory have shown, distance from an event does not necessarily make it any easier to understand or portray. Nor is it to argue for any equivalency between Chamoiseau's struggle with the legacy of colonialism and Perec's early loss of both parents. As outlined previously, Perec's life is immediately and directly changed by the Nazi persecution of the Jews through the loss of his mother and other members of his extended family. Chamoiseau, on the other hand, is much more distant from the beginnings of colonial violence and slavery in Martinique. His life is influenced by its consequences in a much less direct way; they shape the conditions of his life rather than intervening to alter its course. Despite these important differences, both Perec and Chamoiseau are working to portray the after-effects of historical violence that they themselves did not witness, though their lives can only be understood in its context. Their autobiographies thus focus on the ways in which they come to apprehend events that occurred beyond the bounds of their conscious memory. In doing this, they offer models of transmission of traumatic memory, in particular inter-generational movements of the memory of violence.

The Transmission of Trauma between Generations

There has been increasing interest in the means of transmission of traumatic memory between generations in recent years, in particular in the field of Holocaust Studies, perhaps as the result of the fact that survivors are passing away, and their children, or those born shortly after the war, are reflecting on the issues involved in taking on the role of preserving the memory of the experiences of the previous generation.[82] Marianne Hirsch has been an influential theorist in this field, coining the term 'postmemory' to describe the way memories of the Second World War and of other historical traumas are transmitted in a particularly vivid way from one generation to the next. Perhaps in part because Hirsch formulates the concept of 'postmemory' in a specifically comparative perspective, applying it to traumas other than the Holocaust, it has been used in recent years in postcolonial studies.[83] However, there are other theorists who have also done stimulating work on the transmission of traumatic historical memory, and I want now to open up a dialogue between these different models of transmission, which overlap in striking ways.

In the 1970s, psychoanalysts Nicholas Abraham and Maria Torok developed the concept of 'the phantom', their term for a painful memory that is passed from generation to generation. They write: 'what haunts are not the dead, but the gaps left within us by the secrets of others'.[84] When someone dies having experienced something unspeakable, the memory of this unarticulated experience passes from parent to child, though Abraham and Torok acknowledge that the means of this transmission are difficult to understand. Its effects, however, can be discerned in the way the child seems to be inhabited by experiences they never knew, which he or she might unconsciously re-enact.[85] The model they develop is intended to be a general one, not specific to any one history, but it resonates with many of the concepts developed by theorists of the transmission of Holocaust memory specifically. These lay emphasis on the charged relationship between parent and child, and the way painful histories are transmitted silently and not through straightforward narration. Ilse Grubrich-Simitis sums up this altered relationship between parent and child when she remarks that the trauma of the Holocaust is so great that it cannot be held within one mind but spills over, making the boundaries of the self permeable, so that the interaction with children becomes part of the way parents articulate or avoid articulating their past.[86] Their relationship with their children is then deeply implicated in their own process of coming to terms with the past. Because of this, their past experiences come to have a shaping power over their children's lives.

There are strong echoes between both Abraham and Torok's concept of the phantom, theories of transmission of Holocaust memory and Louise Hardwick's concept of 'the scene of recognition' in the Francophone Caribbean *récit d'enfance*, which builds on Maeve McCusker's work on the 'primal scene' in Francophone Caribbean *récits d'enfance*, where the child first discovers the history of slavery and their parents' unwillingness to speak of it.[87] Though these bodies of theory are developed in very different contexts, each lays emphasis on the role of silence and the charged relationship with parents in the transmission of memory of violence. Hardwick uses this term to refer to the moment when the child asks his parents about some aspect of the legacy of slavery. She draws attention to the way the child's questions are often rebuffed or answered in a fragmentary fashion, so that what is passed on from parent to child is an inability to articulate the violence of the past, and hence make sense of its relationship to the present.

At the end of the essay where Abraham and Torok first outline the concept of the phantom, they write that 'it is reasonable to maintain that the "phantom effect" progressively fades during its transmission from one generation to the next and that, finally, it disappears'.[88] But, as they note with surprise, 'this is not at all the case when shared or complementary phantoms find a way of being established as social practices'. Rather than tapering off, the shaping power of unconscious memories retains its strength through the generations and can even migrate from an interpersonal context to a broader social context. I want to argue here that a comparative reading of *Une enfance créole* and *W ou le souvenir d'enfance* alongside these bodies of theory suggests that the memory of colonial violence, particularly the violence of slavery, retains its strength as a traumatic memory passing through the generations. This can be seen in three aspects signalled by each text: the child learns about the facts of the violent past indirectly, through silence rather than speech; the adult has a sense of exclusion from the historical events which shape his life, and there is a sense that the links between different modes of memory have been damaged.

Hirsch draws out the tensions embedded within the concept, 'postmemory', writing: 'Postmemory is not identical to memory: it is "post"; but, at the same time, I argue, it approximates memory in its affective force and its psychic effects.'[89] Hirsch draws on Jan and Aleida Assmann's work on the links between individual, family and collective social memory to draw attention to the fact that individual memory is always formulated in relation to inter-generational memory, which in turn shapes and is informed by collective and historical memory. Because an individual's memory always extends beyond the boundaries of his or her own life, postmemory is not an exceptional state, but rather an awareness that the links connecting these different kinds of memory have become problematic. It necessitates a conscious attempt 'to *reactivate* and *re-embody* more distant political and memorial structures by reinvesting them with resonant individual and familial forms of mediation and aesthetic expression'.[90]

This attempt to set up a dialogue, or re-forge links between, individual, family and official memory is visible in both texts. One example of it in *W ou le souvenir d'enfance* is the way Perec dwells on the historical and political events that took place on the day he was born. This speaks of an effort to integrate his individual life within family history and official history. Perec writes that he had long thought, mistakenly, that the day he was born was the day of the Nazi invasion of Poland.[91] This is not true, but the underlying idea of his own family history being threatened by a larger history from the beginning of his life still holds: 'Ce qui était sûr, c'est qu'avait déjà commencé une histoire qui, pour moi et tous les miens, allait bientôt devenir vitale, c'est-à-dire, le plus souvent, mortelle' [What is certain is that a story had already begun, a history which for me and for all my people was soon to become a matter of life and for the most part a matter of death].[92] This comment explicitly draws out the connections between a destructive international history and suffering in Perec's family and his own life, and a footnote to it continues this process in a more subtle way.

The footnote gives the newspaper headlines on the day he was born, and so acts as a corrective to the mistaken assumption referred to in the main body of the text. The headlines record a range of events relevant to Perec's family history, including Germany's violation of the Locarno pact and Nazi attacks in Austria.[93] Perec's writing brings his own life into dialogue with an event which is not quite as obviously related to his own history, however. He notes that one of the news stories from those two days was the attempted assassination of the Prime Minister of Yugoslavia. Perec's text gives the spelling as 'Stojadinovitch' but the newspaper has the fourth letter as a 'y' rather than a 'j'. By mis-transcribing the newspaper headline, Perec introduces an element of individual agency into his interaction with this record of an apparently impersonal history. His misspelling also recalls his mistakes with his mother's name and names in his extended family.[94] This linguistic incompetence with names of Eastern European origin is in part a result of the breakdown in linguistic continuities between Perec's generation and that of his parents, a breakdown triggered or exacerbated by the turbulent international histories which the newspaper headlines describe. This passage of text can thus be seen as an example of the process Hirsch describes of reactivation of links between personal, family and collective histories.

This process is also at work in *Une enfance créole*. As explored previously, the body plays a key role in making present the intangible suffering the children experience in school. It is also possible to read images of the wounded body layered with other kinds of record of the past as intended to activate connections between the life of the individual and the 'more distant political and memorial structures' Hirsch refers to. A more extended look at the short piece of verse where the image of the 'registres de cicatrices' [registers of scars] appears illustrates this point:

> Les Maîtres armés
> gravaient État civil en
> stigmates sur les jambes
> mémoire-peau
> registres de cicatrices
> ho douleurs fossiles
> les tibias osent des songes.[95]
>
> [The Teachers, armed,
> engraved the Body Politic
> in stigmata on little legs
> thin-skinned memory
> registers of scars
> ho fossil pains and woes
> tibias dare to dream]

Here the co-presence of slave registers and scars has the effect of setting up a relationship between a living individual body, and the somewhat inert historical document of the slave register. The reference to 'stigmates' reinforces this, and introduces the idea of a wound which moves from body to body, indicates belonging, and refuses to heal. These facets of stigmata resonate with Chamoiseau's conception of the legacy of slavery and colonial violence. Maeve McCusker reads the 'douleurs fossiles' as a reference to 'the painful but deeply embedded or petrified memory' of slavery. 'Douleurs fossiles' could also evoke the pre-colonial indigenous inhabitants of Martinique, almost all of whom were killed early in the colonial era. Fossils are strongly associated with these people in Chamoiseau's work, because remnants in the archaeological record are one of the few ways of reconstructing their history.[96] Here the phrase 'douleurs fossiles' transforms these fossils from an object of geological history to an inner ache within the body. The presence of 'os' within 'fossiles' identified by McCusker, replicates on the formal level the discovery of a bodily structure within what appears to be mineral or stone.[97] As in the 'registres de cicatrices' it introduces the presence of the living body into what is otherwise a mute remnant of the past. This poem then re-embodies elements of the histories of both Africans and indigenous Caribbeans.

The reason these processes of re-embodiment and reactivation of impersonal traces of the past are necessary is because the usual processes of mediation between individual history and family or collective history have come under threat. The situations which create a need for postmemory, the Holocaust and colonialism in the case of the two authors under discussion, disrupt the usual links between parent and child, individual life and historical archive, through death, migration, intergenerational shifts of language and the destruction or falsification of the historical record.[98] In Perec's text, the deaths of his parents in the war break the immediate link between his own life and broader family life. Hirsch's point about the way the historical archive often does not accurately record the details of violent histories is relevant in Perec's case, as his mother's date and place of death are incorrectly recorded.[99] Historical archives are also a problematic mode of access to knowledge about slavery and the colonial past for Chamoiseau, as they were largely produced by the same people and institutions responsible for the violence. More immediately, the family and the education system, two places where memory of the past might be handed on, are hampered in this task by a reluctance to speak of the painful aspects of Martinique's history.

This reluctance to speak of the past and its enduring influence on the present is a key characteristic of the transmission of traumatic memory. Ilse Grubrich-Simitis speaks of a 'pact of silence' maintained by the first generation on their experiences in the camps.[100] Nicholas T. Rand, summing up Nicolas Abraham and Maria Torok's concept of second-generation traumatic memory, writes: 'The phantom represents the interpersonal and transgenerational consequences of silence.'[101] Henri Raczymow, born to Eastern European parents in Paris in 1945, writes that his family's past 'was handed down to me precisely as something *not* handed down to me'.[102] Nadine Fresco argues that rather than learning about the Holocaust from what their parents tell them, members of the second generation struggle to make sense of their parents' silence about large swathes of their past. As a result, their knowledge of their family's past is belated; they can only put together its pieces once they have reached an age where they can seek out information without asking their parents. This knowledge then retroactively transforms their understanding of the family past, without, however, coming as a complete surprise, as the parents' very silence around the past intimates pain.[103] Louise Hardwick brings out a similar dynamic in the Francophone Caribbean *récit d'enfance*, where the child asks a question about some aspect of the legacy of slavery only to be met with an embarrassed silence which heightens their curiosity. They will only understand the reasons for this reluctance to speak of the past by piecing together various puzzling and painful experiences they have of the contemporary traces of the colonial past. Hardwick argues that this process leaves 'fundamental psychic traces'.[104]

This sense of coming to knowledge of a painful history through silences rather than speech is present in both texts. The mute tension around the events of the war is evoked in Perec's description of the anxiety of a woman who was looking after him when the German soldiers who were staying nearby took to playing with the child regularly: 'Elle avait très peur, disait-elle à ma tante qui me le raconta par la suite, que je ne dise quelque chose qu'il ne fallait pas que je dise et elle ne savait comment me signifier ce secret que je devais garder' [She was very afraid, she said to my aunt who subsequently told me, that I might say something I shouldn't say and she didn't know how to get me to understand the secret I had to keep].[105] Here, it is possible to imagine the child picking up on the woman's fear through non-verbal cues and associating it with the presence of the soldiers without being able to articulate why. This sense of the child-self knowing something is wrong but not being sure what is present elsewhere in the text. When writing about his imagined memory of breaking his collar-bone, Perec tells the reader: 'ces thérapeutiques imaginaires, moins contraignantes que tutoriales, ces *points de suspension*, désignaient des douleurs nommables et venaient à point justifier des cajoleries dont les raisons réelles n'étaient données qu'à voix basse' [these fantasy treatments, more like supports than like straitjackets, these marks of suspension indicated pains that could be named; they cropped up on cue to justify an indulgence the actual cause of which was mentioned only in an undertone].[106] The imagined injury is thus figured as a way for the child to make sense of his shadowy knowledge that something about his life has been damaged. The unexplained cossetting and hushed voices noticed by the child act as signs that something is wrong, though it is unspoken.

Silence around the violence of the past has a much less central place in *Une enfance créole*, but it is still present. Though the history of slavery and colonial power structures shape the child's world, there is no scene where his discovery of this history is narrated. Instead, it is present as 'an oblique undertow'.[107] Its unspoken presence chimes with Chamoiseau's comment in a theoretical essay on memory that '[r]ien de ce que j'en sais ne m'a été transmis de manière directe ou volontaire' [nothing of what I know about it was transmitted to me directly or voluntarily].[108] Louise Hardwick notes Chamoiseau's comment in an interview that Creole folk-tales transmit to the child the knowledge that the world is a dangerous place, where the vulnerable must have their wits about them, and even then have no guarantee of safety.[109] In *Une enfance créole*, the child receives knowledge of the island's violent past through the folk-tales of Jeanne-Yvette, a story-teller.[110] Knowledge about Martinique's colonial history and its continuing ramifications in the present is thus passed on indirectly, through silences and fictional stories.

Both authors inherit a memory of violence through silences rather than speech, and both engage in an active enterprise of reconnecting individual, family and official history. The third point of convergence is a somewhat painful knowledge of their own belated position in relation to the events whose memory they inherit. Theorists of second-generation memory of the Holocaust draw attention to this counter-intuitive facet of transmitted memory. Members of subsequent generations occupy an uncertain position in relation to the histories of their parents and ancestors, because they do not fit into the categories of victim or survivor and lack a language for articulating their relationship to the historical events which shape their lives. Fresco quotes one member of the second generation as speaking of 'an almost incommunicable feeling, made up for the most part of jealousy' about those who lived through the genocide.[111] Raczymow speaks of 'the feeling all of us have, deep down, of having missed a train'.[112] There are echoes of this sense of exclusion from the events of history in the adult Gaspard Winckler's comment, 'je fus témoin et non acteur' [I was a witness and not an actor], an idea which recurs when Perec realizes it was his classmate, not he, who broke his collar-bone, and writes, 'L'événement eut lieu, un peu plus tard ou un peu plus tôt, et je n'en fus pas la victime héroïque mais un simple témoin' [The thing happened, a little later or a little earlier, and I was not its heroic victim but just a witness].[113]

There is also an echo of the paradoxical jealousy described by Fresco's interviewee in Chamoiseau's distinction between 'la domination insidieuse' and 'la domination brutale'.[114] These are his terms for distinguishing between the violent colonial oppression of the past and the more subtle psychological oppression of the contemporary period. When he sketches the differences between these two modes, his comment that violent oppression is easier to perceive and to oppose is almost wistful about the clearer role occupied by anti-colonial activists of a previous era. This sense of occupying a belated position in relation to colonial violence could also account in part for the sense of the author as a slightly pathetic figure, present in his brother's remarks about his reluctance to wean from his mother and in the ineffectual alter egos to whom the author is implicitly compared, such as the 'petit pompier' [little fireman] in the preface.[115] The opposition Chamoiseau draws between those who experienced and opposed colonial violence and later figures who merely record its lingering effects echoes Perec's contrast between actors in, and witnesses of, histories of violence.

Reading these two texts comparatively through theories of transmission of traumatic memory thus suggests that the relatively well-developed work on transmission of Holocaust memory can be fruitfully cross-pollinated with scholarship on the inherited memory of slavery and colonial violence. Such a comparative approach brings out the enduring impact on a child of coming into contact with a history of violence through the silences and oblique approaches of adults who have not yet come to terms with it. Hirsch's concept that subsequent generations must re-weave the links between bodily, textual, family and national histories helps make sense of otherwise obscure practices, such as Perec's transcription of a whole set of headlines from the day he was born and Chamoiseau's interweaving of references to slavery and recollections of his experience of school in the 1950s. This comparative reading then bears out each author's suggestion that there are resonances between the history of the Holocaust and colonial histories. It illustrates Abraham and Torok's disconcerted observation that memories of trauma do not necessarily fade with the passing of generations, but can instead migrate from the interpersonal, familial context to the social realm. This move is notable in the texts in the way that Perec's narration of the hampered transmission of knowledge of the camps takes place in domestic settings with members of his extended family or people who have taken the place of his parents, whereas in Chamoiseau's text, the schoolroom, where the children form a collective mass, and the teacher is a condensed portrait of many different teachers, is the arena where the memory of slavery and colonial violence makes itself felt. Although each author's portrayal of their reception of the memory of violence differs in this respect and in others, looking at them together suggests the value of further comparisons of autobiographical writing which confronts the legacies of the Holocaust, colonialism, and other histories of violence.

Reading these texts for marks of trauma shows the power of trauma as a conceptual category in bringing out overlaps between texts recounting a broad range of modes of contact with the violent histories of modernity. Reading for textual tropes of trauma, such as dissociation, silence about painful subject-matter, and fragmentary, non-linear narrative structures reveals points of convergence in these authors' approach to the narration of personal and collective pain, though the source of trauma moves from direct experience of violence (Nabokov) to family bereavement through war and genocide (Perec) to the everyday events in a society whose origins lie in colonial violence (Chamoiseau). Such movements of the source of trauma from the extreme to the everyday have been at the source of some anxiety in recent debate on the subject. This reading suggests that where sources of trauma seem to be so everyday as to threaten the use of the term in extreme situations, it is worth taking a diachronic approach to the experience in question. Crossovers between the bodies of theory on the transmission of Holocaust memory and memory of slavery suggest that movement of traumatic experience across generations is possible, and that as long as the painful history remains unprocessed it will embed itself within social structures, continuing to damage individuals' development.

Theories of trauma and its transmission thus stand to benefit from comparative approaches to texts recounting a range of different histories, as well as providing an illuminating way into the issues of history and memory opened up by these texts. Yet the portrayal of the transmission of memory of painful historical events in Perec and Chamoiseau's texts also suggests a certain tension between their projects and traumatic modes of relationship to the past. The depiction of the previous generation's silences around violent histories implies a degree of criticism of the ways in which these silences create or perpetuate problematic relationships to the past, while the active processes of re-embodiment of connections between personal, family and historical traces of the past speaks of a will to move beyond such problematic relationships, even where such an enterprise can never be entirely successful. Reading *W ou le souvenir d'enfance* and *Une enfance créole* as expressions of a traumatic relationship to the past thus involves reading against the grain of the text to a certain extent. As noted earlier, this is also the case with *Speak, Memory*.

The next chapter will consider in greater detail the aspects of each text which register a tension with traumatic modes of relationship to the past, and will argue that the expression of trauma in these texts is interwoven with attempts to achieve a conscious, active relationship with the past.

Notes to Chapter 3

1. Lawrence D. Kritzman, 'Remembrance of Things Past: Trauma and Mourning in Perec's *W ou le souvenir d'enfance*', *Journal of European Studies*, 35 (2005), 187–200; Eleanor Kaufman, 'Falling from the Sky: Trauma in Perec's *W* and Caruth's *Unclaimed Experience*', *Diacritics*, 28 (1998), 44–53 (pp. 44–49); Barbara Straumann, *Figurations of Exile in Hitchcock and Nabokov* (Edinburgh: Edinburgh University Press, 2008), pp. 33–86.
2. *Unclaimed Experience: Trauma, Narrative and History* (Baltimore, MD: Johns Hopkins University Press, 1996), p. 17.
3. Whitehead, p. 6.
4. Whitehead, p. 162.
5. *Testimony: Crises of Witnessing in Literature, Psychoanalysis and History* (London: Routledge, 1992), p. 57.
6. Luckhurst, p. 88.
7. Luckhurst, p. 81.
8. Brian Boyd, *Vladimir Nabokov: The Russian Years* (Princeton: Princeton University Press, 1993), p. 8.
9. *SM*, 33.
10. *The Magician's Doubts: Nabokov and the Risks of Fiction* (London: Chatto & Windus, 1994), p. 91.
11. *SM*, 146–47.
12. *SM*, 147.
13. Boyd, pp. 7–8; *SM*, 19.
14. *SM*, 19.
15. Straumann, p. 59.
16. *SM*, 200.
17. *SM*, 201.
18. Will Norman, *Nabokov, History and the Texture of Time* (New York: Routledge, 2012), p. 67.
19. *SM*, 54.
20. Wood, p. 97.
21. *SM*, 52.
22. *SM*, 49.
23. *SM*, 17.
24. *SM*, 107–08.
25. *SM*, 58.
26. *SM*, 131.
27. *SM*, 131.
28. *SM*, 16.
29. *DB*, 18. The last phrase literally means 'as if it has taken blood into its mouth', and plays on a saying, 'to take water into one's mouth', which means to swear an oath of silence.
30. Washington, D.C., Library of Congress, Manuscript Division, Vladimir Vladimirovich Nabokov Papers, Box 9; *SM*, 33.
31. *SM*, 200.
32. Wood, p. 101.
33. Wood, p. 84; Straumann, p. 67.
34. *SM*, 10.
35. Kaufman, p. 46
36. Kaufman, p. 46.
37. *W*, 59; Kaufman, p. 45; p. 48.

38. Kritzman, p. 187; p. 188.
39. Kritzman, p. 189.
40. *W*, 84–85.
41. *W*, 19; *W*, 29; *W*, 65; *W*, 83.
42. Elizabeth Bruss, *Autobiographical Acts: The Changing Situation of a Literary Genre* (Baltimore, MD: Johns Hopkins University Press, 1976), p. 149.
43. Philippe Lejeune, *La Mémoire et l'oblique: Georges Perec autobiographe* (Paris: P.O.L., 1991), p. 43.
44. *W*, 59.
45. See Lejeune, p. 1, Paul Schwartz, *Georges Perec: Traces of his Passage* (Birmingham, AL: Summa, 1988), p. 55 and Montfrans, p. 151. Each of these authors quotes the finale of this chapter with very little commentary, in contrast to their practice elsewhere in these works.
46. *Scroll of Agony: The Warsaw Diary of Chaim A. Kaplan*, trans. and ed. by Abraham Isaac Katsh (London: Hamilton, 1966).
47. *Treblinka*, trans. by Helen Weaver (London: Weidenfeld & Nicholson, 1967).
48. *Language and Silence: Essays 1958–1966* (London: Faber, 1967), p. 193.
49. Steiner, *Language and Silence*, p. 193.
50. *Writing History, Writing Trauma* (Baltimore, MD: Johns Hopkins University Press, 2001), p. 77.
51. LaCapra, pp. 76–85.
52. LaCapra, p. 176.
53. *Chemin*, 69.
54. *A bout*, 80, italics in original.
55. *A bout*, 116–17, italics in original.
56. *A bout*, 260.
57. *A bout*, 273–77.
58. *A bout*, 21; 31.
59. *Chemin*, 187.
60. *Chemin*, 52.
61. *Chemin*, 53–54.
62. *Chemin*, 59.
63. *Patrick Chamoiseau: espaces d'une écriture antillaise* (Amsterdam: Rodopi, 2006), pp. 69–72.
64. *Chemin*, 69.
65. *Chemin*, 91.
66. *Chemin*, 201.
67. 'Progress and Controversy in the Study of Posttraumatic Stress Disorder', *Annual Review of Psychology*, 54 (2003), 229–52 (p. 231).
68. 'Genealogy of a Category Mistake: A Critical Intellectual History of the Cultural Trauma Metaphor', *Rethinking History*, 8 (2004), 193–221 (p. 206).
69. *Antan*, 21.
70. *SM*, 47.
71. Straumann, pp. 55–58.
72. *W*, 141.
73. 'The Work of Mourning', *Yale French Studies*, 105 (2004), 56–71 (p. 64).
74. *W*, 142–43.
75. Mireille Ribière, 'L'Autobiographie comme fiction', *Cahiers Georges Perec*, 2 (1986–1987), 25–37 (p. 29); Bernard Magné, *Georges Perec* (Paris: Nathan, 1999), p. 92.
76. *W*, 71–73.
77. *Chemin*, 95–96.
78. *Chemin*, 96.
79. *Chemin*, 103.
80. *Chemin*, 105.
81. McCusker, *Recovering Memory*, p. 68.
82. Marianne Hirsch, *The Generation of Postmemory: Writing and Visual Culture after the Holocaust* (New York: Columbia University Press, 2012), p. 18.
83. For example in McCusker, *Recovering Memory*, pp. 4–6; Claudia Marquis, 'Crossing Over: Postmemory and Postcolonial Imaginary in Andrea Levy's *Small Island* and *The Fruit of the Lemon*',

EnterText, 9 (2012), 31–52; Fiona Barclay, *Writing Postcolonial France: Haunting, Literature, and the Maghreb* (Lanham: Lexington Books, 2011), pp. 45–46.
84. *The Shell and the Kernel: Renewals of Psychoanalysis*, trans. and ed. by Nicholas T. Rand (Chicago: University of Chicago Press, 1994), p. 171.
85. Abraham and Torok, p. 175.
86. Ilse Grubrich-Simitis, 'From Concretism to Metaphor: Thoughts on some Theoretical and Technical Aspects of Work with the Children of Holocaust Survivors', *Psychoanalytic Study of the Child*, 39 (1984), 301–29 (p. 308).
87. *Childhood, Autobiography and the Francophone Caribbean*, pp. 16–22; McCusker, ' "Troubler l'ordre de l'oubli": Memory and Forgetting in French Caribbean Autobiography of the 1990s', pp. 441–43.
88. Abraham and Torok, p. 176.
89. Hirsch, p. 31.
90. Hirsch, p. 33, italics in text.
91. *W*, 31.
92. *W*, 32.
93. *W*, 32–34.
94. *W*, 45; *W*, 57–58.
95. *Chemin*, 98.
96. *Écrire en pays dominé*, p. 118.
97. *Recovering Memory*, pp. 68–69.
98. Hirsch, p. 33.
99. *W*, 57–58.
100. Grubrich-Simitis, p. 308.
101. *The Shell and the Kernel*, p. 168.
102. 'Memory Shot Through with Holes', trans. by Alan Astro, *Yale French Studies*, 85 (1994), 98–105 (p. 103).
103. Nadine Fresco, 'Remembering the Unknown', *International Review of Psychoanalysis*, 11 (1984), 417–27.
104. *Childhood, Autobiography and the Francophone Caribbean*, p. 20.
105. *W*, 73.
106. *W*, 110, italics in original.
107. McCusker, *Recovering Memory*, p. 66.
108. *De la mémoire obscure à la mémoire consciente*, p. 7.
109. *Childhood, Autobiography and the Francophone Caribbean*, p. 5, quoting Patrick Chamoiseau, *Au Temps de l'Antan* (Paris: Hatier, 1988), p. 10.
110. *Antan*, 126–27.
111. Fresco, p. 421.
112. Raczymow, p. 105.
113. *W*, 10; 109.
114. *Écrire en pays dominé*, pp. 17–18.
115. *Antan*, 24; 9–10.

CHAPTER 4

Literary Thinking as Conscious Memory

We saw in the previous chapter that trauma theory provides a powerful interpretive framework for making sense of the silences in these texts, and in particular of their non-linear temporal constructions and images of the wounded body. While the textual devices analysed in the last chapter do seem to fit the patterns of a traumatic response, the idea of the author as an individual who is not fully conscious of his past sits slightly uneasily with the way each text places value on a conscious, active approach to memory. This privileging of conscious memory is present in explicit statements in each text, in metatextual comments which draw the reader's attention to nuances of memory's workings, in the author's wider work and in the way each situates himself in relation to previous writers on memory, most notably Marcel Proust. This chapter seeks to bring out the concept of conscious memory that each author puts forward and to bring it into dialogue with the value each places on establishing indirect, ludic textual pathways to engage the reader. It explores ways of making sense of non-linear temporal structures and indirect approaches to painful subject matter in the light of each author's avowed commitment to conscious memory. It finds that these authors connect conscious memory with specifically literary modes of engagement with the real, which they present and explore through the language of displacement. Mobility then takes on an ambivalent value in each author's thought, as it is connected both with painful historical experiences of travel as subjection and with the freedom that comes from making new mental moves. Reading these authors together points towards the potential held by the concept of mobility to create uneasy fusions of freedom and constraint. Echoes between the genealogy of each author's conception of literary thinking offer one example of the relationships between authors that become visible through moving across and beyond the national frame.

Conscious Memory

Each author places emphasis on the value of conscious approaches to memory of the past in the autobiography and in his wider fictional and theoretical or critical work. The question of the proper mode of relation to the past recurs insistently across Chamoiseau's oeuvre. As we have seen, his autobiographical texts can certainly be read as expressive of the shaping presence of historical trauma in the life of the child-self. Yet, Chamoiseau's critical writing, along with elements of the texts themselves and his wider work, encourages the reader to go beyond this reading. In particular, an essay entitled *De la mémoire obscure à la mémoire consciente* suggests that the relationship he sets up between traumatic and conscious memory is slightly different from that found in contemporary trauma theory. The essay is published as a 'postface' to two novels, *L'Esclave vieil homme et le molosse* and *Un dimanche au cachot*, originally published separately but repackaged in this instance as two volumes which together make up a set Chamoiseau names *Le Déshumain grandiose*.[1] The essay takes as its subject the relationship of contemporary Martinicans to slavery. Chamoiseau's 'mémoire obscure' has strong echoes with concepts of traumatic memory explored in the previous chapter; it is a form of non-memory, an 'exacerbation silencieuse de la blessure' [silent exacerbation of the wound], a 'crispation du psychisme' [contraction of the psyche].[2] The essay, as its title suggests, argues for a conscious and deliberate process of recognising and moving beyond this form of memory. This process does not constitute a rejection of traumatic memory, but rather an imaginative engagement with it: '[La mémoire consciente] imagine cette mémoire obscure dans ses mystères et l'envisage en ses croyances, mais la soumet toujours aux nécessités de la clairvoyance et de l'élucidation qui ne craignent pas l'inconnaissable' [[Conscious memory] imagines this dark memory in its mysteries and contemplates it in its beliefs, but always subjects it to the necessities of a clear-sightedness and clarification which does not fear the unknown].[3] There is a kind of respect here for the otherness of traumatic memory, but this respect is curiously accompanied by an insistence that its otherness be brought into dialogue with another form of relationship to the past, whose association with light and knowledge suggests it is quite distinct from trauma. The verb 'soumettre' is unlikely to be used lightly by Chamoiseau, who is usually at pains to dismantle or destabilize hierarchical relationships. This sentence firmly situates traumatic memory as a bridge toward the more valuable conscious memory. The emphasis on traumatic memory as a tool, and the specific use of the vocabulary of mastery in 'soumettre', is at odds with Caruth's definition of trauma as an event which takes away the individual's ability to master their own experience. It also sounds a dissonant note with the emphasis placed on the importance of not resolving the disruptive presence of trauma in the mind and the text. Though some argue that to undo trauma's status as an unknowable event would be an unethical smoothing over of the challenge it poses to understanding, Chamoiseau seems here to argue the opposite, by calling for the transformation of inarticulate historical pain into knowledge and understanding in the service of social renewal.

The essay suggests that the imagination is crucial in this enterprise, an argument which is supported by its accompaniment by two novels. Chamoiseau uses these works as examples of attempts to move from traumatic to conscious memory. Originally published ten years apart, each is an extended meditation on one aspect of slavery. *L'Esclave vieil homme et le molosse* deals with the capture of a runaway slave by a dog, and *Un dimanche au cachot* interweaves the experiences of a contemporary young girl with the practice of imprisoning slaves in dungeons.

Chamoiseau writes that both of these novels constitute attempts to 'transformer, au plus profond de moi, le crime en expérience' [transform, in the deepest part of me, crime into experience].[4] There are hints of this attempt to transform sites of inarticulate pain into knowledge at the opening of his autobiography too, where the speaker petitions memory: 'Mémoire, passons un pacte le temps d'un crayonné, baisse palissades et apaise les farouches' [Memory, let's make a pact long enough for a sketch, lower your palisades and pacify the savages].[5] These lines suggest an attempt to enter into those parts of the collective past which previous generations fenced off from speech and thought as part of an effort of self-preservation.[6] They also evoke a reversal of the move away from the plantation undertaken by the escaping slave in *L'Esclave vieil homme et le molosse*. If the old man needs to cross those forbidding barriers to escape from the oppression of slavery, contemporary Martinicans need to undertake a reverse journey, crossing the barriers from the outside in, re-entering the experience of slavery in order to gain a measure of understanding of it. Chamoiseau's theoretical reflections on traumatic memory as a stepping-stone to a more conscious, articulate relationship to the past, his extended imaginative recreations of life under slavery, and these opening images of crossing the forbidding mental boundaries all encourage the reader of his autobiographical text to be attentive to the silences which suggest a traumatic relationship to the past, but also to read for the ways in which the text transforms this traumatic legacy into something knowable.

In a comparable way, Perec's work situates the concentrationary universe as knowable. Like Chamoiseau, he uses imagery of physical boundaries to both raise and contest the idea that the world of the camps is definitively sealed off from knowledge and understanding. In his review of *L'Espèce humaine*, Robert Antelme's memoir of his time in a Nazi camp, Perec praises the way Antelme's writing allows the reality of the camps to emerge slowly, and he expresses disapproval of the way other writers who describe the camps give the impression that it is 'un monde total, refermé sur lui-même, et que l'on restitue en bloc' [a whole world, shut in on itself, and which can be recreated in its entirety].[7] He criticizes the idea that the world of the camps is in some sense fundamentally different to the everyday world: 'Il n'y a pas deux mondes,' he writes, 'mais seulement des hommes qui tentent désespérément de nier les autres' [There aren't two worlds, but only people who seek desperately to deny others].[8] Though silence is deployed to indicate the difficulty of articulating his grief over his mother, these comments on Antelme's article suggest that while his personal grief might be traumatic, he does not believe that the historical circumstances which caused it lie beyond knowledge or comprehension. Rather, he emphasizes the importance of seeing the concentrationary universe as available to understanding and even familiar in some of its aspects, and of striving to transmit such a view when writing on the subject.

This effort of overcoming what appears to lie beyond the mind's capacity for memory is present elsewhere in Perec's work. His concept of memory, like that of Nabokov and Chamoiseau, involves a measure of self-criticism and questioning of his own ready-made images of the past. This is expressed in all three texts in metatextual comments on the process of recording the past in writing, but occurs in its most striking form in Perec's text, where he takes a narration of his parents' lives written fifteen years previously and systematically points out its flaws and inaccuracies in a set of footnotes.[9] The notes are longer than the text itself, indicating the value the author places on the process of criticizing the blank spots and omissions in one's own memory. The effort of filling in the blank spaces in one's memory of the past perhaps helps make sense of some of Perec's more puzzling excursions into memory, such as the list of apparently banal memories in *Je me souviens*.[10] Here, although the memories recovered do not always seem of any immediate value, the process of retrieving them nonetheless demonstrates the possibility of extending the boundaries of memory through conscious effort. Though, in some ways, what is recovered through conscious memory only points up the foundational absence of clear memories of his parents, this emphasis on memory as a conscious effort recurs across Perec's literary criticism and wider work, as well as in the autobiography itself.

The focus on details of the past, an emphasis on memory as effort and an unwillingness to situate historical violence as beyond the bounds of understanding are also found in Nabokov's work. The development of the conscious mind's ability to perceive the past and present accurately is a major theme across Nabokov's work, and it goes hand in hand with a turning away from the activity of the unconscious mind. Nabokov's privileging of conscious memory emerges in three ways across the different iterations of *Speak, Memory*: in the important role he gives to the accurate record of details of the past, in his satire of the propensity to recreate new versions of the past according to one's current mood and interests, and in the models of memory he inherits from his parents. The importance of accuracy with regard to the details of the past can be seen in the triumph associated with minor corrections and additions between the various versions of the text, from the change of 'spectacles' to 'cigarette case' to the matching of a certain shade with 'Rose Quartz' in a dictionary of colours.[11] Evidence of the preparatory notes for the writing of the first full-length version of the autobiography also testify to the importance of detail. Here Nabokov drafts a letter to a scientific colleague, inquiring about the species and genus of monkeys used by organ grinders at the turn of the century in Russia, for an episode described in a sentence or two in his text.[12] The attention given to these minor changes suggests the value attached to recording accurately the details of the past, and of testing one's own memory against external sources.

In the episodes where Nabokov describes his parents, it becomes clear that this detail-oriented approach to memory is inherited from them.[13] The autobiography thus presents the author's parents as models of good memory, but it also mocks those who fail to take this attentive approach to recalling the past. Mademoiselle O is the main focus for this satire in the autobiography. When Nabokov goes to visit her as an adult, she has forgotten how miserable her time in Russia was, and happily narrates moments of tenderness between herself and her charges which Nabokov suggests never happened.[14] What is mocked here is a slightly solipsistic approach to the past, where the mind generates images which reflect the self and its current concerns rather than attending to the past as it was. The author himself comes in for similar mockery in the final revision of Chapter Three, which opens with an image of an unseeing relationship to the past: 'An inexperienced heraldist resembles a medieval traveler who brings back from the East the faunal fantasies influenced by the domestic bestiary he possessed all along rather than by the results of direct zoological exploration.'[15] Nabokov is referring to his inaccurate memory of the family crest, which he recalled as two bears holding up a chessboard, but which he found was quite different when he managed to consult an external source. There is a suspicion here of the mind's power to shape one's image of the past, and value is placed on attention to the mind's ruses and blind spots.

We can see that this questioning approach to the activity of one's own mind is important to Nabokov through the way he excoriates models of memory which argue that the mind cannot be fully understood. His disapproval of the idea of unconscious memories becomes clearest in his notorious dislike of Freud's work. Toward the end of *Speak, Memory* he remarks acerbically, 'incidentally, what a great mistake on the part of dictators to ignore psychoanalysis — a whole generation might be so easily corrupted that way!'[16] Here he draws attention to the ethical problems associated with the idea that one can carry out actions while remaining unaware of, or helpless to change, one's reasons for doing so. Will Norman points out the connection made between psychoanalysis and cruelty to the vulnerable in *Bend Sinister*, where the murder of the protagonist's child takes place as part of psychoanalytic research, and in *Lolita*, where Humbert argues his treatment of Dolores is determined by the untimely ending of a youthful love affair.[17] Nabokov's satire of the implications of unconscious memory draws attention to its potential influence on ethics and even politics, as well as on individual attempts to recover the past. Freud is a very conspicuous target for his critique of the idea of unconscious memory, but this critique is also present in his approach to Marcel Proust, whose ideas are taken up and nuanced in each of the texts under discussion.

Rewritings of Proust

The value placed on conscious memory in each author's metatextual comments and wider work is echoed by rewritings of famous Proustian scenes. Proust is present in each autobiography as a stimulating, and at times contested, presence. In each case, the author takes aspects of Proust's work and re-shapes them so that voluntary, conscious memory takes ascendance over involuntary memory. Nabokov's autobiography draws on Proust's novel through attention to the role of the senses in recollection of the past, evocations of synaesthesia and magic lantern pictures, the use of Bergsonian vocabulary of immersion in pure time, and an episode where a book from childhood brings back memories of the past, to name a few salient points of convergence between the two authors. However, while engaging closely with Proust's work, Nabokov departs from the model of involuntary memory. Will Norman points out that the end of Chapter Two, where Nabokov dismisses the visions of the dead which come to him in dreams, celebrating instead those achieved through high levels of concentration, is a movement away from Proust's valuing of involuntary memory.[18] More generally, we can see the horror of sleep expressed in *Speak, Memory* as symptomatic of the text's turning away from unconscious and involuntary modes of being.

Nabokov's narration of falling asleep as a child can be read as a rewriting of the famous opening of Proust's novel. Like the invalid referred to at the beginning of the novel, he enjoys the time when he can still see a line of light beneath the door of his bedroom while Mademoiselle O is awake and is dismayed when she puts out her light and it disappears.[19] Whereas Proust's invalid is unsure about the provenance of the light, thinking perhaps it is morning, Nabokov's child-self knows every detail of Mademoiselle O's night-time routine. This contrast between Proust's invalid's sleepy confusion about when his servants will come to help him and the child's detailed knowledge of his governess's every movement concentrates in miniature the difference between Proust's attentiveness to states of semi-awareness and Nabokov's devotion to detailed, conscious awareness.

The opening of *Combray* and the image of a sleeping man is also used by Perec to mark his distance from Proust, though in a novel rather than the autobiography. He writes a novel entitled *Un homme qui dort* in a nod to the famous lines near the beginning of the *Recherche*:

> Un homme qui dort tient en cercle autour de lui le fil des heures, l'ordre des années et des mondes. Il les consulte d'instinct en s'éveillant et y lit en une seconde le point de la terre qu'il occupe, le temps qui s'est écoulé jusqu'à son réveil; mais leurs rangs peuvent se mêler, se rompre.[20]
>
> [A sleeping man holds spooled around him the thread of hours, the order of years and worlds. He consults them instinctively as he wakes up and reads there in a moment the point of the earth he occupies, the time that has passed until his awaking; but their places can get mixed up, break.]

The novel, which describes the lost wanderings of a young man in Paris, can be seen as an exploration of the unspooling of 'le fil des heures, l'ordre des années et des mondes'. This ambivalent engagement with the opening of *Du côté de chez Swann* continues in a piece of writing Perec envisaged but never completed, where he would record all the different bedrooms he had slept in 'une sorte d'autobiographie vespérale' [a kind of evening autobiography]. There are obvious echoes between this idea and the beginning of Proust's work, and Perec states that it is intended to be a development of the sixth and seventh paragraphs of the novel, but the fragments of writing Perec undertook for the project, like Nabokov's narration of falling asleep, abandon Proust's exploration of states of half-awareness in favour of detailed, dispassionate knowledge, with the use of technical vocabulary, such as 'recenser' [to take an inventory], to describe the project, and musings about whether to list the bedrooms according to location or theme.[21]

Because of this evidence of engagement with Proust elsewhere in Perec's work, it is possible to read the two mentions of Venice in *W ou le souvenir d'enfance* as further echoes of the *Recherche*. These are placed in prominent positions in the text, one in the first fictional chapter and the other in the first autobiographical chapter. In both instances, Venice is associated with an element of the past returning or seeming to return. In the fictional chapter, the narrator, who has been searching for evidence that his experience in W really happened, is sitting in a restaurant in Venice when he thinks he sees a man he recognizes: 'Je me suis précipité sur lui, mais déjà balbutiant deux ou trois mots d'excuse. Il ne pouvait pas y avoir de survivant' [As

I rushed towards him, I was already stammering my apologies. There could be no survivor].[22] Venice is then the scene of an abortive moment of memory, where the narrator's sudden hope that the destruction he witnessed in W has not been total is dashed. The second mention of Venice occurs in the next chapter, where the author writes that he had invented the W story at the age of thirteen and had forgotten about it until he remembered it suddenly in Venice one evening.[23] This kind of memory is quite distinct from Proustian memory. It is a verbal recollection and is fragmentary; the author remembers the title of the story but very little else, in contrast to the sense of wholeness and sensory engagement associated with Proustian involuntary memory. The previous narration of the fictional narrator's mistaken identification of the man in the restaurant also resonates with this episode, preparing the reader to see it as another moment of abortive memory. These two references to Venice mark the autobiography's distance from a model of memory which allows re-immersion in the past.

Chamoiseau also engages closely with imagery and concepts from Proust's exploration with memory while working to nuance them for his particular context, though Proust's presence in his text is more attenuated than it is in *Speak, Memory* or *W ou le souvenir d'enfance*. Wendy Knepper identifies the child's delight in tasting the sweets his mother makes as a rewriting of the madeleine episode, drawing attention to the way the child's sensory delight also functions as an initiation into language, as the child eats the words his sister writes in icing on the cakes.[24] Language, associated with voluntary memory in Proust's work, is here fused with the sensory pleasure of the sweet taste. Knepper points out that recalling this taste brings back a different period to the author's mind in a way that connects his own memory with that of his generation, so that sensory memories become a way into a collective as well as an individual past.[25]

We might also see the imagery of magma hardening that follows shortly after this episode as an echo of Proust's geological imagery. As explored in the first chapter, Chamoiseau uses geological imagery of magma, crusts and caves to suggest the landscape of memory and the self. There are echoes between this imagery and Proust's metaphor of the different periods of a life as flows of magma which fuse together, but the distinctions between the two authors' use of such imagery are telling. Chamoiseau's emphasis on a crust forming over a more labile state draws attention to the distinction between the surface level of adult selfhood and the older and more vital mode of childhood perception which it masks, in contrast to the more fluid interaction proposed between different layers of self in Proust's novel. Chamoiseau's emphasis on the difference between the crust and the lava beneath could be read as an adaptation of Proust's metaphor to the neo-colonial context, where the distinction between different layers of selfhood is imposed from without to a greater degree than is the case in Proust's work. In Chamoiseau's emphasis on the enduring value of childhood modes of perception, and his denial that attainment of adulthood marks progress, this metaphor also gestures toward the need to actively peel back the crust of adult perception. Along with the lines which follow this excerpt, which criticize the complacency and inaccuracy of adult perception, there is a suggestion that childhood ways of thinking should be actively preserved and recovered, which is absent from Proust's evocation of blending between different layers of selfhood and his emphasis on the unpredictable nature of the return of previous modes of perception.

Each author then reshapes and reworks elements of Proustian conceptions of memory in order to privilege conscious, deliberate approaches to recovery of the past, and to call into question the value of memories which return unbidden. The connection between Proust's conception of memory and models of traumatic memory explored in the previous chapter might seem obscure, but Proust's involuntary memory can, and has, been read as a form of traumatic memory. Richard Terdiman argues that the traumatic qualities of Proustian involuntary memory become more apparent if one focuses on the way they are experienced and disregards the way the narrator describes them after the fact. Though these moments of recall are described as pleasurable, the experience of them is unsettling because of its power. Terdiman draws these moments into dialogue with the models of traumatic memory that were emerging at the beginning of the twentieth century, noting echoes between involuntary memory and emerging Freudian concepts of traumatic recall.[26] Traumatic memory and involuntary memory both suggest that the individual is not fully in possession of his past. At any moment, an apparently everyday scene or sensation can bring a moment of the past flooding back. In each case, the moment in question is re-experienced in all of its vividness. Moments of involuntary memory disrupt the wholeness of identity, producing 'a feeling of inexplicable and irresistible surrender, of a fantastic penetration by the irrational'.[27] In rewriting scenes from Proust's novel, these authors are working against a model of the self that can be overcome by 'a fantastic penetration of the irrational'.

All three of these authors are at pains to demonstrate their allegiance to a model of memory which argues that the past can be known through the activity of the conscious mind, and detracts from the value of unconscious modes of relationship to it. This is a major concern across each writer's oeuvre, and is worked out through relatively unconventional approaches to the recovery of the past, such as Nabokov's almost maniacal focus on detail, the trouble Perec takes to come up with what seem to be insignificant memories, and Chamoiseau's reworking of the trauma paradigm so that conscious memory masters traumatic recall. In each author, models of the past which neglect or reject a conscious approach to memory are criticized with some vehemence and carry political connotations, as we see in Chamoiseau's emphasis on the necessity of moving beyond unconscious memory of the colonial past, in Perec's criticism of modes of narration of the Nazi camps which depict them as unknowable, and in Nabokov's linking of psychoanalysis with totalitarianism.

Each author gives the reader many reasons to read his autobiographical work as motivated by an approach to memory which values conscious and deliberate recollection. Yet, as explored in the previous chapter, there are significant elements in each text which suggest that memories which cannot be fully known, understood or expressed are at work within it and are even a determining element in its structure. In the light of this gap between declared allegiances and textual practice, how is the reader to understand marks of trauma in the text? One way of reading this contradiction is to argue that these authors place such emphasis on conscious memory precisely because unconscious, involuntary recollections drive their autobiographical enterprise and wider approach to the past. I want to look now at the ways in which traumatic modes of relationship to the past are intertwined with attempts to move beyond them. Such duality is present in the temporal structures of *Speak, Memory* and *Une enfance créole* and in the portrayals of the wounded body by Perec and Chamoiseau.

The non-linear temporal structures of *Speak, Memory* and *Une enfance créole* can be read either as marks of foundational traumas or as deliberate attempts to allow the past its strangeness. The work of Johannes Fabian on the temporality of anthropological writing is helpful in understanding the rationale for the use of non-linear temporal structures as part of a conscious practice of memorial writing. Fabian points out that there is a gap between the time during which the anthropologist experiences the culture he is studying, and the time when he writes up his experiences. Fabian argues that this leads to what he calls 'a denial of co-evalness', where the culture under study is consigned to the past. This becomes even more problematic when it is replicated at the level of national discourse, where the cultures studied by anthropologists are spoken of as occupying an earlier stage in human history than the countries which colonized them. According to Fabian, the way the anthropologist occupies the first person and the present, while the people described are spoken of in the third person and the past, contributes to a suppression of their voices.[28]

Fabian was not writing about autobiography, but many of the issues he examines are relevant to autobiographical writing which seeks to record and preserve a cultural and linguistic inheritance and memorialize a lost parent. Autobiographical discourse is also characterized by a temporal gap between the present of writing and the experiences described. Memorial writing runs the risk of suppressing the voices of the loved ones mourned, and of making them mere characters within the author's repertoire. In addition to this, the depiction of a lost linguistic and cultural community for an audience who does not share this heritage creates a risk of reifying it. In the unpredictable relationships Nabokov and Chamoiseau create between past and present within the autobiographical text, each author displays a commitment to allowing his past, his ancestral language and culture, and his loved ones, their strangeness. Though this might seem close to trauma theory's conception of the traumatic event as something that cannot be assimilated into the mind or a conventionally linear narrative, there are important distinctions between the two models. Whereas in trauma theory the individual cannot assimilate the painful event, whether they wish to or not, reading these temporal structures through Fabian's work suggests that even if the past could be assimilated to the present, maintaining its isolation serves a purpose. Where trauma theory sees fragmentation as a sign that the individual cannot make coherent sense of their past, this reading sees distinctions between past and present as a sign of a clear understanding of the nuances of their separation.

Separation between Different Temporal Periods

As we have seen, in theories of trauma, experiencing an overwhelming event will lead to disrupted temporality because the moment of trauma will return over and over again, preventing the individual from experiencing it as 'past'. This will continue unless the individual is able to find a way to process the overwhelming experience and leave it behind. Literary theories of trauma emphasize the great difficulties involved in this process. If nothing is done, the traumatic moment will always remain unassimilated. In Fabian's model, the process is the opposite. He argues that the conventions of anthropological work lead writers to elide the strangeness of the past and of other people to the present and the self, and that a conscious effort must be made to preserve distinctions between the two. In addition to this, in Fabian's model the past is not formed of a single moment or experience but rather a whole period. Trauma theory often uses the metaphor of the overwhelming experience as a small, hard object, embedded in the amorphous material of the mind, like a bullet or a piece of shrapnel. These metaphors suggest the way one traumatic event can puncture the mind. Fabian's analysis, on the other hand, sees past and present as swathes of time, rather than focusing on single moments in the past. As noted in the first chapter, in Perec's text there is no real sense of a time 'before' his contact with violent history and loss of his parents. As a result, his text does not set up an interaction between different periods of his life in this way, but the sense of the past as a swathe of time rather than a condensed moment is present in Nabokov's use of miniatures and Chamoiseau's use of fractals as devices which draw different temporal periods into dialogue while preserving their separateness.

The Use of Miniatures

Nabokov deploys miniature, cameo portraits to embed one temporal period within another without dissolving the borders between them. This is particularly the case in references to America during Nabokov's evocation of his Russian childhood. One example of this is when Nabokov relates how as children his mother and her siblings called one particular bog 'America' because of its inaccessibility and mystery.[29] This comment is part of a description of the country estates where Nabokov spent his childhood. The reference to America orients the reader's perspective away from pre-revolutionary Russia to the America of the 1950s and 1960s, where we know Nabokov now resides. However, this leap into the future is made through an initial move into the past (his mother's childhood). The association of America with inaccessibility and mystery has the effect of making the present of writing strange by allowing the Russian past to shimmer through it. Layers of time are superimposed here, as Nabokov's mother's past influences his child-self's present, which turns out to foreshadow his adult-self's present. This is also one of many instances of a cameo image from one time taking on vast proportions in another. A comparatively tiny America was part of Nabokov's childhood home, while part of his adulthood was spent in an America of much larger dimensions.

A similar effect is achieved when Nabokov writes about fairground toys called 'американские жители' (American inhabitants) or Cartesian devils in English.³⁰ Again the adjective 'American' is only used by the Russian children to mean strange, outlandish, mysterious, but Nabokov allows this prophetic reference to his eventual *terre d'asile* both to create a link between past and present and to bring the two into an estranging relationship with each other. He says that although the children only used the word 'American' to mean strange, the figures inside the coloured bottles resemble contemporary American citizens going up and down a skyscraper's elevators at evening light. Americans in elevators in the 1950s and 1960s, whom Nabokov presumably sees in the present of writing, are thus shrunk to be held within coloured bottles bought at a fairground in St Petersburg in the first decade of the century, while this seemingly trivial toy from the Russian past is expanded to take on the dimensions of a skyscraper in the American present. Here, present, past and future are bound into unpredictable relationships with each other, where a pinpoint moment from the past can expand into a constellation of moments in the present or future, or the huge, looming realities of the present can be shrunk into a patch of wetland or a toy figure in a bottle in the past. Though these images suggest a degree of interpenetration between the different periods of the author's life, the idea of boundaries between different times is preserved through the depiction of the 'America' bog as one area of the park, or the coloured glass which forms a boundary between the Cartesian devils and the children. Nabokov's use of miniatures contributes to his project of maintaining the strangeness of different temporal periods to each other, even as he embeds one within another.

Fractals

A fractal is a mathematical term for a shape or structure that is self-similar when observed at different levels. An example of a fractal in nature is the way a floret of broccoli has the same form as a head of broccoli, or the way a single segment of a fern has the same shape as a whole fern. Chamoiseau entitles one of the sections of *A bout d'enfance* 'Fractales et impossibles' and Louise Hardwick writes that this may be a way of connecting the autobiography with African culture.³¹ Fractals, like the imagery of spirals and sedimentation used elsewhere in the text, allow Chamoiseau to create recurrence that incorporates renewal within the text. We see this in the way the first sentence of *A bout d'enfance* works as a description of a single moment, but also describes the structure of the text as a whole. The sentence reads: 'Un jour, bien des années avant l'épreuve du mabouya, le négrillon s'aperçut que les êtres-humains n'étaient pas seuls au monde: il existait aussi des petites-filles' [One day, many years before the ordeal of the mabouya, the little black boy realized that human-beings were not alone in the world: there were also little-girls].³² 'Êtres-humains' is the child's word for other male children. Although we do not find this out until much later in the text, 'l'épreuve du mabouya' refers to the touch of the feet of a certain kind of lizard on Chamoiseau's chest. The touch of the mabouya, which was associated with death in Martinican pre-Colombian culture, is supposed eventually to be fatal to whoever receives it.³³ Chamoiseau undergoes this ordeal as a punishment for spending too much time gazing at Gabine la Lune. This sentence then directs the reader's attention to the time between the discovery of love and contact with death, the liminal period of adolescence which is the subject of the volume as a whole. This specular relationship between the fragment and the whole, where the fragment echoes the larger structure of which it is part, yet remains distinct and complete in itself, provides a model of integration which takes account of the relationship between the part and the whole without blurring the distinctions between them or placing more value on one than another. This is apt, considering that the autobiography seeks to record the contribution childhood makes to adult life, while preserving the distinct nature of childhood experience. It leaves the reader with the impression that Chamoiseau's autobiographical writing aims to explore how singular events or periods can be expanded or condensed, mapped or mirrored from past to present. Rather than integrating life's changes into a smooth continuum, it examines the kinds of structures and perspectives which allow for fruitful relationships between distinct temporal realities.

As we saw in the previous chapter, *Speak, Memory* and *Une enfance créole* are both structured to a significant extent by the obsessive return to moments of loss which remain unassimilated into the larger body of the autobiographical narrative. In the use of miniatures and fractals, however, a different model of the relationship between past and present emerges. In this model, the interaction between different temporal periods is figured as productive rather than ruminative. Nabokov's miniature images of America within his Russian childhood embed very different periods within one another without collapsing distinctions between them. Chamoiseau's fractals gesture towards relationships between the whole and the part where the autonomy of both is preserved. Read through Fabian's analysis of time in anthropological writing, such devices can be seen as part of an attempt to preserve the strangeness of the past without depicting it as beyond the bounds of expression or memory. They thus indicate greater mastery over past experience than the structures of haunting analysed in the previous chapter. These two models of interaction between past and present — one indicating mastery over the portrayal of the past, the other helplessness before it — do not cancel each other out but rather gesture toward the variegated response of these authors to the past, and the partial success of commitments professed elsewhere to conscious approaches to memory.

The Wounded Body

Fabian's work helps make sense of the somewhat jarring temporal structures in each text, but what of the images of the wounded body in the work of Chamoiseau and Perec? As explored previously, these play an important role in making the intangible psychic pain of personal and collective traumas visible to the reader. Read closely, bodily marks also connect the author's literary work with the lives of previous generations. In this way they go some way toward working against the linguistic and cultural discontinuities that otherwise distance these authors from the family and the collective past. Chamoiseau uses textual images of bodily marks to open up a dialogue between the written word and the landscape of Martinique.

As noted previously, the schoolroom, like the plantation in créoliste thought, is a concentrated space where cultural loss and rebirth go hand in hand. This link between destruction and survival is made clear in the last words of *Chemin-d'école*. Chamoiseau writes about himself from the point of view of Gros-Lombric, a composite character who represents Creole culture:

> Il lui aurait fallu [à Gros-Lombric] un vieux don de voyance pour deviner que — dans ce saccage de leur univers natal, dans cette ruine intérieure tellement invalidante — le négrillon, penché sur son cahier, encrait sans trop savoir une tracée de survie.
> *Répondeurs*:
> Conteurs, contez…!
> Oh, la place est belle![34]
>
> [He [Gros-Lombric] would have needed the ancient gift of second sight to divine that — in this sacking of their native world, in this crippling inner ruination — the little black boy bent over his notebook was tracing, without fully realizing it, an inky lifeline of survival …
> *Répondeurs*:
> Storytellers, on your mark!
> Ho: off you go!]

Here, the wounds inflicted by the republican school-system and the healing that occurred afterward are fused. The French characters which Chamoiseau writes on his exercise book are foreign to him, and cut him off from the world of his childhood, but once his writing career begins, they will provide a way out of foreign consciousness into a creative space where childhood and adulthood can intermingle. The response of the 'répondeurs' affirms the continued links between the writing project and the oral tradition in which it claims its roots. Maeve McCusker points out that we can read 'encrait' as 'ancrait' here, and it is worth examining in more detail the connection between the cerebral act of writing, rootedness in the physical world and the body.[35]

Chamoiseau links the outline of letters on the page with the *tracées*, the paths used by the dominated people of Martinique, whose significance he and Raphaël Confiant explore in *Lettres créoles: tracées antillaises et continentales de la littérature, 1635–1975*. They see the *tracées* as preserving those parts of the history of Martinique which have remained unwritten. The communicative power of the *tracées* is emphasized, and they function as a kind of alternative writing, one that does not carry with it submission to the values of the colonizer:

> La chose est frappante: à côté des routes coloniales dont l'intention se projette tout droit, à quelque utilité prédatrice, se déploient d'infinies petites sentes que l'on appelle tracées. Élaborées par les Nègres marrons, les esclaves, les créoles, à travers les bois et les mornes du pays, ces tracées disent autre chose. Elles témoignent d'une spirale collective que le plan colonial n'avait pas prévue.[36]
>
> [It is striking that near colonial roads whose trajectory is cast straight ahead, useful and predatory, little paths called *tracées*, fan out endlessly. Fashioned by slaves, runaway slaves and creoles through the woods and hills of the country, these *tracées* speak of something else. They are witness to a collective spiralling which the colonial plan had not reckoned on.]

By describing his childhood writing as 'une tracée de survie', Chamoiseau opens up a channel between the marks he makes on the page and the marks made by previous generations on the soil. The child's writing becomes a sign of integration within a larger tradition of memory, rather than a sign of his alienation from his original language and culture. This continuum is extended to include marks on the body of the author. We see an echo of the image of the 'infinies petites sentes' in his description of his writing hands:

> L'homme d'à-présent regarde ses mains. Elles écrivent. Stationnent sages sur un clavier. Elles se souviennent en cicatrices. Elles n'ont plus mémoire des douleurs d'un yo-yo qui écorche ou qui racle un os. [...] Elles se sont amollies, presque devenues précieuses. Seules de minuscules traînées blanchâtres ou de rose coquillage, de fines rayures, témoignent d'un temps d'intense humanité où elles se voyaient expédiées au-devant d'un yo-yo...[37]

> [The present-day man looks at his hands. They are writing. Pausing quietly on a keyboard. They remember through their scars. They no longer recall the way a yoyo hurts when it grazes or scrapes a knuckle [...] They have become soft, almost precious. Only tiny tracks and delicate grooves, either whitish or shellfish-pink, witness to a time of intense humanity when they were sent ahead of a yoyo.]

The mention of 'cicatrices' suggests a connection with the *tracées* because they are both formed by cutting into something, either the soil or skin. 'Miniscules traînées' and 'fines rayures' echo 'petites sentes'. Both the marks on Chamoiseau's skin and the *tracées* are figured as fragile, with the delicacy of the paths thrown into relief by the 'utilité prédatrice' of the colonial roads. The use of the verb 'témoigner' echoes the description of the *tracées* quoted from *Lettres créoles* above in that it ascribes communicative power to non-verbal phenomena. Finally, the reference to 'coquillage' is significant, given that a shell is also something left over once the living form that caused it to be created has died. A shell, like the paths, is a non-linguistic trace of life. The mention of the author's hands pausing on the keyboard collapses the distinction between narrating and narrated self, and so overcomes the splitting of the self normally required by the written form.

In this way, Chamoiseau interweaves his writing, his body and Martinique's landscape and makes it clear that his autobiographical project does not set out to trace a straight line between past and present, nor to circle around an irrecoverable, traumatic past, but rather aims to reflect on the ways in which his present constantly echoes and renews aspects of his past and the wider history of Martinique. The identification of his first steps into the literate world as the 'encr[age]' of 'une tracée de survie', inscribes his writing as part of a continuum of resistance that is rooted in the earth, yet open to transformation and movement. As well as making psychic pain visible then, bodily marks also make visible the incompleteness of severance from the personal and collective past.

Blasco Ibañez, Maffeo Barberini and Michel Leiris: Scars, *Bandes* and Inheritance

Perec connects literary activity, bodily marks and the lives of previous generations, especially his parents, through the inter- and intra-textual networks he weaves with the word *bande*. The *bandes* are connected with the fine balance between display and concealment of pain in Perec's writing, and represent the dangers and potential of integration within a literary or professional community. There is a link between Perec's life and his father's time as a soldier through an association between *bandes* and military uniform. Perec writes that although the diagonal scar on his lip is important to him, 'elle n'est pourtant pas considérée comme un "signe particulier" sur ma carte d'identité, mais seulement sur mon livret militaire, et je crois bien que c'est parce que j'avais moi-même pris soin de le signaler' [though it is not entered as a "distinguishing mark" on my identity card, only on my army passbook, and I think that's only because I bothered to point it out].[38] The puttees link Perec's professional life as a writer and his father's short time as a soldier through two connections made between woven *bandes* and the act of writing. The first occurs when Perec recalls a memory he has of making paper doilies in school:

> on disposait parallèlement des bandes étroites de carton léger coloriées de diverses couleurs et on les croisait avec des bandes identiques en passant une fois au-dessus, une fois au-dessous. Je me souviens que ce jeu m'enchanta, que j'en compris très vite le principe et que j'y excellais.[39]
>
> [we laid out, side by side, narrow strips of thin cardboard of various colours and wove identical strips crosswise, once over, once under. I remember being delighted by this game, that I quickly understood how it worked and was very good at it.]

Bernard Magné points out that this is a very precise description of the structure of *W ou le souvenir d'enfance*, whose various narrative strands also overlap at certain defined points.[40] This reference is situated in such a way that it is both half-hidden and displayed prominently, in a footnote to the main text at the end of the chapter. Because it is the last piece of writing the reader encounters before moving on to the section where Perec recounts his final parting from his mother, it is set apart from the text that surrounds it on either side.

This tension between display and concealment also arises in the second link made between the image of the *bandes molletières* and literary life, as it dwells on images of lengths of material which display a certain professional identity by concealing the body. This link is made when Perec records his fascination with a technique used by professional or semi-professional skiers to attach their skis to their feet. This passage comes directly before Perec recalls receiving the injury which left him with a scar in the shape of a *bande*. This is his description of the skier's technique:

> ce système extraordinairement complexe de laçage, utilisant une lanière unique mais démesurément longue, passée et repassée autour de la chaussure un nombre incalculable de fois selon un protocole apparemment immuable dont le déroulement me faisait l'effet d'une cérémonie capitale (aussi capitale, aussi

décisive que put m'apparaître, plus tard, le laçage de la ceinture dans *les Arènes sanglantes*, de Blasco Ibañez, ou la métamorphose vestimentaire du cardinal Barberini en Urbain VIII dans *le Galilée* du Berliner Ensemble) et qui assurait au skieur l'indissoluble union de ses skis et de ses chaussures, multipliant autant les risques de fracture grave que les chances de performances exceptionnelles.[41]

[that amazingly complex lacing system [...] which involved the use of a single but inordinately long thong threaded over and under the boot innumerable times in an apparently unalterable routine, the execution of which seemed to me to be a cardinal ceremony (as cardinal, and as decisive, as the lacing of the Matador's belt in Blasco Ibañez's *Blood and Sand* later seemed to me to be, or the sartorial transformation of Barberini into Urban VIII in the Berliner Ensemble's production of *Galileo*), and giving the skier that indissoluble union of ski and boot increased to the same degree the risk of a serious fracture and the chance of an outstanding performance.]

The skier's use of a constraint to attain improved performance echoes the use of strict compositional rules to stimulate innovative literary works by members of the *Ouvroir de littérature potentielle*, a literary group to which Perec belonged.[42] The opposition of the risk of serious injury to the potential for high achievement resonates with tensions present in the use of Oulipian constraints.

We can also see this reference to the risk of injury as uniting a connection to Perec's father with an allusion to a literary forefather, Michel Leiris. Later in the autobiography, Perec writes that Leiris was one of the authors who allowed him to experience 'la jouissance [...] d'une parenté enfin retrouvée' [enjoyment [...] of having in the end found kin again].[43] When Perec mentions the 'laçage de la ceinture' [the lacing of the belt] in Blasco Ibañez's bull-fighting novel, he is referring to the moment when the torero's servant wraps an extended length of material around his waist. This is supposed to afford him some measure of protection from any potential injury from a bull's horn, and Ibañez writes that it would not be unwrapped until the bullfighter had won the fight or been killed in the attempt.[44] This resonates with the preface to *L'Age d'homme*, where Leiris writes that he would like autobiographical writing to be like bull-fighting, where the danger of death confers 'une réalité humaine' to the torero's art, and prevents it from being mere show.[45] For Leiris, the image of the torero in the 'terrain de vérité' of the bull-fighting arena, acts as a symbol of self and world bound into a relationship where neither dominates completely.[46]

In the connection between Leiris's autobiographical work, Perec's writing and his father's military life, Perec creates an overlap between his literary and family connections. These intersecting networks are extended to include the life and death of Perec's mother through the reference to Urban VIII. Perec elsewhere in the text displays an interest in St Cecilia's hagiography, writing that, because his mother was known as Cécile in France, he has always known that St Cecilia is the patron saint of music and that the cathedral in Albi is dedicated to her.[47] Because of this comment, and, of course, the similarity in names, the fictional figure of Caecilia Winckler can be read as a kind of imagined version of Perec's mother. In a typically indirect move, Perec draws attention to the parallel between St Cecilia's association with music and the opera career of Caecilia Winckler, but leaves unspoken the more painful link. Like Caecilia Winckler, St Cecilia did not die instantaneously, but experienced a long, slow death.[48] She was first condemned to be boiled to death, and when this had no effect, she was to be beheaded in the bath of hot water. The executioner struck three times without managing to behead her, and then he fled. Cecilia lived for three days before dying.[49] With this information, Perec's statement that Caecilia Winckler 'ne mourut pas sur le coup' comes to seem a veiled reference to the executioner's blows.[50] The reference to a pope named Urban in the parentheses above could be read as another oblique hint at this painful history, as Urban I, according to some accounts, buried St Cecilia in defiance of the Roman authorities who forbade the burial of those sentenced to execution.[51]

The reference to Urban VIII could then be an attempt to include Perec's mother in the network which holds his father, Leiris and his own writing. The otherwise gratuitous reference to the Berliner Ensemble strengthens this impression. In an interview, Perec remarked that he scattered German words and references to Germany throughout *W ou le souvenir d'enfance* as a way of gesturing towards the role Germany played in his parents' lives.[52] Perec's reference to Urban VIII can be seen as one of the very indirect ways in which his text attempts to remedy the fact that his mother does not have a final resting-place. Display and concealment once more enter into tension here. On the one hand, Perec's oblique allusion to the burial of a woman who shares his mother's name works against the erasure of all traces of her life, and so is connected with display. But the triple temporal displacement, where Perec's mother is hidden behind St Cecilia, who lived in the twelfth century, and St Cecilia is hidden behind Urban VIII, who was pope in the seventeenth century and in this context is a character in a Brecht play, works very effectively as concealment.

If the tension between display and concealment crops up again and again in Perec's treatment of the *bande*, it is because artful concealment is part of Perec's display of his literary identity. Just as, in the text, soldier, bull-fighter, pope and skier all don lengths of material which hide the body in order to display a committed professional identity, so Perec's ability to mask the most painful parts of his history and his methods of dealing with them speaks of his skill as a writer. The semi-hidden nature of the textual networks reinforces the literary nature of the text in a second way: it means the reader can only understand certain aspects of the text if she approaches it as a specifically literary document, paying close attention to any recurrence of certain words and images. The example of the *bande* demonstrates how one word and the images it denotes reach outwards to include the lives of other people (Perec's parents), separate literary voices (Ibañez, Leiris, Brecht), and a range of different kinds of writing (Hebrew writing, Oulipian writing, theatre, popular fiction). These different kinds of writing and the various allegiances they express are all condensed into the single diagonal scar on Perec's upper lip, a mark which comes to gesture toward the connections between the author and his parents which remain to a limited extent, as well as to the literary networks which allow the author to re-negotiate a relationship between self and world in the aftermath of bereavement.

The bodily marks Perec and Chamoiseau depict in their text do act as fixed marks of traumas which cannot entirely be erased or redeemed. Their prominent role within each text gestures toward a turning away from the verbal articulation of the pain of severance from a personal, family and collective past. However, as 'figures en quelque sorte doubles', these marks are polysemic.[53] As well as acting as a record of ineradicable pain, they also go some way toward linking the author's creative practice with the lives of previous generations. Though these links remain problematic and tenuous, the corporeal writing of the scars acts as a kind of alternative language which is capable of holding lives separated by linguistic and historical discontinuities. The tenuous qualities of such links emerge in the faintness of the marks on the author's body and in the way their links with previous generations are semi-hidden in marginal locations within the text. The scars hold within one mark the legacy of trauma and the muted possibility of moving beyond it.

Connections between the Oblique and the Ludic

Throughout this chapter we have seen the intertwining of traumatic, ruminative memory and conscious, productive modes of relation to the past. This intertwining is present in the co-existence of a haunted present and fruitful connections to the past in *Speak, Memory* and *Une enfance créole*, and in the polysemy of the bodily marks in *Une enfance créole* and *W ou le souvenir d'enfance*. The traumatic and the productive are even more tightly interwoven when it comes to these authors' approaches to the place of the oblique in artistic activity. Comparisons between different kinds of games and literary activity suggest that the process of becoming conscious of the interaction between memory and perception is not simply relevant to these authors' approach to historical questions, but is at the very heart of literary endeavour. Further, these depictions of games suggest that one becomes conscious of the workings of one's own mind, not through reflection on it, but rather through journeys outwards through other minds and modes of perception. Such outward journeys lead individuals back to their starting-point with a deepened awareness of the way they apprehend the world. The connection between roundabout pathways and a more conscious awareness of the workings of one's own mind perhaps suggests another way of reading the oblique approaches to painful topics explored in the previous chapter. Yet though these ludic, indirect routes are associated with conscious forms of memory and thought, they are also paradoxically connected with imagery of the traumatic historical displacements which make conscious approaches to the past difficult. There is a tension between displacement as a painful historical experience and its presence as a metaphor for productive reading and writing in these texts. The reader faces here what Barbara Straumann calls the 'murky interface' between lived experiences of exile or displacement and their recurrent use as a trope for aesthetic production, an interface which is connected in these texts with the intertwining of traumatic and conscious modes of relationship to the past.[54]

Each author uses a depiction of games to explore in miniature the dynamic between the creator and interpreter of a text. They conceive of reading and playing as activities where perception is transformed, using metaphors of displacement to evoke such transformations, and emphasising the value of deception in bringing them about. This is especially the case with Nabokov and Perec. The last section of the penultimate chapter of *Speak, Memory* concerns Nabokov's lifelong fascination with chess puzzles. He emphasizes the difference between the chess puzzle and the chess game, and the proximity of the chess puzzle to art: 'Inspiration of a quasi-musical, quasi-poetical, or to be quite exact, poetico-mathematical type, attends the process of thinking up a chess composition.'[55] He emphasizes the way the manipulation of the pieces of the puzzle gives concrete form to mental activity, speaking of the 'manipulation of carved figures, or of their mental counterparts'.[56] There is an analogy here between the chess figures and words on the page, whose position acts as a trace or expression of mental activity. Nabokov goes on to describe the composition of one puzzle that gave him particular delight. It was designed to fool someone experienced with chess puzzles into thinking that it had a complicated solution. Having pursued this avenue fruitlessly, the solver would look again at the problem and realize it had a very simple solution. Nabokov emphasizes that creating and solving a chess puzzle are inherently relational activities, although they are usually accomplished alone. In this way they echo the relational dimension of the (usually) solitary activities of reading and writing, a comparison Nabokov makes explicitly slightly later:

> It should be understood that competition in chess puzzles is not really between White and Black but between the composer and the hypothetical solver (just as in a first-rate work of fiction the real clash is not between the characters but between the author and the world) so that a great part of a problem's value is due to the number of 'tries' — delusive opening moves, false scents, specious lines of play, astutely and lovingly prepared to lead the would-be solver astray.[57]

Here the relationship between composer and solver contains an ambivalent mix of hostility and pedagogy. The composer sets out to deceive the solver not simply by placing false clues in his way, but by playing on habits of perception the solver is likely to have. Thus, Nabokov says that his favourite puzzle would not be interesting to a beginner because they would immediately see the simple solution, not knowing of more elaborate possibilities. Nabokov's puzzle only becomes delightful when played by a more advanced player who is likely to try a very elaborate solution, only to return to the beginning when this solution fails. Doing the chess puzzle leads the solver to become more aware of the movements of his own mind, the filters which influence his apprehension of the world. By the end of the puzzle, the solver will also have gained a deeper appreciation of the composer's cunning. He or she will see the way the composer has integrated the likely movements of the solver's mind into the very structure of the puzzle, producing a sense of simultaneous closeness and distance between the two minds. The relationship between the two is an ambivalent one, as we see in this quotation, where Nabokov compares the movements of the deceived solver's mind to those of

> somebody on a wild goose chase [who] might go from Albany to New York by way of Vancouver, Eurasia and the Azores. The pleasant experience of the roundabout route (strange landscapes, gongs, tigers, exotic customs, the thrice-repeated circuit of a newly-married couple around the sacred fire of an earthen brazier) would amply reward him for the misery of the deceit.[58]

Here, the solver's elaborate mental efforts are suggested through a metaphor of displacement which evokes both the trouble of pursuing the false solution and the enriched experience of the puzzle it brings. The earlier coupling of chess puzzles and literary art suggests that in both, pleasure arises from deceit and revelation of deceit because of the heightened degree of consciousness such movements from states of confusion to clarity create. This process of seeing through the artist or composer's tricks can be connected with the effort to achieve conscious modes of memory, especially when one considers that it is the solver's faulty mapping of previous problems on to this one that causes the confusion, and when one recalls Nabokov's comments about autobiography as a process of becoming conscious of unnoticed patterns scattered throughout one's life. Such roundabout mental journeys are then figured as part of the process of becoming conscious of the workings of one's own mind. As we have seen, conscious memory offers a way of mastering a traumatic past. Yet exile is a significant part of what has made the past traumatic, so to use displacement as a metaphor for conscious memory interweaves the source and the cure for traumatic memory.

Nabokov would seem to be aware of this duality, because he links his creation of the chess puzzle with his frantic search for an exit visa from wartime France. This was an anxious time for the family, as Nabokov could have been called up to serve as a soldier at any time, which would have left his wife and son vulnerable as foreign Jews. The oblique solution to the chess puzzle emerges from a time in Nabokov's life when straightforward ways out of a dangerous situation were not available to him. This resonates with one possible source for Nabokov's use of chess as a metaphor for art, Viktor Shklovsky's 1923 *Ходъ коня: сборник статей* [The Knight's Move: Collected Essays]. Shklovsky uses the way the knight is obliged to move in an L-shape as a metaphor for conventions in art. He writes: 'конь не свободенъ — он ходитъ в бок потому, что прямая дорога ему запрещена' [the knight is not free — he moves sideways because going straight ahead is forbidden to him].[59] Here the oblique pathways of art are connected with a context of constraint. In Nabokov's autobiography this constraint is present within the puzzle itself and in the circumstances in which he created it. That Nabokov intended the connection between the solution to the chess problem and the obtaining of a passage out of Europe can be seen in the way he has the chapter close on the dual image of the completed chess problem and the successfully obtained exit visa. The intention to combine the two is also present in Nabokov's misdating of the composition of the problem to May, 1940, the month of his departure from Europe, when Boyd writes that it was actually composed in November, 1939.[60] Janet Gezari points out that this misdating evidently held some significance for Nabokov because he preserved it in his 1970 book, *Poems and Problems*, where the two chess problems mentioned in *Speak, Memory* appear at the beginning and the end of the book.[61] Boyd picks up on this conflation of chess and life when he refers to America as 'the solution to the problem of exile' and there is evidence in Nabokov's notes for the autobiographical project that he intended the work to point towards the chess solution as a coming together of strands developed over its course.[62] Because Nabokov interweaves the composition of the chess problem with his account of his desperate attempts to leave

France, the metaphorical movements of the chess-solver's mind become charged with the weight of historical displacements triggered by war.

Though impossible to prove, it is possible Perec's model of the relationship between puzzle-maker and puzzle-solver in his 1978 novel *La Vie mode d'emploi* is influenced by aspects of Nabokov's work and perhaps even by a reading of *Speak, Memory*. Perec embeds hidden quotations from Nabokov's work in *La Vie mode d'emploi*,[63] and David Bellos suggests that the way the author moves from room to room of the apartment block using the knight's move might have been influenced by Perec's reading of Nabokov's first English-language novel, *The Real Life of Sebastian Knight*.[64] Bellos also tells us that in the 1960s Perec was reading *The Defense*, Nabokov's 1930 novel concerning an obsessive chess player.[65] In 'Quelques-unes des choses qu'il faudrait tout de même que je fasse avant de mourir', Perec lists 'Faire la connaissance de Vladimir Nabokov' [Meet Vladimir Nabokov].[66] This wish is the last one of the list, and is numbered thirty-seven. Thirty-seven was a significant number for Perec for several reasons: it is connected with palindromes because it is the reverse of his date of birth, 7 March. Another connection with palindromes is that he was 37 in 1973, the year he started his autobiography. In *Les Enfants du capitaine Grant*, the children search for their shipwrecked father by following the 37th parallel south around the world. The ship in *W ou le souvenir d'enfance*, the *Sylvandre*, sends a distress signal from the 37th parallel south and the work itself ends at its thirty-seventh chapter.[67] Nabokov would have been thirty-seven in the year that Perec was born. Perec's reading of and admiration for Nabokov's work suggests he might have been influenced by his explorations of the connections between ludic activity and literature. In any case, the echoes between the description of the relationship between puzzle-maker and puzzle-solver in *La Vie mode d'emploi* and Nabokov's exploration of chess puzzles in *Speak, Memory* are striking.

One of the main relationships in Perec's novel is that between Bartlebooth, an eccentric millionaire, and Gaspard Winckler, a master craftsman whom he employs to make jigsaw puzzles of watercolours he has painted in locations around the world over a period of twenty years. Bartlebooth spends a further two decades completing the puzzles in the order in which he did the paintings. Once completed, the images are removed from the puzzle by a special chemical process, and then bleached white. Winckler's craft is a deceptive one, where he cuts the puzzle pieces to trick Bartlebooth into seeing them incorrectly. This deception culminates in the last scene of the novel, where Bartlebooth dies in front of a puzzle with only one piece unfilled. The gap is in the shape of an X but the only remaining piece is in the shape of a W, reflecting the power of the creator to frustrate the puzzle-solver's quest for totality and completion.[68]

The novel opens with a preamble where the author meditates on the relationship between those who create jigsaw puzzles and those who solve them. He makes clear that he has in mind the artful crafting of individual puzzle pieces one at a time, rather than machine-cutting. Where puzzles are made piece by piece, the craftsman can anticipate the solver's view of them and take advantage of this to nudge him to see them in a certain way.[69] In the novel, Winckler takes advantage of this, playing on the likelihood of Bartlebooth's missing slight variations between familiar shapes and the actual pieces he has in front of him. To solve the puzzles, Bartlebooth has to learn to perceive the pieces in a new way:

> Bartlebooth devait, pour trouver cet angle à vrai dire presque mais pas vraiment tout à fait droit, cesser de le considérer comme la pointe d'un triangle, c'est à dire faire basculer sa perception, voir autrement ce que fallacieusement l'autre lui donnait à voir.[70]

> [To find that angle which was in fact almost but not quite a right angle, Bartlebooth had to stop seeing it as the tip of a triangle, that is to say he had to completely change how he perceived, to see otherwise what the other led him falsely to see.]

Here, Bartlebooth has to stop mapping familiar, ready-made mental images (such as that of the right angle or the triangle) on to what he sees before him. This process of perceiving the slight divergence between what he expects to see and the actual shapes of the puzzle-pieces entails becoming aware of that which filters his vision of the surrounding world. Because the tricks in the puzzles have been carefully placed there by Gaspard Winckler, he also learns about the other man's expectations of his habits of perception. As in Nabokov's description of the chess puzzles, then, doing the jigsaw puzzle is a relational activity with an ambivalent mix of pedagogy and hostility. Like the chess puzzle, it is an apparently solitary activity which actually leads to a charged interaction between two minds. Like words on the page and positioned chess pieces, puzzle pieces are physical traces of the activity of the creator's mind, and the ambivalent mix of freedom and constraint with which the reader approaches a text echoes that portrayed in the relationship between Winckler and Bartlebooth. As we have seen, the deceptive quality of Winckler's art is depicted as both the product of a degree of hostility toward the millionaire and as something which leads Bartlebooth into an enriched awareness of the workings of his own mind and that of Winckler. The portrayal of this relationship thus opens up the dual role of misdirection and oblique pathways in written texts, which have the potential to entrap the reader and to enrich her.

Perec's evocation of the interaction between Bartlebooth and Gaspard Winckler is also suggestive of concrete historical displacements and the threat of violence, though in his case these displacements are not quite as obviously autobiographical as they are in *Speak, Memory*. He writes about Bartlebooth struggling to fit a piece into a gap, because the gap seems to him to have the shape of 'une sorte d'Inde noire à laquelle Ceylan serait restée attachée' [a kind of black India if Ceylon had remained attached to it].[71] In fact, the piece which fits in the gap is pale grey and not black, and, if tilted by ninety degrees, is in the shape of England and not India. These references to incorrect perception of space, seeing India instead of England, call up colonial histories and their connections with competing modes of perception of national spaces. Such connotations could be seen as coincidental or unimportant were it not for another allusion embedded in this passage. The puzzle Bartlebooth is doing when he runs into the India/England confusion is of a New Zealand port on the Coromandel coast. Though Perec does not mention it, the Coromandel peninsula borders the Firth of Thames. The picture then portrays a real-life example of the reverse of Bartlebooth's misperception; instead of looking at

England and seeing India, the place name suggests a history of someone looking at New Zealand and seeing England. Together the evocation of these different national spaces suggests the concrete, political issues involved in the perception and naming of space. Although Perec's description of the interaction between Winckler and Bartlebooth seems to emphasize a process internal to the mind, he simultaneously suggests the external, collective implications of movements between different ways of seeing. In this way, the jigsaw puzzle is depicted as an interaction between two minds which has echoes of interactions between different nations and peoples.

These allusions to English colonial history begin to take on autobiographical import when one recalls the history of the imagined island in *W ou le souvenir d'enfance*. All of the stories offered as potential histories of W emphasize that it was colonized by Westerners, and one of the origin stories says that it was founded by White Anglo-Saxon Protestants, or Wasps, a group to which Bartlebooth is also said to belong.[72] Manet van Montfrans points out the connection between the category of Wasps and the Nazi concept of an Aryan race. He argues that the conflation of class and ethnicity associated with the concept of Wasps is present in a much more extreme form in the Nazi system, where 'lower races' are deprived of all social power.[73] This conflation of race and class finds an echo in the oppression of the Athletes by the authorities in the W story, which has echoes of both Nazi and colonial histories. Because of the way Perec intertwines these separate histories elsewhere in his work, the references to English colonial practices in the Coromandel scene carry with them connotations of the racial discrimination which introduced upheaval into his family history and led to the death of his mother.

Nabokov suggests the ludic qualities of the interaction between reader and author through an exploration of chess puzzles; Perec does the same in his portrayal of the dynamics at work when a jigsaw puzzle is solved; Chamoiseau looks at deception and play in his evocation of childhood games of marbles. Marbles offer a way of exploring the concept of the 'détour', developed in more theoretically-oriented work by Édouard Glissant.[74] Celia Britton, in her reading of Glissant, describes the detour as 'tactical and ambiguous', 'essentially an indirect mode of resistance that "gets around" obstacles rather than confronting them head on, and [which] arises in response to a situation of disguised rather than overt oppression and struggle'.[75] It is then appropriate as a response to the insidious influence of Martinique's colonial legacy on the developing mind of the child.

The child finds an old playground where other children play marbles after school when he begins to try new routes on the walk home from school. These wanderings are a way for him to explore the surrounding area as he becomes more independent, and, as in the case of Nabokov and Perec, confronting new experiences in the outside world leads the child to a greater knowledge of the workings of his own mind:

> Le détour s'effectue en silence, retiré en toi-même, vigilant en toi-même, à l'écoute de toi-même. Opérer un détour c'est comme rentrer en soi: dans l'étrangeté plus ou moins inquiétante de l'entour, on ne dispose plus que du rempart de soi.[76]
>
> [You make a detour in silence, withdrawn into yourself, on the alert inside yourself, attentive to yourself. Taking a detour is like examining one's

conscience: in unfamiliar and more or less disquieting surroundings, one can rely only on oneself.]

Here, physical movement outwards into unfamiliar surroundings is coupled with a corresponding movement inwards and a deepened awareness of the way the self filters the relationship with the outside world. The value placed on indirect routes here is echoed in the depiction of the children playing marbles in the old schoolyard. The game of marbles acts as a miniature version of a world where the child has to be on his guard against hostile forces and use knowledge of the local environment to resist them. He learns that the way to win is not to aim directly at the target, but rather to feign nonchalance and to aim as if one is only testing one's opponents.[77] He also learns that such indirect paths become more sure through imaginative appreciation of the possibilities of apparently useless material:

> Ainsi donc: le plus court chemin n'était pas le plus clair, et le plus long ne valait pas mieux. Il te fallait transformer en alliés les roches, les graviers, les trous-fourmis, les cacas-rats, les graines-job et la poussière.[78]
>
> [So: the shortest path wasn't the safest, and the longest wasn't any better. You had to make allies of the stones, the gravel, the ant-hills, the rat turds, the hard little seeds called Job's-tears, and the dust.]

In another fractal structure, the ruts in the ground made by the marbles form twisting paths which echo both the child's wanderings in the town and those of the *tracées*, whose significance was explored in the previous section. They are thus connected to the strategy of resisting colonial oppression, not by fighting against it directly, but by working around it in indirect ways. There is a fusion of form and content here as Chamoiseau's entry into theoretical issues through a childhood memory of playing marbles is itself an example of an oblique approach.

Chamoiseau's description of the tracks of the children's marbles also opens up a dialogue between mental and physical movements. Louise Hardwick brings this out in her exploration of the significance of *la drive* in contemporary Francophone *récits d'enfance*. Hardwick notes that the kind of wanderings suggested by the verb *driver* are connected to the metropolitan French term *dérive*, or drifting, which was used by the *Internationale situationniste* in the 1950s and 1960s to describe a free, imaginative, non-utilitarian approach to moving through the modern city.[79] Incidentally, Bellos suggests that Perec's privileging of sideways approaches in *La Vie mode d'emploi* might also have been influenced by the *Internationale situationniste*.[80] There are differences between Perec's model of puzzle-solving and Chamoiseau's exploration of *la drive*, but both modes place value on roundabout, gratuitous journeys. Hardwick brings out the conjunction of aesthetic explorations and movement through physical space in *la drive* when she writes that it is 'a metaphorical act of poetry to wander through the streets, alert to a world of endless possibilities, which childhood opens up and adulthood closes down'.[81] The evocation of such wanderings is 'crucial to the consolidation of an indigenous literature' because it portrays both internal exploration of the child's own imagination and growth in knowledge of the physical surroundings of the Caribbean. The child's roundabout routes through the town then connect to the project of working against the alienation produced by living in a place where colonial history has shaped the kinds of physical, mental and literary moves available.

Yet, like the indirect approaches evoked in the work of Perec and Nabokov, the detour is not unequivocally positive. As already noted, it arises in a situation of insidious oppression and is a kind of last-ditch alternative when direct opposition to oppression is not possible. Rather than seeking to achieve a positive result, it aims more to maintain an element of doubt or instability within an oppressive system. It 'is itself marked with the alienation it is trying to combat'.[82] Because it takes place within straitened circumstances, it is not always obvious when or how a detour has been successful. Celia Britton gives the example of the way apparently illogical speech or writing could either be a sign of resistance to colonial rationality or evidence of a failure to maintain a coherent sense of self in oppressive circumstances.[83] This uncertainty is present on a miniature level in the child's doubt about whether he will hit the target, and his need always to be on his guard against unexpected interruptions of his game. The echo between the marbles' twisting paths and the *tracées*, and the way the games take place on an abandoned school playground, link the detour with marginal practices of resistance which might afford alternative paths through or around the colonial system, but which do not truly threaten its centre.

Britton's comment about the detour being 'marked by the alienation it is trying to combat' could also be applied to the explorations of ludic activity conducted by Nabokov and Perec. Their models of the interaction between puzzle-makers and puzzle-solvers suggest a degree of alienation from one's own mind as a preliminary step to attaining a more conscious awareness of the interaction between perception and memory. The solver must see his or her mind through someone else's eyes by falling into the composer's traps, a deception which eventually leads to a deepened awareness of one's habits of perception. This process of seeing one's mind from another point of view can be connected to the autobiographical enterprise, where the writer looks at his life from another person's point of view (his imagined reader's) in the hope of reaching a new vision or understanding of it. The reader of these autobiographies also goes on a roundabout journey through engaging with these texts, which construct elaborate pathways between the author's life and its relationship to other histories, which play on the reader's sense of the distinctions between fact and fiction, the personal and the literary, past and present, self and other. As we saw in the previous chapter, there are good reasons for seeing these texts' oblique approaches to the past as products of trauma. Yet these explorations of the ludic also suggest that oblique approaches are valued by these authors as a mode which enhances conscious perception. As in Glissant's detour, the traumatic qualities of oblique approaches and their relationship to conscious memory are not easily disentangled. Their interpenetration can be seen in the links forged between salutary mental movements and painful historical displacements. Readings of these texts are enriched when both aspects of oblique approaches are held in tension. Seeing such approaches as solely the products of trauma can obscure the ethical and political ramifications of the conscious construction of roundabout pathways towards painful historical episodes. The importance of such roundabout pathways in the apprehension of such histories gestures towards the value of the literary in approaching modernity's histories of migration. The ambivalent relationship between author and reader which leads the reader to see herself seeing things differently offers one way of exploring modes of awareness of the border-crossing histories whose traces inhabit local and national space. The need for the reader to actively embark on the complex journeys made possible by the text allows for a degree of opacity between author and reader, where the afterlives of histories of migration are not yielded easily but are apprehended through a transformation of the reader's vision. Finally, the recurrent metaphor of literary experience as a form of mental displacement points to the importance of reflection on the place of narratives of displacement within the literary sphere, as to think about the literary is to think about the ways in which we understand mental and physical displacements and the tensions between them.

Notes to Chapter 4

1. Patrick Chamoiseau and Édouard Glissant, *L'Esclave vieil homme et le molosse: roman* (Paris: Gallimard, 1997); Patrick Chamoiseau, *Un dimanche au cachot* (Paris: Gallimard, 2007).
2. *De la mémoire obscure à la mémoire consciente*, p. 20.
3. *De la mémoire obscure à la mémoire consciente*, p. 20.
4. *De la mémoire obscure à la mémoire consciente*, p. 22.
5. *Antan*, 22.
6. *De la mémoire obscure à la mémoire consciente*, p. 7.
7. Georges Perec, *L.G.: une aventure des années soixante* (Paris: Seuil, 1992), p. 95.
8. *L.G: une aventure des années soixante*, p. 107.
9. *W*, 42–58.
10. Georges Perec, *Je me souviens* (Paris: Hachette, 1978).
11. *SM*, 5; 21–22.
12. Washington, D.C., Library of Congress, Manuscript Division, Vladimir Vladimirovich Nabokov Papers, Box 9.
13. *SM*, 25–26.
14. *SM*, 80.
15. *SM*, 35.
16. *SM*, 235.
17. Norman, pp. 106–07.
18. Norman, pp. 67–68.
19. *SM*, 81–82; Marcel Proust, *A la recherche du temps perdu*, 16 vols (Paris: Gallimard, 1914–1927), I, (1919), p. 12.
20. Proust, p. 14.
21. *Espèces d'espaces*, pp. 31–35.
22. *W*, 10.
23. *W*, 14.
24. *Antan*, 91.
25. Knepper, pp. 132–36.
26. Terdiman, pp. 208–19.
27. Terdiman, p. 213.
28. *Time and the Other: How Anthropology Makes its Object* (New York: Columbia University Press, 2002).
29. *SM*, 58.
30. *SM*, 186.
31. 'Telling Tales: Childhood and Autobiography in the Francophone Caribbean' (unpublished doctoral thesis, University of Oxford, 2009), p. 56.
32. *A bout*, 13.

33. *À bout*, 258–59.
34. *Chemin*, 202–03.
35. McCusker, *Recovering Memory*, p. 73.
36. Chamoiseau and Confiant, p. 13.
37. *À bout*, 95.
38. *W*, 141–42.
39. *W*, 76.
40. 'Les Sutures dans *W ou le souvenir d'enfance*', *Cahiers Georges Perec*, 2 (1986–1987), 39–57 (p. 53).
41. *W*, 141.
42. Association Oulipo, *La Littérature potentielle: créations, re-créations, récréations* (Paris: Gallimard, 1973), pp. 20–21.
43. *W*, 193.
44. Blasco Ibañez, *Les Arènes sanglantes* (Paris: Calmann-Lévy, 1923), pp. 36–37.
45. Michel Leiris, *L'Âge d'homme, précédé de de la littérature considérée comme tauromachie* (Paris: Gallimard, 1946), p. 10.
46. *L'Âge d'homme*, p. 75; p. 219.
47. *W*, 55.
48. *W*, 80.
49. *Ælfric's Lives of the Virgin Spouses, with Modern English Parallel-Text Translations*, ed. by Robert Upchurch (Exeter: University of Exeter Press, 2007), pp. 73–85 (p. 85).
50. *W*, 80.
51. *Lives of the Virgin Spouses*, p. 79; p. 85.
52. *Entretiens et conférences*, I, pp. 194–95.
53. *W*, 15.
54. Straumann, p. 11.
55. *SM*, 226.
56. *SM*, 226.
57. *SM*, 227–28.
58. *SM*, 229.
59. Ходъ коня: сборник статей (Moscow: Helicon, 1923), p. 10.
60. Boyd, pp. 514–15.
61. 'Chess and Chess Problems', in *The Garland Companion to Vladimir Nabokov*, ed. by Vladimir Alexandrov (New York: Garland, 1995), pp. 44–54 (pp. 46–47).
62. Boyd, p. 514.
63. *La Vie mode d'emploi*, p. 1364.
64. Bellos, pp. 508–09.
65. Bellos, p. 344.
66. *Je suis né* (Paris: Seuil, 1990), p. 109.
67. van Montfrans, p. 149; p. 162.
68. *La Vie mode d'emploi*, p. 1279.
69. *La Vie mode d'emploi*, pp. 655–56.
70. *La Vie mode d'emploi*, p. 1078.
71. *La Vie mode d'emploi*, p. 1077.
72. *W*, 91–92.
73. van Montfrans, p. 217.
74. Édouard Glissant, *Le Discours antillais* (Paris: Seuil, 1981), pp. 27–38.
75. *Édouard Glissant and Postcolonial Theory: Strategies of Language and Resistance* (Charlottesville: University Press of Virginia, 1999), p. 25.
76. *Chemin*, 135.
77. *Chemin*, 140.
78. *Chemin*, 139.
79. 'Telling Tales', p. 261.
80. Bellos, pp. 280–81.
81. 'Telling Tales', p. 261.
82. Britton, *Édouard Glissant and Postcolonial Theory*, p. 26.
83. Britton, *Édouard Glissant and Postcolonial Theory*, p. 27.

CONCLUSION

This book began with Chamoiseau's written evocation of the moment he touches the books in the wardrobe. It seems fitting, then, to look at what happens after the child opens the books. The adult author recalls how the child read before he learned to read:

> Le négrillon recomposait les livres à partir des images. Il imaginait des histoires et s'efforçait de les retrouver dans les textes imprimés toujours indéchiffrables. [...] Il sut s'élancer d'une image jusqu'à atteindre une autre en s'y adaptant bien. On eut l'impression qu'il faisait mine de lire; en fait, il lisait vraiment ce que sa délirante imagination y projetait à chaque fois.[1]

> [The little boy would rewrite the books according to the pictures, inventing stories that he then would try to find in the printed (and still indecipherable) text. He discovered how to launch himself from one picture and carry on until he reached the next one. [...] He seemed to be pretending to read, when in fact he really was reading what his frenzied imagination projected each time upon the page.]

The child's way of reading is as risky as it is rewarding. He launches himself into the indecipherable spaces between the pictures, risking the gaps and his family's scepticism. In spite of this, Chamoiseau is unequivocal about the value of this practice: 'en fait, il lisait vraiment' [in fact he really was reading]. The risks are worth the reward of engaging with material that challenges him to create meaning. This encounter draws stories from his imagination whose origin lies partly within him and partly in the books under his gaze. It is a creatively provisional, and provisionally creative practice. It will give way to a new way of reading when the child learns the letters of the alphabet, but the value placed on knowing an inner world better through engagement with the unknown will remain.

The reading practices of the author of this book also involve risky movements between specificities. These movements require rapid adjustments between take-off and landing, as the points of departure and arrival differ greatly. Like the young Chamoiseau, comparatists will be familiar with raised eyebrows within their professional families. Yet, as in the case of Chamoiseau, this novice form of reading has value in telling us more about the moves available to the critical imagination. The challenge of such a form of reading is to find a way of moving between images and writing settled in very different geographical, historical and cultural niches. It raises the question of the relationship between the specific works of these authors and the wider context from which they emerge. The four tropes which have been examined in this book — home, the space between languages, the traumatic and the ludic — all serve as ways to maintain tension between the history of the self and wider histories.

As explored in the first chapter, the interior space of the home can be mapped on to many other spaces, from interior, mental spaces like the inner life of the child, to larger, collective spaces such as that of the nation. Images of the home's boundaries then call up questions about what is interior and exterior to the self, the family and the nation. This contemplation of individual buildings roots wider questions about the boundaries of the self, the family and the nation in a specific geographical location and moment in time. The border-crossing histories which reshape the adult author's view of his childhood home become present in images of windows and walls: the 'Coiffeur Dames' sign on the house on rue Vilin; the filigree pattern on the window through which Nabokov witnesses killings; the burning walls of Chamoiseau's wooden home. In these images, safety and danger, the public and the private, the first language and later languages are intertwined.

This interstitial intertwining of languages is present in these authors' style, as we saw in the second chapter. In Perec's *W ou le souvenir d'enfance*, Chamoiseau's *Une enfance créole* and Nabokov's first foray into autobiography, 'Mademoiselle O', we see what Françoise Lionnet calls 'the becoming-transnational' of French studies, as each author creates a text which calls for readings attentive to the resonances of other languages within French, and the resonances of French within other languages.[2] This 'becoming-transnational' is something that occurs in the present of writing (and of reading) and which shapes the literary future, but these authors also reach back into the past of the French literary tradition, drawing attention to nineteenth-century attempts to write near and distant places in the light of the colonial migrations of that era.

The migratory present of French literature and the way each author creates texts which can be read on a variety of levels, depending on how many languages the reader speaks, imply a variegated literary space, formed by different histories whose co-presence both calls for and raises questions about comparison and the ethical dilemmas it brings. The dual engagement with specificity and generality is present in the way these texts approach the trauma of personal loss. These authors all draw attention to specific images of marks of trauma while mapping these fixed images on to various contexts, as Perec does through the diagonal scar on his upper lip. Through movements between echoes of trauma resonating at different generational distances from the event itself, connections become visible between Nabokov's witnessing of murders in turn-of-the-century St Petersburg, Perec's slow apprehension of his parents' death through the hushed voices of relatives, and Chamoiseau's loss of his first language in the frightening world of the school. The way such movements offer insights into both these texts and the theories developed to conceptualize literary expressions of trauma suggests the value of following these authors in the imaginative connections they draw between their own histories and those lived through by other people.

The slanted line on Perec's upper lip inscribes personal and cultural loss, but also gestures towards a practice of writing where oblique approaches are valued as a means of renewing perception. The dual meaning of the scar is one element which complicates attempts to fit these authors' works too neatly into a trauma paradigm which their emphasis on the value of conscious memory resists. The slanted line, first conceived by Viktor Shklovsky as an image for the oblique paths of literary art, itself circulates in surprising ways from Shklovsky to Nabokov and then to Perec. In this view literary thinking encourages the reader to think again, to look at the familiar in new ways. Through the loose connection Perec and Chamoiseau share to the *Internationale situationniste*, we see this approach shifting and being adapted to a neo-colonial context. The knight's move, which becomes the twisting paths of the marbles in Martinican soil, speaks both of trauma and of conscious memory, of estrangement in its painful political and salutary literary guises. It is the most condensed expression of these author's approach to the past, which fuses regret over severance from an ancestral culture and language with an exploration of the modes of cultural belonging possible in the light of family histories of state oppression, migration and translation.

The unlikely genealogy running from Shklovsky to Chamoiseau raises the question of what it means to group different literary works. This question is considered playfully and seriously by Perec in an essay entitled 'Notes brèves sur l'art et la manière de ranger ses livres' [Brief Notes on the Art and Craft of Sorting Books]. Unlike Jules Verne's Captain Nemo, Perec writes, most readers cannot pack up twelve thousand books into a submarine and plunge twenty thousand leagues under the sea.[3] Such a bold step would allow the reader to resolve once and for all the question of which books she needs and how to arrange them. As it is, we are faced with what Perec calls 'une humanité qui s'obstine à penser, à écrire, et surtout à publier' [a world in which people carry on thinking, writing, and, above all, writing books].[4] As Perec points out, a library that one does not continually tidy becomes messy: entropy at work on the bookshelf.[5] Both Perec and Chamoiseau draw attention to the counterpoint of chance and design in the coming together of different books, pointing to the limits of ordering systems, their tendency to be overtaken by fortune. If there is value in thinking about how to put books together, it lies in the questioning of ordering principles rather than in the hope of establishing a finally satisfactory system.

This book has been undertaken in sympathy with Perec's essay, with a preference for a messy bookshelf over a tidy one, but still curious about how one might organize a bookshelf if one were to go about such a task. The ordering principle I have experimented with is one which places national, linguistic and geographical borders at the centre of its enquiry rather than around it. This is a different ordering principle from those currently employed in much Modern Languages research and teaching. Linguistic boundaries generally frame the study of each individual Modern Language, and within each language, geographical borders create further sub-divisions. We see these kinds of divisions and sub-divisions, for example, in *The Year's Work in Modern Language Studies*.[6] There are excellent reasons for such an approach, not least the need for scholars to have linguistic and (inter-)cultural competence to understand a given piece of writing. Yet such a framework does not lend itself easily to investigations of what it means for authors to move across linguistic and geographical spaces, nor for thinking through the implications of one language being spoken in a range of different geographies, questions which are important in the light of ongoing histories of migration and language change which entangle separate linguistic and geographical spaces.

My experimentation with another ordering principle offers one way of thinking through such questions. This study performs its own kind of knight's move, where, by looking outward from French studies to comparative literature, I can look back to French studies with a renewed perspective. The work of David Damrosch is helpful in performing these moves. Damrosch notes that for a long time, 'comparatists almost always worked across linguistic as well as national borders, ceding to national literature specialists their long-held primacy in their "national language" of choice, even when that language was spoken in various nations'.[7] He notes that such disciplinary divisions rested on the idea of an equivalency between language and nation, an idea which 'was almost always a fiction, and [...] is becoming more and more tenuous'.[8] Looked at one way, and especially in its second chapter, this study answers Damrosch's call for a constructively monolingual comparative criticism. In its explorations of these authors' use of French to write a life shaped by language change, this book brings out the range of relationships possible to one language and the different ends to which it is put depending on how, where and when the author comes to it. Looked at another way, *Memory Across Borders* does work across languages. By looking at the different languages present in the writing of one text (a single version for Perec and Chamoiseau; multiple versions for Nabokov), the study elaborates a model of comparative criticism attentive to the multiple languages and cultural affiliations present within one text, rather than seeing texts as the product of one literary culture which can be compared with another. Looked at a third way, the study goes beyond Damrosch's call for comparative criticism that would work within one language. By bringing together Chamoiseau and Perec, it offers an example of comparative criticism that works within one nation as well as one language, drawing attention to the way a national literary tradition can be complicated from its centre as well as from its supposed peripheries. Looking back to French Studies from these various modes of comparative criticism, the French language comes to lose its guise as a national language, even one which is complicated by a postcolonial periphery, and instead emerges as a 'variegated world language'.[9] The word 'variegated' is important here: this is not a space in which any kind of movement is possible. Rather it is created by histories of immobility, pain and oppression whose resonances continue to hamper movement within it to this day. Precisely because of the histories which both create and fragment French-language literary space, careful experimentation is needed to establish ethical ways of moving between its different points.

The readings of home, style, trauma and the ludic here demonstrate that there is no one border of French literary culture across which an author can definitively step. Rather, French centres and peripheries are intertwined in the lives and texts of these authors; they meet, clash and are remade in the home, in the self, in language, in the writing of memory and the memory of writing, where they come up against and are changed by the other languages and histories that shape the authors' lives. Nor are moves into or out of French literary space definitive. Rather, as we see in the example of Nabokov, who ends his autobiography with an image of his family walking through the streets of Saint-Nazaire towards the ship which will take them to America, French literary space can be passed through and left behind, only to resonate through his English-language writing in his repeated returns to the governess who is the subject of the first autobiographical sketch. Perec's W island, which disrupts any stable hierarchy or division between 'old' and 'new' worlds, offers another image of the way even French-language life-writing by a lifelong Parisian can undercut its own origins in a national centre. Another kind of shifting in and out of French literary space takes place in Chamoiseau's text, with its switches from French to Creole and the ambivalence about whether the translations given are for a French metropolitan reader or a fellow Martinican. The work of these authors is part of the 'becoming-transnational' precisely because it complicates the boundaries between French literary expression and what lies outside it.

These authors' movements into the French language, or the way the language travels to them, are closely connected to the history of portrayals of that language as inherently civilized. Nabokov speaks French as part of the legacy of the Russian nobility's eighteenth-century adoption of French, an adoption that was part of a continent-wide phenomenon of French becoming 'the European language of diplomacy, aristocratic society, science, learning and literature'.[10] French took on this role partly because of French speakers' successful projection of the language as the natural idiom of civilized thought, education and manners whose word order uniquely predisposed it to the clear expression of abstract concepts and logical argument.[11] It is the same conception of the French language which drives the colonial policies which lead the *Maître* to impose French on the young Chamoiseau in a mid-twentieth-century school in Martinique, and which leads Perec's Aunt Esther to speak of her move from Eastern Europe to Paris as a move 'from the ghetto to the light'.[12] Specifically, Esther Bienenfeld said that one lifetime was not enough to make such a move. Her comment draws attention to the way the promise of assimilation held out with various degrees of privilege and violence to the Nabokov, Perec and Chamoiseau families creates lives which straddle two or more linguistic and cultural communities. What is created through moves towards the 'light' of France, whether forced, willed or somewhere in between, is a particular relationship to the language expressed in writing practices whose resonances this book has begun to explore. The connections between the individual francophonie of each author point towards often unremarked continuities between the older, European francophonie, where French operated as an aristocratic lingua franca, and its more recent institutional incarnation as a state policy of maintaining links between France and its former and current colonial possessions. It further points to connections between the belief in the 'universal' qualities of the French language which underlie both versions of francophonie, and the idea of France as offering the promise of assimilation to immigrants irrespective of religious or national background, whose tensions are explored in the metropolitan French writing of Georges Perec. Such connections suggest it is worth paying further attention to the ramified effects of the projection, migration and return of images of the French language within and without Europe, at the centre of the metropole as well as beyond its borders.

Consideration of this long history of francophonie has a place within a model of transnational French studies adequate to the challenges of reading beyond the nation while keeping in sight its material and ideological power. Even the very brief summary above of the particular image of France which leads each author to French and the image of France which emerges from each author's work will indicate the degree to which the 'becoming-transnational' of French writing is intimately connected with specific French national policies and events, the *départmentalisation* of Martinique in Chamoiseau's case, 1920s and 1930s immigration rules in Perec's case, the 1940 invasion for Nabokov. If I argue for a comparative literature both within and beyond the French language, it is not because I think the nation-state has become irrelevant. As seen in the controversy over the *littérature-monde* manifesto, every attempt to rethink the literary sphere associated with the French language runs the risk of replicating the centripetal hierarchies which, in a practical sense, govern the production of French-language literary works. As much as these authors' work sits uneasily in national frames and calls to be read beyond them, in its witness to the way the nation can hurt and kill, it is a warning against ignoring its power. In Chamoiseau's image of the falling whip meeting a vulnerable Caribbean body, in the blow of the ski inscribing the movement of Hebrew writing above Perec's mouth, in Nabokov's memory of anxiety over the violence of the French police as he walks through a Parisian park with his child, a fragile form of memory emerges.[13] This is a memory which crosses the borders of the nation to look back to migrations and histories of violence which complicate the author's current allegiances. It crosses the borders of self and other as it becomes an exploration of what binds and separates one generation from the next and in doing so crosses linguistic borders. Opening these books and encountering these border-crossing memories challenges the critic to explore the spaces between specificities, to find a way to read them together and to rethink the place of borders in literary study.

Notes to the Conclusion

1. *Chemin*, 200–01.
2. 'Introduction', in *Francophone Studies: New Landscapes*, ed. by Françoise Lionnet and Dominic Thomas (*Modern Language Notes*, 118:4 (2003), 783–86 (p. 784)).
3. *Penser/Classer*, p. 33.
4. *Penser/Classer*, p. 34.
5. *Penser/Classer*, p. 38.
6. There is increasing questioning of this framework, as, for example, in the announcement of a new Liverpool University Press series, 'Transnational Modern Languages', <http://liverpooluniversitypress.co.uk/collections/series-transnational-modern-languages> [accessed 15 May 2016].
7. 'Global Comparatism and the Question of Language', *PMLA*, 128 (2013), 622–28 (p. 623).
8. Damrosch, pp. 623–24.
9. Charles Forsdick, 'Between "French" and "Francophone": French Studies and the Postcolonial Turn', *French Studies*, 59 (2005), 523–30 (p. 528).
10. Gésine Argent, Vladislav Rjéoutski and Derek Offord, 'European Francophonie and a Framework for its Study', in *European Francophonie: The Social, Political and Cultural History of an International Prestige Language*, ed. by Vladislav Rjéoutski, Gésine Argent and Derek Offord (Berne: Peter Lang, 2014), pp. 1–33 (p. 2).
11. Gésine Argent, Vladislav Rjéoutski and Derek Offord, 'European Francophonie', in *European Francophonie*, ed. by Rjéoutski, Argent and Offord, p. 13.
12. Bellos, pp. 16–17.
13. *Chemin*, 103; *W*, 142–43; *SM*, 240.

BIBLIOGRAPHY

Manuscript Sources

New York, The New York Public Library, The Henry W. and Albert A. Berg Collection of English and American Literature, Vladimir Nabokov Papers

Washington, D.C., Library of Congress, Manuscript Division, Vladimir Vladimirovich Nabokov Papers, Boxes 9 and 10

Primary Works

ANTELME, ROBERT, *L'Espèce humaine* (Paris: Gallimard, 1957)
ASSOCIATION OULIPO, *La Littérature potentielle: créations, re-créations, récréations* (Paris: Gallimard, 1973)
BAUDELAIRE, CHARLES, *Selected Poems*, trans. by Geoffrey Atheling Wagner (London: Falcon, 1946)
—— *Les Fleurs du mal*, ed. by Jacques Dupont (Paris: Flammarion, 1999)
BERBEROVA, NINA, *Курсив мой* (Munich: Fink, 1972)
CÉSAIRE, AIMÉ, *Cahier du retour au pays natal*, ed. by Abiola Irele (Ibadan: New Horn, 1994)
—— *Discours sur le colonialisme* (Paris: Présence Africaine, 1955)
CHAMOISEAU, PATRICK, *À bout d'enfance* (Paris: Gallimard, 2005)
—— *Antan d'enfance* (Paris: Gallimard, 1990)
—— *Au Temps de l'Antan* (Paris: Hatier, 1988)
—— *Chemin-d'école* (Paris: Gallimard, 1996)
—— *Childhood*, trans. by Carol Volk (London: Granta, 1999)
—— *Un dimanche au cachot* (Paris: Gallimard, 2007)
—— *De la mémoire obscure à la mémoire consciente* (Paris: Gallimard, 2010)
—— *Écrire en pays dominé* (Paris: Gallimard, 2002)
—— *L'Empreinte à Crusoé* (Paris: Gallimard, 2012)
—— and RAPHAËL CONFIANT, *Lettres créoles: tracées antillaises et continentales de la littérature: Haïti, Guadeloupe, Martinique, Guyane 1635–1975* (Paris: Gallimard, 1999)
—— and ÉDOUARD GLISSANT, *L'Esclave vieil homme et le molosse* (Paris: Gallimard, 1997)
—— *Les Neuf Consciences du Malfini* (Paris: Gallimard, 2009)
—— and JANICE MORGAN, 'Re-imagining Diversity and Connection in the Chaos World: An Interview with Patrick Chamoiseau', *Callaloo*, 31 (2008), 443–53
—— *School Days*, trans. by Linda Coverdale (London: Granta, 1997)
—— *Solibo magnifique* (Paris: Gallimard, 1988)
—— *Texaco* (Paris: Gallimard, 1992)
CONDÉ, MARYSE, *Le Cœur à rire et à pleurer: contes vrais de mon enfance* (Paris: Robert Laffont, 1999)
CONFIANT, RAPHAËL, *Ravines du devant-jour* (Paris: Gallimard, 1993)
—— <http://www.potomitan.info/dictionnaire/b.pdf>, consulted 21 November 2015
DANTE ALIGHIERI, *De vulgari eloquentia*, trans. and ed. by Steven Botterill (Cambridge: Cambridge University Press, 1996)

Deguy, Michel, *A ce qui n'en finit pas: thrène* (Paris: Seuil, 1995)
Didion, Joan, *The Year of Magical Thinking* (London: Fourth Estate, 2005)
Éluard, Paul, *Le Dur Désir de durer: le temps déborde* (Paris: Seghers, 1960)
Gille, Élisabeth, *Un paysage de cendres* (Paris: Seuil, 1996)
Hoffman, Eva, *Lost in Translation: A Life in a New Language* (London: Vintage, 1998)
Ibañez, Blasco, *Les Arènes sanglantes* (Paris: Calmann-Lévy, 1923)
Kaplan, Chaim, *Scroll of Agony: The Warsaw Diary of Chaim A. Kaplan*, trans. and ed. by Abraham Isaac Katsh (London: Hamilton, 1966)
Khodasevich, Vladimir, *Некрополь* (Moscow: Vagrius, 2001 [1939])
Kofman, Sarah, *Rue Ordener, rue Labat* (Paris: Galilée, 1994)
Leiris, Michel, *L'Age d'homme, précédé de de la littérature considérée comme tauromachie* (Paris: Gallimard, 1946)
Modiano, Patrick, *Dora Bruder*, ed. by Bruno Doucey and Marc-Henri Arfeux (Paris: Gallimard, 2004)
Nabokov, Vladimir, *Ada or Ardor: A Family Chronicle* (London: Weidenfeld & Nicolson, 1969)
—— *The Annotated Lolita*, ed. by Alfred Appel, Jr. (London: Weidenfeld & Nicolson, 1993)
—— *Collected Poems*, trans. by Dmitri Nabokov, ed. by Thomas Karshan (London: Penguin, 2013)
—— *Conclusive Evidence* (New York: Harper, 1951)
—— *Дар* (St Petersburg: Simpozium, 2000)
—— *Другие берега* (Ann Arbor: Ardis, 1978)
—— *Король, дама, валет* (St Petersburg: Simpozium, 2000)
—— *Lolita* (Harmondsworth: Penguin, 2000)
—— *Машенька* (St Petersburg: Simpozium, 2000)
—— *Отчаяние* (St Petersburg: Simpozium, 2000)
—— *Pnin* (New York: Avon, 1957)
—— *Приглашение на казнь* (St Petersburg: Simpozium, 2000)
—— *Speak, Memory: An Autobiography Revisited* (London: David Campbell, 1999)
—— *Strong Opinions* (London: Weidenfeld & Nicolson, 1974)
—— *The Stories of Vladimir Nabokov* (London: Penguin, 1995)
—— *Защита Лужина* (St Petersburg: Simpozium, 2000)
Nabokoff-Sirine, Vladimir, 'Mademoiselle O', *Mesures*, 2 (1936), 143–72
Pater, Walter, *The Child in the House: An Imaginary Portrait* (Boston: Everett, 1895)
Perec, Georges, *Un cabinet d'amateur* (Paris: Balland, 1979)
—— *Les Choses: une histoire des années soixantes* (Paris: Poche, 2002)
—— *La Disparition* (Paris: Denoël, 1969)
—— *Ellis Island* (Paris: P.O.L., 1995)
—— *Entretiens et conférences*, ed. by Dominique Bertelli and Mireille Ribière, 2 vols (Nantes: Joseph K., 2003)
—— *Espèces d'espaces* (Paris: Galilée, 1974)
—— *Un homme qui dort* (Paris: Denoël, 1967)
—— *L'Infra-ordinaire* (Paris: Seuil, 1989)
—— *Je suis né* (Paris: Seuil, 1990)
—— *Je me souviens* (Paris: Hachette, 1978)
—— *L.G.: une aventure des années soixante* (Paris, Seuil, 1992)
—— *Penser/Classer* (Paris: Hachette, 1985)
—— *Tentative d'épuisement d'un lieu parisien* (Paris: C. Bourgois, 1982)
—— *Thoughts of Sorts*, trans. and ed. by David Bellos (London: Notting Hill Editions, 2011)
—— *La Vie mode d'emploi: romans* (Paris: Poche, 2002)
—— *W ou le souvenir d'enfance* (Paris: Denoël, 1975)

—— *W or the Memory of Childhood*, trans. by David Bellos (London: Vintage, 1996)
PINEAU, GISÈLE, *L'Exil selon Julia: récit* (Paris: Stock, 1996)
PRICE, RICHARD, *The Convict and the Colonel* (Durham, NC: Duke University Press, 2006)
——, and SALLY PRICE, 'Shadowboxing in the Mangrove', *Cultural Anthropology*, 12 (1997), 3–36
PROUST, MARCEL, *A la recherche du temps perdu*, 16 vols (Paris: Gallimard, 1914–1927)
PUSHKIN, ALEKSANDR, *Eugene Onegin: A Novel in Verse*, trans. by Vladimir Nabokov, 4 vols (London: Routledge & Kegan Paul 1964)
ROUSSET, DAVID, *L'Univers concentrationnaire* (Paris: Pavois, 1946)
SEGAL, LORE GROSZMANN, *Other People's Houses* (London: Victor Gollancz, 1965)
TOLSTOY, LEO, Детство, ed. by B. Faden (Oxford: Blackwell, 1975)
UPCHURCH, ROBERT, *Ælfric's Lives of the Virgin Spouses, with Modern English Parallel-Text Translations* (Exeter: University of Exeter Press, 2007)
VEGH, CLAUDINE, *Je ne lui ai pas dit au revoir: des enfants de déportés parlent* (Paris: Gallimard, 1979)
TERAPIANO, IURII, Встречи (New York: Izdatel'stvo imeni Chekhova, 1953)
VERNE, JULES, *L'Île mystérieuse*, 3 vols (Paris: Hachette, 1918–1919)
ZOBEL, JOSEPH, *La Rue Cases-Nègres* (Paris: Jean Froissart, 1950)

Secondary Sources

ABRAHAM, NICOLAS, and MARIA TOROK, *The Shell and the Kernel: Renewals of Psychoanalysis*, trans. and ed. by Nicholas T. Rand (Chicago: University of Chicago Press, 1994)
ALEXANDER, JEFFREY C., 'Toward a Theory of Cultural Trauma', in *Cultural Trauma and Collective Identity*, ed. by Jeffrey C. Alexander (Berkeley: University of California Press, 2004), pp. 1–30
ALEXANDROV, VLADIMIR E., *Nabokov's Otherworld* (Princeton: Princeton University Press, 1991)
——, ed., *The Garland Companion to Vladimir Nabokov* (London: Garland, 1995)
ANDREWS, DAVID, 'Varieties of Determinism: Nabokov among Rorty, Freud and Sartre', *Nabokov Studies*, 6 (2000–2001), 1–33
APTER, EMILY, 'French Colonial Studies and Postcolonial Theory', *SubStance*, 24 (1995), 169–80
—— *The Translation Zone: A New Comparative Literature* (Princeton, NJ: Princeton University Press, 2006)
——'Lexilalia: On Translating a Dictionary of Untranslatable Philosophical Terms', *Paragraph*, 38 (2015), 159–73
ARENDT, HANNAH, *The Origins of Totalitarianism* (London: G. Allen & Unwin, 1958)
ARGENT, GÉSINE, VLADISLAV RJÉOUTSKI and DEREK OFFORD, eds, *European Francophonie: The Social, Political and Cultural History of an International Prestige Language* (Berne: Peter Lang, 2014)
ASHCROFT, BILL, GARETH GRIFFITHS and HELEN TIFFIN, eds, *The Postcolonial Studies Reader* (London: Routledge, 1995)
AZAM ZANGANEH, LILA, *The Enchanter: Nabokov and Happiness* (London: Allen Lane, 2011)
BACHELARD, GASTON, *La Poétique de l'espace* (Paris: Presses universitaires de France, 1957)
BAR-ON, DAN, *Fear and Hope: Three Generations of the Holocaust* (Cambridge, MA: Harvard University Press, 1995)
BARTHES, ROLAND, *La Chambre claire: note sur la photographie* (Paris: Gallimard 1980)
BARCLAY, FIONA, *Writing Postcolonial France: Haunting, Literature, and the Maghreb* (Lanham: Lexington, 2011)
BASSNETT, SUSAN, and HARISH TRIVEDI, 'Introduction: Of Colonies, Cannibals and Verna-

culars', in *Postcolonial Translation: Theory and Practice*, ed. by Susan Bassnett and Harish Trivedi (London: Routledge, 1999), pp. 1–19

BÉHAR, STELLA, *Georges Perec: écrire pour ne pas dire* (New York: P. Lang, 1995)

BELLOS, DAVID, *Georges Perec: A Life in Words* (Boston, MA: David R. Godine, 1993)

BÉNABOU, MARCEL, JEAN-YVES POUILLOUX and JULIA KRISTEVA, eds, *W ou le souvenir d'enfance: une fiction* (Paris: U.E.R., 1988)

BERNABÉ, J., 'La langue comme fétiche'. <http://www.potomitan.info/articles/guerre/fetiche.html>, consulted 3 March 2011

——, PATRICK CHAMOISEAU and RAPHAËL CONFIANT, *Éloge de la créolité/In Praise of Creoleness (bilingual edition)*, trans. by M.B. Taleb-Khyar (Paris: Gallimard, 1993)

BHABHA, HOMI K., *The Location of Culture* (Abingdon: Routledge, 2004)

BLANCHOT, MAURICE, 'Everyday Speech', trans. by S. Hanson, *Yale French Studies*, 73 (1987), 12–20

—— *L'Entretien infini* (Paris: Gallimard, 1969)

BONGIE, CHRIS, *Islands and Exiles: The Créole Identities of Post/colonial Literature* (Stanford: Stanford University Press, 1998)

BOUCHOT, VINCENT, 'L'intertextualité vernienne dans *W ou le souvenir d'enfance*', *Études littéraires*, 23 (1990), 111–20

BOYD, BRIAN, *Stalking Nabokov* (New York: Columbia University Press, 2011)

—— *Vladimir Nabokov: The American Years* (Princeton: Princeton University Press, 1991)

—— *Vladimir Nabokov: The Russian Years* (Princeton: Princeton University Press, 1993)

BOYLE, CLAIRE, *Consuming Autobiographies: Reading and Writing the Self in Post-War France* (Oxford: Legenda, 2007)

BRAIDOTTI, ROSI, *Nomadic Subjectivities: Embodiment and Sexual Difference in Contemporary Feminist Theory*, 2nd edn, (New York: Columbia University Press, 2011)

BRITTON, CELIA, *Édouard Glissant and Postcolonial Theory: Strategies of Language and Resistance* (Charlottesville: University Press of Virginia, 1999)

—— *Language and Literary Form in French Caribbean Writing* (Liverpool: Liverpool University Press, 2014)

BRODSKY, ANNA, 'Nabokov's Lolita and the Postwar Emigré Consciousness', in *Realms of Exile: Nomadism, Diasporas and Eastern European Voices*, ed. by Dominica Radulescu (Lanham: Lexington, 2002), pp. 49–67

BROWN, LAURA S., 'Not Outside the Range: One Feminist Perspective on Psychic Trauma', *American Imago*, 48 (1991), 119–33

BRUSS, ELIZABETH W., *Autobiographical Acts: The Changing Situation of a Literary Genre* (Baltimore, MD: Johns Hopkins University Press, 1976)

BUGROVA, LARISA, *Мотив дома в русской романтической прозе 20-х и 30-х годов XIX века* (Tver': Forum, 2003)

BULLITT, MARGARET M., 'Rousseau and Tolstoy: Childhood and Confession', *Comparative Literature Studies*, 16 (1979), 12–20

BURGELIN, CLAUDE, *Les Parties de dominos chez Monsieur Lefèvre: Perec avec Freud, Perec contre Freud* (Strasbourg: Circé, 1996)

—— *Georges Perec* (Paris: Seuil, 1988)

BUSH, RONALD, 'Tennis by the Book: Lolita and the Game of Modernist Fiction', in *Transitional Nabokov*, ed. by Will Norman and Duncan White (Oxford: Peter Lang, 2012), pp. 265–85

CAMPBELL, JANET, 'Rhythms of the Suggestive Unconscious', *Subjectivity*, 26 (2009), 29–51

CARUTH, CATHY, *Unclaimed Experience: Trauma, Narrative and History* (Baltimore, MD: Johns Hopkins University Press, 1996)

CASSIN, BARBARA, 'The Energy of the Untranslatables: Translation as a Paradigm for the Human Sciences', *Paragraph*, 38 (2015), 145–58

CHAMBERS, IAIN, *Migrancy, Culture, Identity* (London: Routledge, 1994)
CHILDS, PETER, *Modernism* (London: Routledge, 2000)
CONDÉ, MARYSE, and MADELEINE COTTENET-HAGE, eds, *Penser la créolité* (Paris: Karthala, 1995)
CONNERTON, PAUL, *How Societies Remember* (Cambridge: Cambridge University Press, 1989)
CONNOLLY, JULIAN W., ed., *The Cambridge Companion to Nabokov* (Cambridge: Cambridge University Press, 2005)
CONSTANT, ISABELLE, KAHIUDI C. MABANA and PHILIP NANTON, eds, *Antillanité, créolité, littérature-monde* (Newcastle: Cambridge Scholars, 2013)
COOPER, SARA-LOUISE, '"Des fils invisibles nous relient": Comparative Memory in Caribbean Life-writing', *Francosphères*, 5 (2016), 29–43
COUTURIER, MAURICE, *Nabokov, ou, la cruauté du désir* (Seyssel: Champ Vallon, 2004)
DAMROSCH, DAVID, 'Comparative Literature?', *PMLA*, 118 (2003), 326–30
—— 'Global Comparatism and the Question of Language', *PMLA*, 128 (2013), 622–28
DASH, MICHAEL J., *The Other America: Caribbean Literature in a New World Context* (Charlottesville: University Press of Virginia, 1998)
—— 'Caraïbe Fantôme: The Play of Difference in the Francophone Caribbean', *Yale French Studies*, 103 (2003), 93–105
DAVIDSON, PERCY E., *The Recapitulation Theory and Human Infancy* (New York: Teachers College, Columbia University, 1914)
DAVIS, GREGSON, *Aimé Césaire* (Cambridge: Cambridge University Press, 1997)
DEAN, CAROLYN J., 'History and Holocaust Representation', review of *Traumatic Realism: The Demands of Holocaust Representation*, by Michael Rothberg, *History and Theory*, 41 (2002), 239–49
DELEUZE, GILLES, and FÉLIX GUATTARI, *Mille plateaux: capitalisme et schizophrénie* (Paris: Éditions de Minuit, 1980)
DEREWAL, TIFFANY, and MATTHEW ROTH, 'John Shade's Duplicate Selves: An Alternative Shadean Theory of Pale Fire', *NOJ/НОЖ: Nabokov Online Journal*, 3 (2009)
DOLININ, ALEKSANDR, 'Nabokov's Time Doubling: From *The Gift* to *Lolita*', *Nabokov Studies*, 2 (1995), 3–40
DUREAU, YONA, *Nabokov, ou, le sourire du chat* (Paris: L'Harmattan, 2001)
EAKIN, PAUL JOHN, *Fictions in Autobiography: Studies in the Art of Self-Invention* (Princeton: Princeton University Press, 1985)
—— *How Our Lives Become Stories: Making Selves* (Ithaca, NY: Cornell University Press, 1999)
ELLENBERGER, HENRI F., *The Discovery of the Unconscious: The History and Evolution of Dynamic Psychiatry* (New York: Basic Books, 1970)
ELIOT, GEORGE, *The Mill on the Floss* (London: Vintage, 2010)
FABIAN, JOHANNES, *Time and the Other: How Anthropology Makes its Object* (New York: Columbia University Press, 2002)
FANON, FRANTZ, *Peau noire, masques blancs* (Paris: Seuil, 1992)
FEIGEL, LARA, and MAX SAUNDERS, 'Writing Between the Lives: Life Writing and the Work of Mediation', *Life Writing*, 9 (2012), 241–48
FELMAN, SHOSHANA, and DORI LAUB, *Testimony: Crises of Witnessing in Literature, Psychoanalysis and History* (London: Routledge, 1992)
FORSDICK, CHARLES, '"Worlds in Collision:" The Languages and Locations of World Literature', in *A Companion to Comparative Literature*, ed. by Ali Behdad and Dominic Thomas (Oxford: Wiley-Blackwell, 2011), pp. 473–89
—— 'Between "French" and "Francophone": French Studies and the Postcolonial Turn', *French Studies*, 59 (2005), 523–30
FOSTER, JOHN BURT, *Nabokov's Art of Memory and European Modernism* (Princeton: Princeton University Press, 1993)

——'Poshlust, Culture Criticism, Adorno and Malraux', in *Nabokov and his Fiction: New Perspectives*, ed. by Julian Connolly (Cambridge: Cambridge University Press, 1999), pp. 216-35
FORSDICK, CHARLES and DAVID MURPHY, eds, *Postcolonial Thought in the French-speaking World* (Liverpool: Liverpool University Press, 2009)
FRESCO, NADINE, 'Remembering the Unknown', *International Review of Psychoanalysis*, 11 (1984), 417-27
FREUD, SIGMUND, 'The Uncanny', in *The Uncanny*, ed. by Hugh Haughton, trans. by David McLintock (London: Penguin, 2003) pp. 123-61 (first publ. in *Imago*, 5 (1919), 297-324)
——'Mourning and Melancholia', *The Standard Edition of the Complete Psychological Work of Sigmund Freud*, trans. by James Strachey, 24 vols (London: Hogarth Press, 1953-1970), XIV (1957), 243-58
GALLAGHER, MARY, *Soundings in French Caribbean Writing since 1950* (Oxford: Oxford University Press, 2002)
——, ed., *Ici-Là: Place and Displacement in Caribbean Writing in French* (Amsterdam: Rodopi, 2003)
GLISSANT, ÉDOUARD, *Le Discours antillais* (Paris: Seuil, 1981)
——*Introduction à une poétique du divers* (Paris: Gallimard, 1996)
GOLDBERG, DAVID THEO, 'The Comparative and the Relational: Meditations on Racial Method', in *A Companion to Comparative Literature*, ed. by Ali Behdad and Dominic Thomas (Oxford: Wiley-Blackwell, 2011), pp. 357-67
GNOCCHI, MARIA CHIARA, 'Du Flurkistan et d'ailleurs: Les Réactions au manifeste "Pour une littérature-monde en français"', *Francofonia*, 59 (2010), 87-105
GRAYSON, JANE, *Nabokov Translated: A Comparison of Nabokov's Russian and English Prose* (Oxford: Oxford University Press, 1977)
——, ARNOLD B. MCMILLIN and PRISCILLA MEYER, eds, *Nabokov's World: The Shape of Nabokov's World* (Basingstoke: Palgrave, 2002)
GRUBRICH-SIMITIS, ILSE, 'From Concretism to Metaphor: Thoughts on some Theoretical and Technical Aspects of Work with the Children of Holocaust Survivors', *Psychoanalytic Study of the Child*, 39 (1984), 301-29
HAMILTON, TREVOR, *Immortal Longings: F. W. H. Myers and the Victorian Search for Life after Death* (Exeter: Imprint Academic, 2009)
HARDWICK, LOUISE, *Childhood, Autobiography and the Francophone Caribbean* (Liverpool: Liverpool University Press, 2013)
——'Telling Tales: Childhood and Autobiography in the Francophone Caribbean' (unpublished doctoral thesis, University of Oxford, 2009)
HARGREAVES, ALEC G., CHARLES FORSDICK and DAVID MURPHY, EDS, *Transnational French Studies: Postcolonialism and Littérature-monde* (Liverpool: Liverpool University Press, 2010)
HARTMAN, GEOFFREY, *The Longest Shadow: In the Aftermath of the Holocaust* (Basingstoke: Palgrave Macmillan, 1996)
HECK, MARYLINE, *Georges Perec: le corps à la lettre* (Paris: Corti, 2012)
HELLER-ROAZEN, DANIEL, *Echolalias: On the Forgetting of Language* (New York: Zone, 2005)
HEYWOOD, SOPHIE, *Catholicism and Children's Literature in France: The Comtesse de Ségur (1799–1874)* (Manchester: Manchester University Press, 2011)
HIRSCH, MARIANNE, *Family Frames: Photography, Narrative and Postmemory* (Cambridge, MA: Harvard University Press, 1997)
——*The Generation of Postmemory: Writing and Visual Culture after the Holocaust* (New York: Columbia University Press, 2012)
HUDNALL STAMM, BETH, and others, 'Considering a Theory of Cultural Trauma and Loss', *Journal of Loss and Trauma*, 9 (2004), 89-111
HUIZINGA, JOHAN, *Homo Ludens* (London: Paladin, 1970)

JENSON, DEBORAH, 'Kidnapped Narratives: Mobility without Autonomy and the Nation/Novel Analogy', in *A Companion to Comparative Literature*, ed. by Ali Behdad and Dominic Thomas (Oxford: Wiley-Blackwell, 2011), pp. 369–86

JOHNSON, D. BARTON, 'Vladimir Nabokov and Walter de la Mare's "Otherword"', *Nabokov's World: The Shape of Nabokov's World*, ed. by Priscilla Meyer, Jane Grayson and Arnold B. McMillin (Basingstoke: Palgrave, 2002), pp. 71–87

JOHNSON, GEORGE M., *Dynamic Psychology in Modernist British Fiction* (Basingstoke: Palgrave Macmillan, 2006)

JONES, ELIZABETH H., *Spaces of Belonging: Home, Identity and Culture in Twentieth-Century French Autobiography* (Amsterdam: Rodopi, 2007)

JONES, W. GARETH, 'The Nature of the Communication between Author and Reader in Tolstoy's "Childhood"', *Slavonic and East European Review*, 55 (1977), 506–16

JONES, KATHRYN N., *Journeys of Remembrance: Memories of the Second World War in French and German Literature, 1960–1980* (Oxford: Legenda, 2007)

JØRGENSEN, STEEN BILLE, and CARSTEN SESTOFT, eds, *George Perec et l'histoire: actes du colloque international de l'Institut de littéraire comparée, Université de Copenhague du 30 avril au 1er mai 1988* (Copenhagen: Museum Tusculanum, 2000)

KANSTEINER, WULF, 'Genealogy of a Category Mistake: A Critical Intellectual History of the Cultural Trauma Metaphor', *Rethinking History*, 8 (2004), 193–221

KAPLAN, CAREN, *Questions of Travel: Postmodern Discourses of Displacement* (Durham, NC: Duke University Press, 1996)

KARLINSKY, SIMON, ed., *Dear Bunny, Dear Volodya: The Nabokov-Wilson Letters, 1940–1971*, revised and expanded edition (Berkeley: University of California Press, 2001)

KARPINSKI, EVA C., *Borrowed Tongues: Life Writing, Migration and Translation* (Waterloo, ONT: Wilfred Laurier University Press, 2012)

KARSHAN, THOMAS, 'December 1925: Nabokov Between Work and Play', *Nabokov Studies*, 10 (2006), 1–25

—— 'Nabokov and Play' (unpublished doctoral thesis, University of Oxford, 2007)

—— *Vladimir Nabokov and the Art of Play* (Oxford: Oxford University Press, 2011)

KAUFMAN, ELEANOR, 'Falling from the Sky: Trauma in Perec's *W* and Caruth's *Unclaimed Experience*', *Diacritics*, 28 (1998), 44–53

KEELEY, JAMES P., 'Subliminal Promptings: Psychoanalytic Theory and the Society for Psychical Research', *American Imago*, 58 (2001), 767–91

KERN, STEPHEN, *The Culture of Time and Space* (Cambridge, MA: Harvard University Press, 2003)

KNEPPER, WENDY, *Patrick Chamoiseau: A Critical Introduction* (Jackson: University Press of Mississippi, 2012)

KRAVIS, JUDY, *The Prose of Mallarmé: The Evolution of a Literary Language* (Cambridge: Cambridge University Press, 1976)

KRISTEVA, JULIA, *Étrangers à nous-mêmes* (Paris: Fayard, 1988)

KRITZMAN, LAWRENCE D., 'Remembrance of Things Past: Trauma and Mourning in Perec's *W ou le souvenir d'enfance*', *Journal of European Studies*, 35 (2005), 187–200

KUZMANOVICH, ZORAN, 'No Ghosts Walk', in *Transitional Nabokov*, ed. by Will Norman and Duncan White (Oxford: Peter Lang, 2009), pp. 285–305

LACAPRA, DOMINICK, *Writing History, Writing Trauma* (Baltimore, MD: Johns Hopkins University Press, 2001)

LAMBLIN, BIANCA, *La Biographie de Georges Perec par David Bellos: lecture critique* (Paris: Le Jardin d'essai, 2000)

LAMPERT, EUGENE, 'Modernism in Russia', in *Modernism: A Guide to European Literature 1890–1930*, ed. by Malcolm Bradbury and James McFarlane (London: Penguin, 1991), pp. 134–50

LARMOUR, DAVID H. J., ed., *Discourse and Ideology in Nabokov's Prose* (London: Routledge, 2002)

LEJEUNE, PHILIPPE, *La Mémoire et l'oblique: Georges Perec autobiographe* (Paris: P.O.L., 1991)

—— *Le Pacte autobiographique* (Paris: Seuil, 1975)

LE BRIS, MICHEL, and JEAN ROUAUD, eds, *Pour une littérature-monde* (Paris: Gallimard, 2007)

LEFEVERE, ANDRÉ, 'Composing the Other', in *Postcolonial Translation: Theory and Practice*, ed. by Susan Bassnett and Harish Trivedi (London: Routledge, 1999), pp. 75–95

LEWIS, NATHANIEL, *Unsettling the Literary West: Authenticity and Authorship* (Lincoln: University of Nebraska Press, 2003)

LEWONTIN, RICHARD C., STEVEN ROSE and LEON J. KAMIN, *Not in our Genes: Biology, Ideology and Human Nature* (New York: Pantheon, 1984)

LI, XIAOFAN AMY, *Comparative Encounters between Artaud, Michaux and the Zhuangzi* (Oxford: Legenda, 2015)

LIONNET, FRANÇOISE, 'Counterpoint and Double Critique in Edward Said and Abdelkebir Khatibi: A Transcolonial Comparison', in *A Companion to Comparative Literature*, ed. by Ali Behdad and Dominic Thomas (Oxford: Wiley-Blackwell, 2011), pp. 387–408

LINCOLN, SARAH L., 'Conquering the City: The Poetics of Possibility in *Texaco*', *Small Axe*, 15 (2011), 1–21

LIONNET, FRANÇOISE, and DOMINIC THOMAS, 'Introduction', in *Francophone Studies: New Landscapes*, ed. by Françoise Lionnet and Dominic Thomas (*Modern Language Notes*, 118:4 (2003)), 783–86

LITTLE, R., 'World Literature in French; or Is Francophonie Frankly Phoney?', *European Review*, 9 (2001), 421–36

LUCKHURST, ROGER, *The Invention of Telepathy* (Oxford: Oxford University Press, 2002)

—— *The Trauma Question* (London: Routledge, 2008)

MCCUSKER, MAEVE, *Patrick Chamoiseau: Recovering Memory* (Liverpool: Liverpool University Press, 2007)

——, and ANTHONY SOARES, eds, *Islanded Identities: Constructions of Postcolonial Cultural Insularity* (Amsterdam: Rodopi, 2011)

——, '"Troubler l'ordre de l'oubli": Memory and Forgetting in French Caribbean Autobiography of the 1990s', *Forum for Modern Language Studies*, 40 (2004), 438–50

MCNALLY, RICHARD J., 'Progress and Controversy in the Study of Posttraumatic Stress Disorder', *Annual Review of Psychology*, 54 (2003), 229–52

MAGNÉ, BERNARD, *Georges Perec* (Paris: Nathan, 1999)

—— 'Les Sutures dans *W ou le souvenir d'enfance*', *Cahiers Georges Perec*, 2 (1986–1987), 39–57

MALENA, ANNE, *The Negotiated Self: The Dynamics of Identity in Francophone Caribbean Narrative* (New York: Peter Lang, 1999)

MALLARMÉ, STÉPHANE, *Œuvres complètes*, ed. by Henri Mondor and Georges Jean-Aubry (Paris: Gallimard, 1951), pp. 360–68

MANNHERZ, JULIA, *Modern Occultism in Late Imperial Russia* (DeKalb: Northern Illinois University Press, 2012)

MANDEL, MAUD, *In the Aftermath of Genocide: Armenians and Jews in Twentieth-Century France* (Durham, NC: Duke University Press, 2003)

MARQUIS, CLAUDIA, 'Crossing Over: Postmemory and Postcolonial Imaginary in Andrea Levy's *Small Island* and *The Fruit of the Lemon*', *EnterText*, 9 (2012), 31–52

MATTISON, LACI, 'Nabokov's Aesthetic Bergsonism: An Intuitive, Reperceptualized Time', *Mosaic*, 46 (2013), 37–50

MEEKER, JOSEPH W., 'The Comic Mode', in *The Ecocriticism Reader: Landmarks in Literary Ecology*, ed. by Cheryll Glotfelty and Harold Fromm (Athens: University of Georgia Press, 1996), pp. 155–70

MEYER, PRISCILLA, 'Dolorous Haze, Hazel Shade: Nabokov and the Spirits', *Nabokov's World: The Shape of Nabokov's World*, ed. by Priscilla Meyer, Jane Grayson and Arnold B. McMillin (Basingstoke: Palgrave, 2002), pp. 88–100
—— 'Anglophonia and Optimysticism: Sebastian Knight's Bookshelves' in *Russian Literature and the West: A Tribute to David M. Bethea*, ed. by Alexander Dolinin, Lazar Fleishman and Leonid Livak, Stanford Slavic Studies 35 (Stanford: Berkeley Slavic Specialities, 2008), pp. 212–26
MIDDLETON, PETER, and TIM WOODS, *Literatures of Memory: History, Time and Space in Postwar Writing* (Manchester: Manchester University Press, 2000)
MILLER, NANCY K., 'Representing Others: Gender and the Subjects of Autobiography', *differences*, 6.2 (Spring, 1994), 1–27
MILNE, LORNA, *Patrick Chamoiseau: espaces d'une écriture antillaise* (Amsterdam: Rodopi, 2006)
MIZRUCHI, SUSAN L., 'Lolita in History', *American Literature*, 75 (2003), 629–52
MONTFRANS, MANET VAN, *Georges Perec: la contrainte du réel* (Amsterdam: Rodopi, 1999)
MOTTE, WARREN F., and JEAN-JACQUES POUCEL, eds, *Pereckonings: Reading Georges Perec* (New Haven: Yale University Press, 2004)
—— *Playtexts: Ludics in Contemporary Literature* (Lincoln: University of Nebraska Press, 1995)
—— 'The Work of Mourning', *Yale French Studies*, 105 (2004), 56–71
MURPHY, DAVID, 'De-centring French Studies: Towards a Postcolonial Theory of Francophone Cultures', *French Cultural Studies*, 13 (2002), 165–85
—— 'How French Studies Became Transnational; Or Postcolonialism as Comparatism', in *A Companion to Comparative Literature*, ed. by Ali Behdad and Dominic Thomas (Oxford: Wiley-Blackwell, 2011), pp. 408–19
MYERS, FREDERIC W., *On Human Personality and its Survival of Bodily Death* (Longmans: Green, 1903)
NIRANJANA, TEJASWINI, *Siting Translation: History, Post-structuralism, and the Colonial Context* (Oxford: University of California Press, 1992)
NORMAN, WILL, *Nabokov, History and the Texture of Time* (New York: Routledge, 2012)
NORRIDGE, ZOË, 'Comparing Pain: Theoretical Explorations of Suffering and Working Towards the Particular', in *A Companion to Comparative Literature*, ed. by Ali Behdad and Dominic Thomas (Oxford: Wiley-Blackwell, 2011), pp. 208–23
N'ZENGOU-TAYO, MARIE-JOSÉ, 'Literature and Diglossia: The Poetics of French and Creole "Interlect" in Patrick Chamoiseau's *Texaco*', *Caribbean Quarterly*, 43 (1997), 81–101
OLNEY, JAMES, ed, *Autobiography, Essays Theoretical and Critical* (Princeton: Princeton University Press, 1980)
PETIT, LAURENCE, 'Speak, Photographs? Visual Transparency and Verbal Opacity in Nabokov's *Speak, Memory*', *NOJ/НОЖ: Nabokov Online Journal*, 3 (2009)
PETREY, SANDY, 'Language Charged with Meaning', *Yale French Studies*, 103 (2003), 133–45
PIAGET, JEAN, *The Child's Conception of the World*, trans. by Joan and Andrew Tomlinson (London: Routledge & Kegan Paul, 1971)
PÍCHOVÁ, HANA, *The Art of Memory in Exile: Vladimir Nabokov and Milan Kundera* (Carbondale: Southern Illinois University Press, 2002)
PIFER, ELLEN, *Nabokov and the Novel* (Cambridge, MA: Harvard University Press, 1980)
PILKINGTON, ANTHONY EDWARD, *Bergson and his Influence: A Reassessment* (Cambridge: Cambridge University Press, 1976)
POLONSKY, RACHEL, *English Literature and the Russian Aesthetic Renaissance* (Cambridge: Cambridge University Press, 1998)
POLLOCK, GRISELDA, and MAXIM SILVERMAN, eds, *Concentrationary Memories: Totalitarian Resistance and Cultural Memories* (London: I. B. Tauris, 2014)
POPKIN, JEREMY D., *History, Historians and Autobiography* (Chicago: University of Chicago Press, 2005)

PRICE, RICHARD, and SALLY PRICE, 'Shadowboxing in the Mangrove', *Cultural Anthropology*, 12 (1997), 3–36

PRINCE, VALERIE SWEENEY, *Burnin' Down the House: Home in African American Literature* (New York: Columbia University Press, 2005)

QUENNELL, PETER, ed., *Vladimir Nabokov: A Tribute* (New York: William Morrow, 1980)

RACZYMOW, HENRI, 'Memory Shot Through with Holes', trans. by Alan Astro, *Yale French Studies*, 85 (1994), 98–105

RADOMSKAYA, T. I., *Дом и отчесество в русской классической литературе первой трети XIX века: опыт духовного, семейного, государственного устроения* (Moscow: Sovpadenie, 2006)

RADULESCU, DOMINICA, ed., *Realms of Exile: Nomadism, Diasporas and Eastern European Voices* (Lanham: Lexington, 2002)

RAEFF, MARC, *Russia Abroad: A Cultural History of the Russian Emigration, 1919–1939* (Oxford: Oxford University Press, 1990)

REGGIANI, CHRISTELLE., *L'Eternel et l'éphémère: temporalités dans l'œuvre de Georges Perec* (Amsterdam: Rodopi, 2010)

RÉJOUIS, ROSE-MYRIAM, 'A Reader in the Room: Rose-Myriam Réjouis Meets Patrick Chamoiseau', *Callaloo*, 22 (1999), 346–50

RIBIÈRE, MIREILLE, 'L'Autobiographie comme fiction' *Cahiers Georges Perec,* 2 (1986–1987), 25–37

ROBIN, RÉGINE, *Le Golem de l'écriture: de l'autofiction au cybersoi* (Montreal: XYZ, 1997)

—— *Le Deuil de l'origine: une langue en trop, la langue en moins* (Saint-Denis: Presses universitaires de Vincennes, 1993)

—— 'Vous, vous est quoi vous, au juste: méditations autobiographiques autour de la judéité', *Études françaises*, 37 (2001), 111–25

ROCHE, ANNE, *W ou le souvenir d'enfance de Georges Perec* (Paris: Gallimard, 1997)

ROTHBERG, MICHAEL, *Multidirectional Memory: Remembering the Holocaust in the Age of Decolonization* (Stanford: Stanford University Press, 2009)

RUSHDIE, SALMAN, *Imaginary Homelands: Essays and Criticism 1981–1991* (London: Penguin, 1991)

RUTLEDGE, DAVID S., *Nabokov's Permanent Mystery: The Expression of Metaphysics in His Work* (London: McFarland, 2010)

SAID, EDWARD W., 'The Mind of Winter: Reflections on Life in Exile', *Harper's Magazine*, September 1984, 49–55

SANSAVIOR, EVA, and RICHARD SCHOLAR, eds, *Caribbean Globalizations, 1492 to the Present Day* (Liverpool: Liverpool University Press, 2015)

SCHWARTZ, PAUL, *Georges Perec: Traces of his Passage* (Birmingham, AL: Summa, 1988)

SCHWEIGER, HANNES, 'Global Subjects: The Transnationalisation of Biography', *Life Writing*, 9 (2012), 249–58

SEYHAN, AZADE, *Writing Outside the Nation* (Princeton: Princeton University Press, 2001)

SHAMDASANI, SONU, 'Automatic Writing and the Discovery of the Unconscious', *Spring*, 54 (1993), 100–31

SHERINGHAM, MICHAEL, 'Attending to the Everyday: Blanchot, Lefebvre, Certeau, Perec', *French Studies*, 54 (2000), 187–99

—— *French Autobiography: Devices and Desires: Rousseau to Perec* (Oxford: Clarendon Press, 1993)

—— 'Space, Identity and Difference in Contemporary Fiction: Duras, Genet, Ndiaye', in *French Global: A New Approach to Literary History*, ed. by Susan Rubin Suleiman and Christie McDonald (New York: Columbia University Press, 2010), pp. 437–52

SHKLOVSKY, VIKTOR, *Ходъ коня: сборник статей* (Moscow: Helicon, 1923)

SILVERMAN, MAXIM, *Palimpsestic Memory: The Holocaust and Colonialism in French and Franophone Fiction and Film* (New York: Berghahn, 2013)

SIMMONS, ERNEST J., 'Tolstoy's Childhood', *Russian Review*, 3 (1944), 44–64
SIMON, SHERRY, 'Translating and Interlingual Creation in the Contact zone: Border Writing in Quebec', in *Postcolonial Translation: Theory and Practice*, ed. by Susan Bassnett and Harish Trivedi (London: Routledge, 1999), pp. 58–75
SISSON, JONATHAN B., 'Nabokov's Cosmic Synchronization and "Something Else"', *Nabokov Studies*, 1 (1994), 155–77
SOKOLOW, JAYME A., '"Arriving at Moral Perfection": Benjamin Franklin and Leo Tolstoy', *American Literature*, 47 (1975), 427–32
SPARGO, CLIFTON R., *The Ethics of Mourning: Grief and Responsibility in Elegiac Literature* (Baltimore, MD: Johns Hopkins University Press, 2004)
SPIVAK, GAYATRI CHAKRAVORTY, *The Wellek Library Lectures: Death of a Discipline* (New York: Columbia University Press, 2003)
STARK, JARED, 'Traumatic Futures: A Review Article', *Comparative Literature Studies*, 48 (2011), 435–52
STEINER, GEORGE, *Extraterritorial: Papers on Literature and the Language Revolution* (London: Faber, 1972)
—— *Language and Silence: Essays 1958–1966* (London: Faber, 1967)
STEINER, JEAN-FRANÇOIS, *Treblinka*, trans. by Helen Weaver (London: Weidenfeld & Nicholson, 1967)
STEWART, SUSAN, *On Longing: Narratives of the Miniature, the Gigantic, the Souvenir, the Collection* (Baltimore, MD: Johns Hopkins University Press, 1984)
STRAUMANN, BARBARA, *Figurations of Exile in Hitchcock and Nabokov* (Edinburgh: Edinburgh University Press, 2008)
STUART, DABNEY, *Nabokov: The Dimensions of Parody* (Baton Rouge: Louisiana State University Press, 1978)
SULEIMAN, SUSAN RUBIN, 'The 1.5 Generation: Thinking About Child Survivors and the Holocaust', *American Imago*, 59 (2002), 277–95
TAYLOR, CHARLES, *Sources of the Self: The Making of Modern Identity* (Cambridge: Cambridge University Press, 1989)
TERDIMAN, RICHARD, *Present Past: Modernity and the Memory Crisis* (Ithaca, NY: Cornell University Press, 1993)
TEVERSON, ANDREW, and SARA UPSTONE, eds, *Postcolonial Spaces: The Politics of Space in Contemporary Culture* (Basingstoke: Palgrave Macmillan, 2011)
TOKER, LEONA, *Nabokov: The Mystery of Literary Structures* (Ithaca, NY: Cornell University Press, 1989)
DE TOLEDO, CAMILLE, *Visiter le Flurkistan, ou, les illusions de la littérature-monde* (Paris: Presses universitaires de France, 2008)
TURIN, GASPARD, 'Listes perecquiennes et filiation contemporaine: entre *hybris* et mélancolie', *Cahiers Georges Perec*, 11 (2011), 43–59
UNWIN, TIMOTHY A., *Jules Verne: Journeys in Writing* (Liverpool: Liverpool University Press, 2005)
VISWANATHA, VANAMALA, and SHERRY SIMON, 'Shifting Grounds of Exchange: B. M. Srikantaiah and Kannada Translation', in *Postcolonial Translation: Theory and Practice*, ed. by Susan Bassnett and Harish Trivedi (London: Routledge, 1999), pp. 162–82
VENUTI, LAWRENCE, *The Translator's Invisibility* (London: Routledge, 1995)
VILLENEUVE, L., 'Dwelling Space in Post-war French Fiction: Camus, Sollers, Perec' (unpublished doctoral thesis, University of Oxford, 2008)
VISSER, IRENE, 'Trauma Theory and Postcolonial Literary Studies', *Journal of Postcolonial Writing*, 47 (2011), 270–82
WACHTEL, ANDREW BARUCH, *The Battle for Childhood: Creation of a Russian Myth* (Stanford: Stanford University Press, 1990)

WALCOTT, DEREK, *What the Twilight Says: Essays* (London: Faber, 1998)
WELCHMAN, JOHN C., *Rethinking Borders* (Basingstoke: Macmillan, 1996)
WEST, DONALD JAMES, *Psychical Research Today* (London: Duckworth, 1954)
WHITEHEAD, ANNE, *Memory* (London: Routledge, 2009)
—— *Trauma Fiction* (Edinburgh: Edinburgh University Press, 2004)
WINNICOTT, DONALD W., *Playing and Reality* (London: Tavistock Publications, 1971)
WITTLIN, JOSEPH, 'The Sorrow and Grandeur of Exile', *Polish Review*, 2 (1957), 99–112
WOOD, MICHAEL, *The Magician's Doubts: Nabokov and the Risks of Fiction* (London: Chatto & Windus, 1994)
WYLLIE, BARBARA, review of *The Models of Space, Time and Vision in V. Nabokov's Fiction: Narrative Strategies and Cultural Frames* by Marina Grishakova, *Partial Answers*, 7 (2009), 155–58
YOUNG, ROBERT J. C., *Colonial Desire: Hybridity in Theory, Culture and Race* (London: Routledge, 1995)

INDEX

Abraham, Nicholas 104
America 4, 11, 23, 49, 65, 123–25, 133, 144
Antelme, Robert 116
Assmann, Aleida 105
Assmann, Jan 105

Bachelard, Gaston 14, 17, 20, 24
Bandes molletières 128–31
Barberini, Maffeo 128–29
Barthes, Roland 22
Bartlebooth 134–36
Baudelaire, Charles 43, 72–77
Beckett, Samuel 6
Berberova, Nina 44
Berlin 10, 11, 48, 81, 86, 89
Bolsheviks 67, 88
Boyd, Brian 86, 87, 88, 133
Britton, Celia 60, 136, 138
Bruss, Elizabeth 91

Carroll, Lewis 2
Caruth, Cathy 85, 90, 101, 115
Césaire, Aimé 73
Chamoiseau, Patrick:
　life:
　　Career 28
　　Mother 46, 96–97, 38–39
　　Father 95
　works:
　　A bout d'enfance 12, 96, 124
　　Antan d'enfance 12, 28, 99–100
　　Chemin-d'école 12, 74, 97–98, 126
　　Un dimanche au cachot 115
　　Une enfance créole 8, 12, 17, 27, 31, 32, 33, 36, 41, 42, 43, 49, 57, 60, 68, 94, 100, 101–02, 105, 106, 108, 110, 122, 125, 131
　　L'Esclave vieil homme et le molosse 115–16
　　Lettres créoles 126–27
　　De la mémoire obscure à la mémoire consciente 115
　　Texaco 4, 60, 68
chess puzzles 132–34, 136
children's literature 1–4, 40
Colomina, Beatriz 42
comparative method 14, 144–46
La comtesse de Ségur 2–4
concentration camps 3, 35–36, 88, 107, 110, 116, 121
Condé, Maryse 3
Confiant, Raphaël 19

Connerton, Paul 38
Coppée, François 75
Coverdale, Linda 66
Créole:
　Language 2, 8, 12, 18, 28, 30, 54, 55–56, 57, 59–61, 62, 63–69, 74, 94, 99
　Culture 19, 30, 34–35, 38–39, 46, 47, 55, 73, 95, 97, 98, 108, 126, 145

Damrosch, David 144
Dante Alighieri 54, 58
Defoe, Daniel 2
Le détour 136–38
La drive 137
Dumas, Alexandre 2
Dumas, Louise-Céssette 2

Eakin, John Paul 9
Eliot, George 31

Felman, Shoshana 85, 86
Forsdick, Charles 6
Fort-de-France 1, 28, 35, 46
Fabian, Johannes 122, 123, 125
Faulkner, William 73
first language, concept of 53–61
fire 27–29, 30, 46
fractals 124–25
Francophonie 6, 57, 145
French language, boundaries of 53–61
Fresco, Nadine 107

Gare de Lyon 24, 90
Gezari, Janet 133
Glissant, Édouard 60, 64, 136, 138
Gautier, Théophile 43
Grubrich-Simitis, Ilse 104, 107

Hardwick, Louise 19, 104, 108, 124, 137
Hargreaves, Alec G. 6
Hartmann, Geoffrey 23
Hebrew 11, 54, 56–57, 61, 62, 69, 102, 130, 146
Herzen, Aleksandr 22, 30
Hirsch, Marianne 104, 105, 106, 107, 109
Holocaust 3, 5, 19, 80, 91–93, 94, 99, 100
　comparative approaches to 9–10, 104–11

Ibañez, Blasco 128, 129

Ionesco, Eugène 6
Inheritance 22, 61, 122, 128–31
Internationale situationniste 137, 143

jigsaw puzzles 134–36

Kansteiner, Wulf 99
Kaplan, Caren 8, 11
Kaplan, Chaim 92
Kaufman, Eleanor 90
Kern, Stephen 41–42
Knepper, Wendy 120
Kritzman, Laurence D. 91
Kuropatkin, Aleksei 89

LaCapra, Dominick 93–94, 97, 99
Laub, Dori 85
Lefevere, André 62
Lejeune, Philippe 92
Leiris, Michel, L'Age d'homme, précédé de de la littérature considérée comme tauromachie 129–30
lists 77–79
literary community 5, 9, 10, 13, 62, 71
Lloyd Wright, Frank 41
Lubartów 61
Luckhurst, Roger 86

Maeterlinck, Maurice 75
Magné, Bernard 102, 128
Mallarmé, Stéphane 43, 75
Marbles 55, 66, 72, 80, 136–38, 143
McCusker, Maeve 19, 104, 107, 126
McNally, Richard 99
miniatures 38, 123–24, 125
mobility 2, 6–8, 17, 49, 53, 90, 101, 103, 114
van Montfrans, Manet 136
Motte, Warren 101
Murphy, David 6
de Musset, Alfred 75

Nabokov, Sergey 87–88
Nabokov, Véra 11
Nabokov, Vladimir:
  life:
    brother, see Nabokov, Sergey
    birth 22, 24, 29, 44
    birth of son 11
    departure from Russia 11
    departure from France 11, 133, 144
    father 10, 11, 22 37, 58, 63, 67, 69, 86–87, 89, 90, 95
    marriage 11
    mother 33, 37–38, 41, 42, 44, 58, 63, 86, 89, 100, 123
    synaesthesia 55 118
    uncle Ruka 4, 88
  works:
    The Defense 134
    Другие берега 54, 59
    The Real Life of Sebastian Knight 134
    Speak, Memory 3–4, 8, 17, 20, 22, 23, 31, 33, 36, 41, 43, 44, 49, 57–58, 74, 75, 80, 87, 90, 93, 110, 117–18, 120, 122, 125, 131–33, 134, 135
    'Mademoiselle O' 4, 74, 80, 142
naming 65, 69–71, 136

October Revolution 4, 5, 9, 10, 18, 21, 44, 67, 75

Paris 2, 10, 11, 12, 18, 23–27, 48, 49, 62, 69, 73, 77, 81, 86, 107, 119, 145, 146
Pater, Walter 31
Perec, Georges:
  life:
    Birth 41, 56, 70, 77, 105–06, 109, 134
    cousin Henri 35
    aunt Esther 12, 36, 145
    departure from Paris 32
    Mother 2, 3, 4–5, 11–12, 18, 23–25, 30, 129,
    Father 2, 11, 12, 35, 61, 69–71, 128–30
    Membership of the Ouvroir de littérature potentielle 129
  works:
    Les Choses 40
    Ellis Island 23
    Espèces d'espaces 23–24, 40–41
    Un homme qui dort 101, 119
    'Quelques-unes des choses qu'il faudrait tout de même que je fasse avant de mourir' 40, 134
    'Notes brèves sur l'art et la manière de ranger ses livres' 143
    Quel petit vélo à guidon chromé au fond de la cour? 12
    La Vie mode d'emploi 25–26, 134, 137
    W ou le souvenir d'enfance 2, 8, 17, 23, 24, 39, 71, 77, 79, 90, 92–93, 100, 101, 105, 110, 119, 120, 128, 130, 134, 136, 142
Petit, Laurence 22
Petrey, Sandy 6–7
Petrograd 11, 21, 48, 59
photography 22
Piaget, Jean 14, 31, 33
Pineau, Gisèle 33
Poland 3, 61, 62, 105
postmemory 104–07
Price, Richard 29
Proust, Marcel 114, 118–22
Prudhomme, Sully 75
Pushkin 37, 59

Rabelais, François 72
Raczymow, Henri 107, 109
Radomskaya, T. I. 37
Rand, Nicholas T. 107
Rothberg, Michael 10

Russia 4, 11, 18, 21, 29, 30, 33, 49, 58–59, 62, 67, 75, 77, 81, 86, 88, 117, 123
Rue Vilin 23–27, 35, 41, 49, 142
Russian 4, 10, 11, 18, 21, 49

Said, Edward 8, 9, 31–32
scars 101–06, 127, 128–31
Shklovsky, Viktor 133, 142
Silence 1, 2, 85, 86–87, 90, 93, 96, 99, 104, 105, 107–09, 110, 114, 116, 136
Simon, Sherry 53, 54, 57
Slavery 13, 19, 94, 98, 103–10, 115–16
Spivak, Gayatri Chakravorty 14
St Cecilia 129–30
Steiner, George 8, 92
Steiner, Jean-François 92
Stevenson, R. L. 2
Stojadinovitch, Milan 106
Straumann, Barbara 88
Suleiman, Susan Rubin, 32
Switzerland 75

Terdiman, Richard 43, 121
Torok, Maria 104–05, 107, 110

Tolstoy, Lev 34
translation theory 14, 53, 64–65
trauma:
    controversy over use of term 99
    inter-generational transmission of 104–11

Urban I 130
Urban VIII 129–30

Venuti, Lawrence 62
Verlaine, Paul 75
Verne, Jules 2, 3, 72, 78–80, 143
Verne, Jules, *Les Enfants du capitaine Grant* 134
Villeneuve, Lisa 25–26, 41
Viswanatha, Vanamala 53

Whitehead, Anne 23
Winckler, Caecilia 129–30
Winckler, Gaspard:
    in *La Vie mode d'emploi* 134–35
    in *W ou le souvenir d'enfance* 3, 57, 90–91, 97, 109
Wood, Michael 87

Yiddish 11, 54, 56–57, 62, 69

www.ingramcontent.com/pod-product-compliance
Lightning Source LLC
LaVergne TN
LVHW061252060426
835507LV00017B/2037